Spatial Change and Interregional Flows in the Integrating Europe

Contributions to Economics

Giuseppe Gaburro (Ed.)
Ethics and Economics
1997. ISBN 3-7908-0986-1

Frank Hoster/Heinz Welsch/
Christoph Böhringer
CO_2 Abatement and Economic Structural Change in the European Internal Market
1997. ISBN 3-7908-1020-7

Christian M. Hafner
Nonlinear Time Series Analysis with Applications to Foreign Exchange Rate Volatility
1997. ISBN 3-7908-1041-X

Sardar M.N. Islam
Mathematical Economics of Multi-Level Optimisation
1998. ISBN 3-7908-1050-9

Sven-Morten Mentzel
Real Exchange Rate Movements
1998. ISBN 3-7908-1081-9

Lei Delsen/Eelke de Jong (Eds.)
The German and Dutch Economies
1998. ISBN 3-7908-1064-9

Mark Weder
Business Cycle Models with Indeterminacy
1998. ISBN 3-7908-1078-9

Tor Rødseth (Ed.)
Models for Multispecies Management
1998. ISBN 3-7908-1001-0

Michael Carlberg
Intertemporal Macroeconomics
1998. ISBN 3-7908-1096-7

Sabine Spangenberg
The Institutionalised Transformation of the East German Economy
1998. ISBN 3-7908-1103-3

Hagen Bobzin
Indivisibilities
1998. ISBN 3-7908-1123-8

Helmut Wagner (Ed.)
Current Issues in Monetary Economics
1998. ISBN 3-7908-1127-0

Peter Michaelis/Frank Stähler (Eds.)
Recent Policy Issues in Environmental and Resource Economics
1998. ISBN 3-7908-1137-8

Jessica de Wolff
The Political Economy of Fiscal Decisions
1998. ISBN 3-7908-1130-0

Georg Bol/Gholamreza Nakhaeizadeh/Karl-Heinz Vollmer (Eds.)
Risk Measurements, Econometrics and Neural Networks
1998. ISBN 3-7908-1152-1

Joachim Winter
Investment and Exit Decisions at the Plant Level
1998. ISBN 3-7908-1154-8

Bernd Meyer
Intertemporal Asset Pricing
1999. ISBN 3-7908-1159-9

Uwe Walz
Dynamics of Regional Integration
1999. ISBN 3-7908-1185-8

Michael Carlberg
European Monetary Union
1999. ISBN 3-7908-1191-2

Giovanni Galizzi/
Luciano Venturini (Eds.)
Vertical Relationships and Coordination in the Food System
1999. ISBN 3-7908-1192-0

Gustav A. Horn/
Wolfgang Scheremet/
Rudolf Zwiener
Wages and the Euro
1999. ISBN 3-7908-1199-8

Dirk Willer
The Development of Equity Capital Markets in Transition Economies
1999. ISBN 3-7908-1198-X

Karl Matthias Weber
Innovation Diffusion and Political Control of Energy Technologies
1999. ISBN 3-7908-1205-6

Heike Link et al.
The Costs of Road Infrastructure and Congestion in Europe
1999. ISBN 3-7908-1201-3

continued on page 268

Johannes Bröcker · Hayo Herrmann
(Eds.)

Spatial Change and Interregional Flows in the Integrating Europe

Essays in Honour of Karin Peschel

With 39 Figures and 26 Tables

Springer-Verlag
Berlin Heidelberg GmbH

Series Editors
Werner A. Müller
Martina Bihn

Editors
Professor Dr. Johannes Bröcker
Technical University of Dresden
Institut für Wirtschaft und Verkehr
Mommsenstraße 13
D-01062 Dresden, Germany
E-mail:
johannes.broecker@mailbox.tu-dresden.de

Dr. Hayo Herrmann
University of Kiel
Institute for Regional Research
Olshausenstraße 40
D-24098 Kiel, Germany
E-mail:
hayoherrmann@bwl.uni-kiel.de

ISBN 978-3-7908-1344-9

Cataloging-in-Publication Data applied for
Die Deutsche Bibliothek – CIP-Einheitsaufnahme
Spatial change and interregional flows in the integrating Europe: essays in honour of Karin Peschel; 26 tables / Johannes Bröcker; Hayo Herrmann (eds.). – Heidelberg; New York: Physica-Verl., 2001
ISBN 978-3-7908-1344-9 ISBN 978-3-642-57552-5 (eBook)
DOI 10.1007/978-3-642-57552-5

Originally published by Physica-Verlag Heidelberg in 2001

Softcover Design: Erich Kirchner, Heidelberg

SPIN 10783707 88/2202-5 4 3 2 1 0 – Printed on acid-free paper

Preface

This Festschrift has been created to honour Karin Peschel on occasion of her 65th anniversary on October 25th, 2000. It was a sincere desire of the authors and the editors, who are all indebted to Karin Peschel in their research work, to express their deep gratitude.

We gladly took up the idea to prepare this volume, since we have been closely associated with Karin Peschel for many years of her academic life. We first met her in the early 1970s, when she was Professor and we were students of economics at the university of Kiel. In 1975/76, as director of the Institute for Regional Research, she offered us the opportunity to work in the fields of spatial theory and regional science, which started our academic career.

The editors express their particular thanks for realizing this Festschrift to all friends and colleagues of Karin Peschel, who have contributed to this volume, for their readiness to participate and for the promptness of their delivery. Furthermore, we like to thank the *Physica Verlag* for their co-operation, as well as Hans-Jürgen Krupp, president of the *Landeszentralbank in der Freien und Hansestadt Hamburg, in Mecklenburg-Vorpommern und Schleswig-Holstein*, who provided the necessary funds for the publication. For their assistance in compiling the final draft, we are indebted to Markus Hirschfeld, *Institute for Regional Research*, and to Gabriele Keidel and Werner A. Müller, *Physica*.

Kiel, July 2000 — Johannes Bröcker, Hayo Herrmann

For Karin Peschel

by Johannes Bröcker

After the war Karin Peschel, a daughter of a Saxon industrialist, was stranded in Western Germany where she decided to study economics in Münster. She was probably ambitious to follow her family's tradition to go into business, not at all expecting that this decision would end up in a successful academic career. In that days this was a courageous decision: for one thing female students of economics were even rarer than in our student days. More serious, however, was the fact that she was lacking any means for financing her study after her family had lost everything. So, Karin found work as a secretary, were she learnt a lot of useful skills. It is still impressive to see her typing one of her numerous letters: she comes up with the printout before others have even started thinking.

At that time, Münster was emerging as a seedbed for German academic careers, to a large extent due to the influence of Karin's academic advisor, Andreas Predöhl. She became a research assistant in his Institute of Transport Economics after she had graduated in 1960, and received her doctoral degree in 1963 with a thesis on the competitive framework for rail and road transport in Europe. After a brief interlude in the University of Erlangen-Nürnberg, she moved on to Karlsruhe, to become assistant professor in Rolf Funck's Institute for Economic Policy Research. Soon after habilitation, in 1971, she was appointed as professor of economics in the University of Kiel.

So far, Karin's main research field was transport economics. In her doctoral thesis she already reviewed the results of the modern French school of public utilities regulation, and later, in a joint publication with Rolf Funck, applied these concepts to proposals for reforming road transport taxes. These ideas were not yet common in Germany in those days. Many economists were still suspicious of arguments from theoretical welfare economics. Some of the suggestions about tax reform were then farsighted, and they still are today. We assume that it was from authors like Allais that Karin learnt to trust in good theory, but to brush off all theory, whatever elegant, which seems of no practical use.

After her move to Kiel, Karin was appointed as head of the Institute for Regional Research, founded by Reimut Jochimsen. Here she initiated a research programme aiming at an understanding of the spatial dimension of trade and integration in Europe. This subject was put into her "scientific cradle" by Andreas Predöhl, who has put a focus on the spatial structure of international trade. Karin's reasoning centred around the agglomerating forces enhanced by integration, as suggested along the regional economics tradition, and the equilibrating forces as proposed by neoclassical main stream international trade theory. Typical for her approach is to search for empirical answers as to which of these tendencies dominates under which conditions. Even from contradicting theories she accepts whatever seems plausible rather than trying to reconcile them into a single consistent framework like that of modern economic geography. She would frankly admit to have neither the formal education nor the theoretical ambitions to accomplish such a feat. The countervailing forces are obvious; hence, let us try to measure them.

A closely related issue is the role of distance in trade and factor flows. Much of her own and her associates' research aimed at looking behind the imprecise notion of distance and to measure the impact of different aspects of economic distance on spatial interaction and on trade in particular. It is still puzzling why this impact is so strong and apparently not decreasing over time, even though today transport costs are only a small fraction of trade value, transport and communication technologies improve so dramatically, and artificial and institutional barriers – though not vanished – have significantly declined. Karin's empirical work has shed much light on this issue, without claiming that the puzzle has finally been solved.

When Karin was appointed as head of the Institute in Kiel, she found favourable conditions to realise her goals due to the newly established research programme "Scandinavia and the Baltic Sea area" initiated by Jürgen Rohwedder and financed by the German Research Foundation. The Baltic Sea area became not only one of her favourite research subjects, but also her main "activity space". By now, Karin is a pivotal node in the network of regional scientists in Northern Europe, knowing – as we say in German – "god and the world". She never confined the Baltic Sea area to the western countries. Already in the 1970s she – in co-operation with Rolf Funck – established close contacts with regional scientists in Russia and Poland. For Karin, who always had close connections with her relatives in East Germany, the peaceful revolution in the east was like waking up from a nightmare, setting free new energy. She immediately started knitting the regional science network on the other side of the Baltic Sea, formerly belonging to the Soviet block. Furthermore, in 1993, the EuroFaculty was founded as a support programme to upgrade university education in economics, social sciences and laws in the Baltic states. Notwithstanding the enormous problems and inconveniences, Karin supported the project actively from the very beginning, and the result in terms of a first generation of excellently educated young economists graduating in Tartu is impressive.

Beyond those already mentioned, Karin's scientific work was devoted to a lot of further issues. We name a few just briefly. One is the theory of income distribution, on which she only published once some 30 years ago, but which was continuously one of her main fields in teaching. Another is economic development in general and the labour market in particular in Schleswig-Holstein. The Institute periodically reports to the Schleswig-Holstein parliament on the labour market situation. One of her present research fields is the regional impact of cultural activities; her interest was stimulated by an advisory report she submitted on a renowned music event in Schleswig-Holstein, sponsored by the government.

As already mentioned, Karin has a pragmatic attitude towards theory. She regards theory as irrelevant, if it is not applicable to practical problems. And solving problems is exactly what she aims at. Impatience is her driving force, impatience with unsolved problems and the failure of contemporaries to push for solutions. One of the problems Karin was increasingly confronted with as an university teacher was the pessimistic perspective of the university itself. To Karin it was – and still is – impossible for the traditional concept of the German university to fulfil two conflicting goals at the same time: to educate a small elite according to the standards of international scientific research and to prepare a large number of students – up to one third of an age group – for practical professional life. Facing the necessity of change, she took over the responsibility as rector of the university of Kiel from 1992 to 1996. Of course, the impact of a rector on the reform process is restricted, but Karin's achievements are noteworthy, from restructuring teachers' education to introducing modern management techniques into the old fashioned university administration.

Even though Karin has formally retired when her duties as rector ended, she has not with regard to her scientific work and her numerous other activities. Hence, this volume is not primarily meant to report and evaluate what has been achieved during the last four decades. Rather, it is a report on current work in the fields, in which Karin is still actively involved, and it is written by those colleagues and friends with whom she is holding contacts in research, editorial work, conferences et cetera. The editors apologize that the book became so voluminous. This is because we got such an overwhelming response to our suggestion to edit a Festschrift at Karin's 65th anniversary. This witnesses the high appreciation she receives in the scientific community.

On behalf of the large number of scholars, of her colleagues and friends we express our deep gratitude for her dedication to her work, for her courage, farsightedness and sincerity. We want to profit from it also in the future.

Contents

Erratum

Page XI: Part II got an incorrect headline.
The correct headline should be:
"Innovation and Regional Growth".
This error also occurs on page 87

Contributions to Economics
Bröcker/Herrmann (Editors)
Spatial Change and Interregional Flows in the Integrating Europe
ISBN 3-7908-1344-3 Physica-Verlag Heidelberg 2001

Part I

Economic Integration in the Baltic Rim

Structural Shifts? Sketches of the Regional Economic Development in Denmark

Nils Groes

AKF – Institute of Local Government Studies

Copenhagen, Denmark

1. Introduction

Karin Peschel has always been very interested in the regional interactions across the borders, not least in the Baltic Area. This has resulted in many publications about the topic by Karin Peschel as well as in co-operation and friendships with researchers all over Europe. It has also led to an interest in the regional economic developments in neighbouring countries.

This article ranges over regional economic developments in Denmark during the past 150 years. The question we are trying to expound is: *where* has economic activity in Denmark taken place and *why,* and whether regional income disparities have become greater or smaller (meaning whether we have experienced *divergence* or *convergence*) as well as spatial concentration or not?

As a starting point, we have just assumed that with reasonably the same kind of production function in all parts of the kingdom, we should expect convergence. This is due to trade between the regions and net transfers of capital and labour. Pointing into the same direction is the catch-up hypothesis, according to which existing high technology will spill-over from more advanced to less advanced regions at a faster rate than that at which new technology is developed.

However, regional income disparities exist, and they have even been much greater. How did they arise? Our theory is that new technology can act as a catalyst of *structural shifts* in the economy. New production functions arise in particular parts of the country, leading to divergence, which may again lead to concentration.

There are indications that Denmark actually experienced such a shift towards the end of the 19th century with the breakthrough of industrialisation. Particularly in this period, we have noted signs of divergence, and we see a strong rate of concentration.

During the greater part of the 20th century, Denmark experienced convergence, and the greater equalisation of incomes resulted in fewer relocations in the period.

In addition to new technology, family patterns and market forces, also the public welfare policy contributed to this trend.

The question is whether Denmark experienced a new structural shift towards the end of the past century? Whether new technology has given a few university cities new benefits of scale? Whether we are heading for a new era of divergence and concentration?

Until we have analysed developments in the late 20th century more closely, it is difficult to foretell developments in the 21st.

2. Regional Economic Development 1870-1914

The economic growth in Denmark from the middle of the 19th century was driven by increasing agricultural exports to England and greater employment in the urban sector, particularly within commerce and transport.

Growth was promoted by new infrastructure, with railways and shipping playing a major role. It also meant that growth was concentrated in the towns along the railway and/or with a port. The growth rate was quite spectacular in Copenhagen, which counted as many inhabitants as all provincial towns together. The greater part of the financial sector, wholesale trade and central government administration were also located here. This concentration of market and resources created the basis for industrial expansion. The arguments in favour of spatial economies of scale were highly relevant.

In 1870, the wages of unskilled in Copenhagen were more than 20 % above those in the provincial towns, and the differences among skilled workers were even larger (35 %). The wages in the rural districts were lower than in towns. Farm workers earned 25 % less than unskilled workers in provincial towns (Pedersen 1930, Christensen 1975). In spite of the great changes in the economy, the wage relations between capital and provincial towns remained relatively unchanged till 1905. On the other hand, the wages of unskilled urban workers rose more than those of agricultural workers. However, the trend in agricultural wages from 1859 to 1913 shows sustained growth, unlike the prices of agricultural products and prices of farm properties. And Pedersen has no doubt that the driving force was the migration from the rural districts into the towns. In the 1950s, the migration from rural districts was still relatively modest »therefore, the adult rural population was increasing considerably in these years, and as the farming technology was stagnating, wages were suppressed to the absolute subsistence level«. In the following decades, the migration into the towns was rising, culminating in the decade 1880-1890 with an average migration of more than 15,000 persons a year. At no time before or after that decade has the migration in Denmark reached such proportions. So the rising income and employment opportunities available in the cities produced defection from agriculture, thus increasing agricultural wages. This fits in well with our theory: The mobility of labour contributes to convergence (as well as the Danish growth driven by trade with Great Britain in the studied period fits in well with trade contributing to convergence). The reason why capital did not to the same extent move to the rural areas was because of the infrastructure at the time.

The only part of the period in which there was real divergence was precisely in the 1990s when according to Hansen (1970) industrialisation took hold in Denmark. During that decade, the hourly wages of unskilled urban workers rose more than 50 %, and their annual wages rose more than 40 %, while the wages of rural workers rose just 10 % (Christensen 1975, Pedersen 1930).

Based on Hansen (1983), we may therefore claim that there was a structural shift in the Danish economy in the second half (and particularly towards the end) of the 19th century, and that this shift produced divergence. That the divergence did not become greater was due to the high mobility of labour, which led to concentration. And in the following decade, convergence started in Denmark.

3. Trends Throughout the 20th Century (1914-1993)

Throughout the 20th century, Danish society has been characterised by rapid technological change, both in the production of goods and services, in the transport sector and in family life.

The industrial structure has changed dramatically. The absolutely dominant part of the working population are now pay earners in urban trades. A constantly falling number are employed in the production of goods (agriculture and manufacturing etc.), and increasing numbers are employed in private and public service sectors.

3.1 Migration Patterns

The migration from the countryside to the towns continued in the 20th century. However, the rates of urban growth were declining. Growth continued in the Copenhagen area during the first half of the century but at a reducing rate, until it stopped completely (around 1950). Growth in provincial towns declined as well, but without stagnating completely during the century. In contrast, the population decline in rural districts slowed gradually, and finally stopped (at a level of about 17 % of the population).

Pedersen (1981) has proved the decline in net mobility between counties and in the migration into Copenhagen. He has also tried to link changes in the mobility pattern to changes in unemployment. There is partial match during the studied period from the 1930s until the beginning of the 1970s when both unemployment and net mobility went down. But from that point the correlation stops.

However, there are other reasons for the changed mobility pattern.

- First of all, the regional *income disparities* contracted. As shown by Dilling et al. (1994) there was steady convergence from 1935 to 1990, and the income gap in relation to the capital region was narrowed throughout the period. The reasons will be discussed below, but the importance of just unemployment benefits and other transfers is evident: people no longer have to move even if they are made redundant.
- In addition, car driving and thus *commuting* is gaining importance. Instead of moving when they get a new job, people can decide to commute. As shown by Andersen (1998) they may even choose to move further away from their work, if other preferences have higher priority.
- *Women's paid work* is also part of the reason for the increasing commuting and the declining net mobility. When a household depends on two job incomes, it becomes more difficult to move in pursuit of job opportunities for just one income earner. This article is not designed to analyse the changed work sharing in families, but it is worth noting that, also here, technological development plays a significant role. First, the rising productivity in the labour market has created greater prosperity and thus the opportunity of shorter working hours for those in employment. Secondly, the rising productivity and all sorts of domestic hardware have allowed women to take paid work (without overburdening men!). Cars and durable consumer goods have also allowed families to change their shopping patterns to fewer weekly shopping rounds and less dependence on local shops. All this has led to steadily enlarged shopping and labour market areas.
- *Education opportunities* have steadily improved as well, and more of the young are taking this advantage. Therefore, on the one hand there are more education opportunities for young people in their own counties, on the other there are so many more who want to take education. In several regions (e.g., the island of Bornholm) the net emigration is exclusively accounted for by young people seeking education. For all other age groups there is net migration into the region – it is just not large enough to cancel out the emigration of the young, and a considerable number (of the well educated) remain in the towns which are education centres.

Nevertheless, the proportion of the population living in rural districts has largely been unchanged in the past many years. It may partly be explained by people's wish to be closer to nature and have a more healthy *environment* (Manniche 1999), and partly lower *prices of homes* in rural districts (Hansen 1991), which enable young families to buy their own homes, if only they are ready to commute a little longer.

As yet, new *IT technology* has hardly had much impact on mobility and settlement patterns, but the possibility of spatial separation of the employee's home and the employer's domicile is getting increasingly obvious as people are working at home more and more days a week. Especially, this tendency may increase the acceptable commuting distance.

3.2 Relocation Pattern of Firms

The reasons for the decline in the population's net mobility has another dimension as well: While employees have migrated less, employers have become more mobile, and many of them no longer need to be located in towns.

The regional economic developments towards the end of the 19th century were driven by a surplus of labour in the country and scarcity in the towns, where the new sectors (commerce and manufacturing industries) were in rapid development. These sectors were tied to towns and cities due to their infrastructure requirements: railways and ports. It was in the junctions of this infrastructure that the opportunity of economic development was greatest, and this was where labour migrated to and settled down (close to jobs).

Throughout the 20th century, automobiles gained increasing importance for the transport of persons and goods, making it easier for manufacturing industry to set up facilities in rural districts. Both raw materials and finished goods were carried by truck on the constantly improving road network. And as labour had become more mobile as well (commuting), companies did not have to be located in towns in order to attract the required labour. At the same time, technological development for example in the production structure of manufacturing industry and in wholesale trade meant constantly larger area requirements, and one-storey production facilities situated on less expensive land replaced multi-storey property in central locations.

There is an amazing feature in the development of private car driving and commuting. From the 1970s, supporting public transport as well as regional planning seems to have been an uphill struggle. The public commitment was focused on locating homes and workplaces together (in towns) and keeping the open countryside free of housing and urban trades. The objective was ensuring that employees would be living near their workplaces and public transport. Instead, people are commuting over longer and longer distances, the labour market areas are constantly getting larger (Andersen 1999) and the population in rural districts is maintained, even if the importance of agriculture is constantly declining.

During the second half of the 19th century and the first half of the 20th, workers thus moved into towns (where the capital stock was), contributing to concentration and convergence. From the middle of the 20th century (and until the 1990s), capital moved to the regions in which manpower was available, reducing the concentration but also helping to create convergence.

So industrial employment has increased considerably in Jutland and especially in the rural districts (Jensen, Maskell et al. 1997). Copenhagen's share of well-paid jobs in the growth industries has constantly been higher than Jutland's, but the growth in the very same industries has been higher in Jutland. This trend is not specific to Denmark; it may be rebound all over Europe as proved by Molle (1997), who has also shown that most industries have been less concentrated spatially throughout the period 1950-1990, and that the less advantaged regions in Europe have continuously caught up with the more prosperous.

It should be added, however, that population rates and employment have not risen in the Danish fringe regions (e.g., on the smaller islands), where the new type of infrastructure (cars and road networks) has been of little use.

3.3 Causes of Convergence

The paragraph above illustrates one of the causes of convergence: *the market forces*. It would fit in nicely with our hypothesis (underpinned by trading activity and the mobility of labour and capital) as well as with the catch-up theory. The rate of job growth in Jutland has also raised per capita income, while the opposite trend has prevailed in the capital region.

Also wage developments for different types of labour may have generated convergence. In general, lifetime incomes from 1960 to 1995 improved most for the less educated workers in private employment, and least for the well educated workforce in public employment (Danish Council of Economic Advisers, 1996). Since there are relatively more in the second category in the capital region, this may lead to convergence.

At the same time, the *public welfare policy* has helped ensure convergence. Rising taxes and transfers contribute to levelling out income disparities between the regions (Groes 1997). This development has been thoroughly documented for the last few decades, but may no doubt be traced back to much earlier periods. The social reforms adopted in Denmark from 1933, the introduction of the state pension in 1956 and, in general, the rapid increase in tax revenue and transfer payments after the Second World War (creation of the welfare state) were, in fact, aimed to contribute to eliminating income disparities in the population, and thus significantly reducing regional income disparities. Particularly, the poor fringe areas have enjoyed the benefits of this policy. Inversely, the benefits system and the cash social assistance system have contributed to retaining labour (and population) also in parts of the country with receding demand (thus reducing net mobility).

Overall, the market forces produced convergence in earned income until 1993, and the differences in per capita disposable incomes between local authority districts have narrowed even more. The rate of convergence in disposable per capita income has been almost twice as strong as that of primary per capita income. The politically induced factors such as taxes, transfer payments and equalisation programmes have therefore reinforced the narrowing of the income disparities created by the market forces in the period from 1980 to 1995. Calculations have also indicated that the development in the number of jobs and in transfer payments and taxes as a whole have underpinned convergence in the period from 1980 to 1995 (Danish Ministry of the Interior, 1998).

4. The 1990s

In the 1990s, the trend seems to have been reversed. The general mobility appears to have increased and the population in the capital region has risen in the past few years. A decline from the early 1970s has been turned into a weak growth trend from 1990, which has later been replaced by more significant growth. A major part of the population growth in the capital region in the past decade has been created by the increase among ethnic minorities. In percentage terms this growth has admittedly been greatest in all other regions than the capital region; however measured in absolute numbers it carries heavy weight for several municipalities in the Copenhagen area, even though the increase of population in the last few years includes Danish citizens as well. There has been positive net migration into the capital region from other parts of the country. If, like in Andersen (1999), the labour market area of the capital region is now defined as the entire island of Zealand, a new set of contours are emerging. Net migration – from Jutland and Fyn – into the capital region (Zealand) has grown since 1990, and the population growth since 1995 has largely bypassed North, West and Southern Jutland and Fyn–having been concentrated around the capital and in the eastern part of Jutland.

The capital region has recorded a high rate of employment growth since 1993, also compared to other regions, whereas the growth rate seems relatively low in large parts of Western and Southern Jutland.

We have not yet obtained reliable data for regional income developments after 1995. Preliminary figures, however, do not indicate any divergence. If the growth in real property prices is studied, however, the former geographical pattern will reappear: Prices increased most in the capital region and the large provincial towns, least in the fringe areas. And more in Eastern than in Western Jutland.

The reason for possible divergence in regional incomes after 1993 must for obvious reasons be speculative. But let us try.

There might be two sets of causes resulting in possible divergence after 1993. One being market economic forces, the other being the public welfare policy.

In the market, the growth in private service trades (excluding commerce, transport and finance) has risen steadily. In fact, the private service trades are now employing more than the entire manufacturing industry, but distributed on a host of different trades – ranging from domestic service and repairs to private and business services for which high education is required.

There are several indications that the high technology segments of the private service trades have their home base close to a few universities (in data science and technology, natural sciences, medicine and economics). But in addition, the technological environments tend to be self-reinforcing. Also, people without formal qualifications in the mentioned disciplines may obtain jobs in such companies (for instance in the IT industry). There, they may be offered the training and learning that will enable them to contribute to the development and growth of these environments. Inversely, the rural local districts in general and the fringe local districts in particular have hardly been the obvious choice when new high technology firms were choosing a location.

Based on this line of thought, the capital region, and one or two university cities in Jutland (Aarhus and Aalborg) must have the best prospects of economic prosperity, based on growth in the high technology service sector, which also attracts people by offering relatively high (and steeply rising) earnings opportunities.

The development in public transfers may also help explain the hypothesis of divergence in Denmark since 1993. (Per capita) wages have risen more than transfer payments, and the employment rate has risen significantly at the same time, while the number of claimants of transfer payments has fallen in step with the economic upturn. So contrary to the situation until 1993, the public welfare policy may from that point have contributed to rising economic inequality and greater regional divergence.

5. Conclusion

In 1908, the German emperor, Wilhelm II, declared that the airship was the greatest invention of this (the 20th) century, and Count Zeppelin its greatest inventor. This was disproved, however. His statement shows how wrong things may go for those who want to foretell the future without knowing about technological developments.

We do not know whether there has been a shift in Denmark's long term economic trend – whether the development of the high technology service sector will gain momentum to such an extent that the regional economic trends will change. And if so, whether this development will remain tied to a few university cities.

We do not know either how public policies will develop in future – or internationalisation and immigration.

Before pondering further over the future, we had therefore better provide appropriate figures for and carry out a closer analysis of the structural developments of the past decade. This would be well in line with the attitude of Karin Peschel.

The experience of the past two centuries indicates that many forces are pulling towards convergence between regions when the regional production functions (including the qualifications of labour) are reasonably the same. Trading activities and the mobility of labour and capital contribute to this movement. Thus, concentration is a function of income disparities among other factors. And catch-up mechanisms assist in making the regional production functions more similar when technology (and skills) are transferred between the regions.

But once in a while structures are shifted and disparities are increasing. New technology is developed in a few regions and contributes to divergence. It happened in the late 19th century and is perhaps happening again?

References

Andersen AK (1999) Commuting and Shopping Areas. Paper presented at a Seminar on Regional and City Research, Svinkloev, Denmark, September 29-30, 1999

Andersen AK (1998) Decomposition of the Change in the Amount of Commuting in Denmark 1980-1995. AKF Forlaget, Copenhagen

Barro RJ, Sala-i-Martin X (1991) Economic Growth in a Cross Section of Countries. Quarterly Journal of Economics 106: 407-443

Barro RJ, Sala-i-Martin X (1992) Convergence. Journal of Political Economy 100: 223-251

Barro RJ, Sala-i-Martin X (1995) Economic Growth. McGraw-Hill, New York

Christensen JP (1975) Lønudviklingen inden for Dansk Håndværk og Industri 1870-1914 (Development in Earnings Within Danish Trade and Manufacturing Industries 1870-1914). Akademisk Forlag, Copenhagen

Danish Ministry of the Interior (1998), The Expert Commission. Markedskræfter og Politisk Styring (Market Forces and Political Government), Copenhagen

DORS (1996) Danish Council of Economic Advisers (ed), Dansk Økonomi (Danish Economy)

Dilling-Hansen M, Petersen KR, Smith V (1994) Growth and Convergence in Danish Regional Incomes. Scandinavian Economic History Review 17: 54-76

Dixit AK, Stiglitz JE (1977) Monopolistic Competition and Optimum Product Diversity. American Economic Review 67: 297-308

Fujita M, Krugman P, Venables A (1999) The Spatial Economy. The MIT Press, London

Groes N (2000) Strukturbrud i Kongeriet? (Structural Shifts?) Draft Memo, forthcoming. AKF Forlaget, Copenhagen

Groes N (1997) Inequalities and Mobility in the Danish Welfare State. In: Peschel K (ed) Regional Growth and Regional Policy Within the Framework of European Integration. Physica, Heidelberg, pp 142-175

Groes N (1997) Uligheder i Danmark (Inequalities in Denmark). AKF Forlaget, Copenhagen

Hansen AC (1991) Den Geografiske Omfordeling (The Geographic Redistri-bution). AKF Forlaget, Copenhagen

Hansen SA (1970) Early Industrialization in Denmark. University of Copenhagen, Institute of Economic History, Copenhagen

Hansen SA (1983) Økonomisk Vækst i Danmark, 1720-1914 og 1914-1983 (Economic Growth in Denmark, 1720-1914 and 1914-1983), 3rd edn. University of Copenhagen, Institute of Economic History, Akademisk Forlag, Copenhagen

Jensen TP, Maskell P, Arnberg S, Hansen MB, Ranis T (1997) Erhvervslokalisering og Vækst (Business Location and Growth). AKF Forlaget, Copenhagen

Kærgård N (1991) Økonomisk Vækst. En Økonometrisk Analyse af Danmark 1870-1981 (Economic Growth. An Econometric Analysis of Denmark 1870-1981). Studies from the University of Copenhagen, Economic Institute. No. 33, Copenhagen

Lucas RE Jr. (1988) On the Mechanics of Economic Development. Journal of Monetary Economics 22: 3-42

Manniche J (1999) Landdistrikter og Lokaludvikling på Bornholm. Udvik-lingsbetingelser og–Muligheder (Rural Districts and Local Development at Bornholm. Conditions and Possibilities). Paper presented at a Seminar on Regional and City Research in Svinkloev (Research Centre of Bornholm), Denmark, September 29-39, 1999

Molle W (1997) The Regional Economic Structure of the European Union: An Analysis of Long Term Developments. In: Peschel K (ed) Regional Growth and Regional Policy Within the Framework of European Integration. Physica, Heidelberg, pp 66-86

Pedersen PO (1981) De Lange Svingninger i Økonomien og Deres Betydning for den Regionale Udvikling (The long-run Fluctuations in the Economy and their Importance for the Regional Development). Sydjysk Universitetscenter, Esbjerg

Pedersen J (1930) Arbejdsløsheden i Danmark (Unemployment in Denmark). The Institute of History and Economics. Gyldendalske Boghandel. Nordisk Forlag, Copenhagen

Romer PM (1986) Increasing Returns and Long-Run Growth. Journal of Political Economy 94: 1002-1037

Sala-i-Martin X (1996) Regional Cohesion: Evidence and Theories of Regional Growth Convergence. European Economic Review 40: 1325-1352

Regional Economic Integration in the Baltic Rim: Towards a European Region after Ten Years of Transition?

Andreas P. Cornett

University of Southern Denmark

Sønderborg, Denmark

1. Introduction

A view back in history proves that the Baltic Sea region was one of the centers of trade in commerce in Europe. The Vikings and later the Hanseatic League, a loose confederation originally of north German cities, gradually developed into a trading system covering most of Northern Europe with its stronghold in the Baltic Sea area. The League reached its peak of influence in the 14th century with a maximum of nearly 100 cities as members, but lost importance gradually. By 1630, most of the towns had deserted the alliance, but the spirit of the Hanse is still alive today, mainly as a framework for twin-city agreements. The Baltic Rim continued to be a regional area of commerce with intensive links between the countries and to the European Hinterlands.

This situation changed fundamentally after the second world war, when the Iron Curtain divided the region into two different economic and political systems, the state-trade dominated East *European Council of Mutual Economic Assistance (CMEA)* and the market based Western Europe, with increasing global economic orientation. For almost three decades the peripheral position of the Baltic Rim was reinforced by the artificial division of the latter into the European Community based arrangements and the *EFTA,* the *European Free Trade Agreement.*

The first division lasted until 1995 when finally Sweden and Finland became EU members as well. In a commercial and trade perspective, the economic frontier was slightly removed through trade agreements, the development of economic links and global trends towards free trade and liberalization since the 1970s.

The significant change, opening up for regional cooperation and integration took place after the Fall of the Iron Curtain in 1989, and the regained independence of the three Baltic states, Estonia, Latvia and Lithuania 1991.

The purpose of this article is to give an assessment of the political, economic and spatial aspects of reintegration of the transition economies into the West European economic and political system in general, and of the significance of this process for the Baltic Rim region as one of the geographical regions in Europe (European Commission 1994) most directly effected by the dissolution of the former two-bloc system.

After a short theoretical introduction and a survey of economic and political indicators of integration, a brief overview of economic and political integration in the Baltic Rim leads to an analysis of economic links in the region, focusing on trade and FDI. The final Section reconsiders the issue whether the Baltic Rim constitutes a functional region or not, and will briefly address the question to what extent the Baltic Rim region can be compared with other geographical regions in Europe.

In a European context the Baltic Rim region is a peripheral part of Europe, located at the fringe of the economic and political center of Europe. Until the beginning of the 1990s, it suffered from both the political and the economic division of Europe. Neither one has been solved yet, but significant progress has been made with regard to political and economic change. Politically the principles of democracy have become the guiding principle in all countries, and they are all members of the OSCE *(Organization for Security and Cooperation in Europe)*, the former CSCE and the *Council of Europe*. Apart from Russia, the Baltic Rim countries are members of the EU, or have applied for membership, and are included in the EUs pre-accession strategies. Nevertheless, huge differences prevail with regard to income, labor-market and economic performance

Examining economic and demographic structure of the region two features are evident, the division into high and low income countries, coincidentally to the division between old market economies and transition economies. The second important characteristics is that three of the countries adjacent to the Baltic Sea are large countries, where only a minor part belongs to the geographical Baltic Rim region (The Baltic Institute 1994).

2. Theoretical Outline

Evaluating regional integration in a specific geographical area not bound together by formal agreement or institutional links is a difficult task. The selection of relevant indicators depends to a high degree on the concept of integration applied and the historic situation analyzed. The first years after the break-up of the iron curtain focus was very much on institutional and political transformation within the former central-planned economies and the change of economic orientation of the involved state-trade economies. One concept applied to the Baltic Rim region was trade blocs, or less formally, integration areas, i.e., "groups of countries which are more highly integrated through trade than others" (Peschel 1993, pp 25-26). The crucial issues involved in this kind of analysis are to obtain relevant and reliable data. The analysis of barriers to economic interaction in general and towards regional integration in particular has to deal with:

"- distance bridging costs such as transport- and communication costs
- linguistic and cultural dissimilarities
- differences in the scope of social and political life
- political influences, deliberately or unintentionally
resulting in the separation of countries" (Peschel 1993, p 26).

Usually, there is a strong correlation between geographic adjacency and strong economic ties. In economic theory this has not always been a part of mainstream economic thinking and analysis (Tichy 1998). Concerning formal economic co-operation in a regional framework like free trade areas, customs unions or more far reaching arrangements, the spatial dimension has always – at least implicitly – been an important aspect (Robson 1987, Balassa 1963/73, WTO 1995). Actually, co-operative frameworks covering non contiguous areas are seldom, and the economic success of scattered trade arrangements like the EFTA has been rather limited. In the period of discriminative trade regimes the potentials of trade creation were also rather limited in Europe (Cornett ed. 1996). In many respects, regional integration is an ambivalent notion, varying from a very general concept that describes cooperation between nations or regions, to very specific social theories of human or organizational behavior.

The two approaches are distinct and are important roots of modern regional integration[1]. Economic theories of integration have their roots particularly in the field of international economics and trade theory (Balassa 1963/73, Robson 1987, Baldwin 1995), the conceptual anchors of the political theories of integration have to be found in various branches of political science (Pentland 1973, Panild 1989, Chryssochoou 1997). The results of these processes in specific regions have to be seen in a spatial context.

2.1 Spatial Integration

Spatial integration is not a commonly used phrase, but rather a kind of summarizing description of a comprehensive notion dealing with an overall assessment of regional changes. Spatial integration includes features like:

- the development of specific geographically defined systems of production such as industrial district, cluster of industries or systems of innovation,
- a system of urban networks defined according to specific functional links,

[1] For further elaboration of the concepts see Cornett (1999a,b).

- the availability of a relevant regional infrastructure linking the analyzed area together,
- last but not least, the intensity of intra regional flows relative to the outside flows can be considered to be the "conditio sine non quo" whether we talk about a spatial integrated area or not.

In particular, the last condition is restrictive. In this notion, the concept of spatial integration has to be understood as the most far reaching concept of integration. In this analysis, the spatial concept is not merely a consequence of the physical environment, but also the result of economic and political integration.

In a continental or regional perspective, we have strong evidence that political and economic integration is "powered" by spatial proximity and adjacency, but at the same time political and economic integration reinforce the other aspect of spatial integration, accessibility.

In a European context, political and economic integration have been twins–but not necessarily Siamese twins. In some periods, economic integration took the lead, in other the political initiative became predominant. Overall neither one can be understood without the other. Together they are important determinants for spatial integration in Europe as a whole and in the Baltic Rim, marked by the division of Europe for almost a half century.

Figure 1: A revised concept of integration

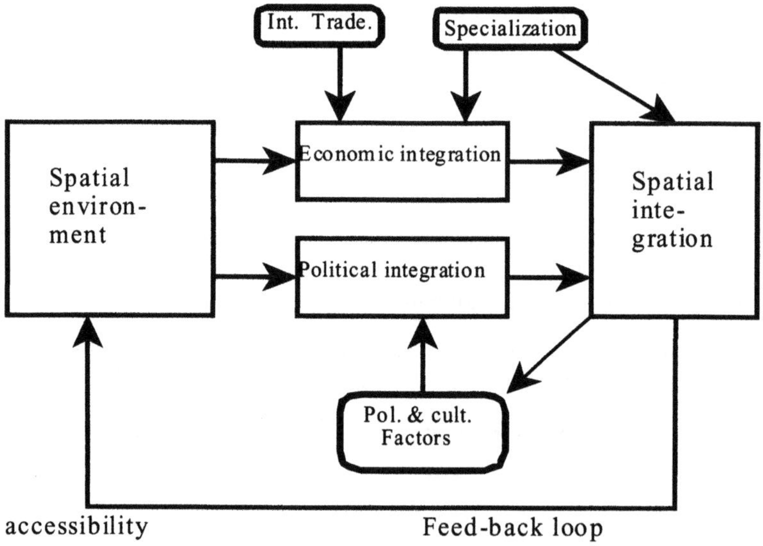

Figure 1 provides a brief summary of this approach focusing on the main factors leading towards spatial integration and the impact of this process on the future development through a feed-back mechanism reinforcing accessibility. The final result could be a kind of "network based" (spatial) theory of integration (Gidlund 1990). Before turning to an investigation of the Baltic Rim region, a closer look at the two pivotal concepts in *Figure 1* seems necessary.

2.2 Economic Integration

The economic concepts of regional integration were originally introduced by Viner (1950) in his analysis of Customs Unions, but the concepts have been expanded in scope to cover most aspects of regional economic cooperation. Traditionally, regional economic integration takes place between relatively similar countries, similar as to economic development or political traditions and institutional frameworks. Most Regional Economic Associations (REA) are dominated by relatively similar countries, although large internal regional differences are not unusual. The process of economic integration between former state trade countries and the established western market economies is a different task. To some extent, the internal aspects of the exercise can be compared with attempts to implement integration frameworks between the restructuring economies in less developed countries. Although there have been many attempts to form regional economic associations between third world countries, their success has been rather limited[2].

The external perspective is simultaneously to (re-)establish links to the industrialized market economies without causing too much damage to national competitiveness, and to avoid new regional disparities. Especially the latter seems relevant for the emerging market economies in Eastern and Central Europe, although they to some extent are similar to frameworks of cooperation used during the existence of the CMEA. A comparison of economic integration in various types of economic systems by Brada, Mendez (1985) showed that the ability to promote inter-member trade largely depended on the environmental factor inter-member distance. Regarding the effectiveness of integration policy, the study showed a relatively poor record for the highly institutionalized EU. The latter can partly be explained by the period of investigation, the early seventies when most trade effects from the implementation of the Customs Union were achieved. Regarding their comparison of the CMEA with the western approaches the most interesting conclusion is:

---

[2] According to Robson (1987), these attempts are usually based on the *classical approach of general trade liberalization* resulting in the formation of Free Trade Areas or Customs Unions, *complementary agreements* (i.e., trade liberalization for certain existing industries) or *joint measures to regulate investment* in new industries aiming to exploit scale economies based on the total regional market.

"Thus, the combined effect of central planning and of integration policy in CMEA causes that integration grouping to under fulfill its potential by about the same amount as the EEC. Consequently, it does not seem that CMEA integration policies or the system of central planning appear to be significant greater barriers to promoting inter-member trade than do politics adopted among integrating market economies" (Brada, Méndez 1985, p 555).

The crucial issues regarding these roads to economic integration are how to ensure that they conform with especially GATT/WTO rules on nondiscrimination and equal treatment, and to avoid probable adverse impacts on Eastern and Central Europe's relations to the European Union. Association agreements between the East and the EU have already proved the importance of these concerns as far as salient sectors of the EU are involved (European Economy 1994). Also, in Western Europe the process of consolidation of the regional economic system is still in flow, and unambiguous solutions have not been found in Western Europe either. Since 1993, the EEA has basically provided the EFTA countries the participation in the Single European Market on equal terms.

Regarding the reintegration of the former state trade economies into the western dominated market economic system, the nature of the issue of complementarity and competitiveness is more complex than it is when dealing with free trade agreements between countries on different levels of development. The theory of economic integration stresses among other things that competitive countries are more likely to receive benefits from regional trade agreements than complementary economies. The analysis of this topic in the European transition process requires a broader approach including also political aspects of integration.

2.3 Political Integration

With regard to the political theories of integration, four approaches are often considered to be the classical schools in the field. They are often labeled as: the federalism, the transaction or pluralistic approach, and the functionalism and the neofunctionalism. In the 1970s, new variants have been added, namely the so-called intergovernmentalism and transgovernmentalism, mainly taking into account the obvious changes real political integration has taken in the period (Chryssochoou 1997, Panild 1989). The schools indicate that no common consensus with regard to a definition of integration exists. Some focus on the process of forming a regional body, others emphasize the stage of integration. In a review of the state of the art of political integration theory after the first "honey-moon" of political integration and the first major draw-backs in real world integration as well as theory-building, Pentland (1973) made the attempt to formulate what he called a common denominator of political integration:

"All it seems possible to say is that international political integration is a process whereby a group of people, organized initially in two or more independent nation-states, come to constitute a political whole which can in some sense be described as a community" (Pentland 1973, p 21).

In particular, the neofunctionalistic approach to regional integration, often addressed as the "theory of Western European integration", was modified and extended as the original versions failed the empirical proof, partly due to real world developments, and partly because of conceptual weaknesses and shortcomings. With regard to the importance of integrative processes for regional development this is probably the most relevant school for the topic discussed in this article.

3. Policy Implications

Since the fall of the Iron Curtain a process of reintegration and redirection in international relations has been the most prominent feature of European economic and political development. After a tentative start, economic as well as political links have intensified. After an almost abrupt change in trade and cooperation patterns in the aftermath of 1989/90, a more gradual process of reintegration took place (Cornett 1999b).

With regard to political integration, relations to NATO and the EU are the most prominent areas of action, but more obvious means of co-operation have also been attempted, i.e., *CEFTA, the Central and East European Free Trade Agreement* or the Baltic Council. Economic and political steps were part of a complementary process towards economic and political reintegration (Cornett, Iversen 1997).

Politically, this two tier strategy consists of both economic and political agreements. The latter can be divided into two groups: (1) security policy (OSCE and NATO) and (2) economic issues, namely the relations towards the EU and the major global economic organizations, i.e., WTO, IMF and the World Bank.

In spite of the fact that economic issues and policy alignments are not settled in all details, the picture is more clear, at least with respect to the regime for trade and other forms of economic exchange. With few exceptions, mainly in the field of textile, iron and steel and agriculture the EU's trade regime towards Eastern and Central Europe has been liberalized in all substantial aspects facilitating the participation in the European Market economic system. This means that we only have few remaining obstacles to trade in the Baltic Rim region, since the above mentioned restriction are in a fading out process or will become more or less obsolete if the EU reform of the Common Agricultural Policy is successful. For merchandise trade, the region (with the exemption of Russia) almost constitutes a homogenous trade area.

Intensified trade relations are usually followed by closer economic ties based on a higher level of commitment, often manifested through foreign direct investment

(FDI) and formal integration in the international production system[3]. In an integrated area – or in a region moving towards integration – FDI can be seen as a second step towards the formation of a (spatial) integrated system of production. The first step is international trade, the third step is a change in the nature of international trade from inter to intra-industry trade.

4. Reintegration and Integration in the Baltic Rim Region in an Economic Perspective

In traditional theory of economic integration, a main distinction goes between trade effects of regional economic associations, namely trade-creation and trade diversion effects, and effects of further integration towards the formation of a common market, including the elimination of all visible and hidden impediments to trade and economic exchange. The purpose of this Section is to provide a brief overview of the level of integration of the regional economic system in the Baltic Rim and to give a first assessment with regard to the intensity of intra-regional links compared to extra-regional interaction.

An assessment of the nature of a system of production, here defined as the relations between individual firms, vertically integrated companies, R&D institutions and the whole range of public policy is not the objective for this contribution. Nevertheless, a tentative evaluation of changes in the system is possible through the analysis of trade and foreign direct investment flows within the region and from the region to the outside. Three types of indicators illuminating the relative importance and the intensity of intra-regional flows are presented:

- gross trade,
- intra-industry trade,
- foreign direct investment.

Trade flows in the Baltic Rim have suffered from the artificial economic borders between the economies in the area. This does not mean that the region historically – at least not for the last hundred years – has constituted a functional, internal coherent region. In the 1970s and 1980s, the region belonged to three different economic associations, the market based EU and EFTA and the CMEA based on non-market principles. The economic border between the two former Regional Economic Associations (REA's) did not have major importance on trade flows for most groups of commodities. The latter was much more important, and it is mainly with regard to trade between the countries belonging to the former "East Block"

[3] A good example of the latter is the international specialization taking place in the textile sector. For a Danish example see Illeris (1998).

and the Scandinavian countries[4] and Germany the redirection of trade in the area took place (Cornett, Iversen 1993).

Table 1 shows that only for the smaller economies the Baltic Rim region has a dominant position with regard to foreign trade. Taking the nature and the size of the German economy into account the importance of the Baltic Rim as a geographical region diminishes further. In the long run the Baltic states will probably move towards a trade pattern more similar to the Nordic countries, and find their historical place in the regional trading system (Laaser, Schrader 1992).

Table 1: Share of intra regional trade as percentage of total trade of Baltic Rim countries since 1992

	1992	1993	1994	1995	1996	1997
Denmark	48.7	44.3	45.4	41.5	42.5	43.7
Estonia	92.0	66.8	74.1	68.0	68.8	69.8
Finland	41.7	37.5	39.4	36.5	35.2	38.0
Germany	8.6	8.8	9.1	9.4	9.3	10.3
Latvia	61.8	46.1	48.0	60.3	48.8	49.6
Lithuania	57.8	45.5	50.1	48.8	46.1	48.9
Norway	35.9	32.4	37.0	37.1	36.9	36.4
Poland	47.4	47.1	50.2	51.6	48.2	47.9
Russia	18.9	24.8	23.5	20.9	21.5	22.7
Sweden	35.5	32.6	33.1	32.7	32.2	32.9
Baltic Rim	17.9	18.0	19.0	18.9	18.9	20.1

Figures based on exports to Baltic Rim countries as percentage of total exports. All figures are based on reported imports from receiving countries. Danish exports to Sweden 1992-1994 are based on Danish exports. For 1992 and 1993 some figures are missing for former state trade countries. Source: IMF 1998.

A country by country analysis proves the dominant position of Germany in the regional trading system. Germany counts for more than 30 % of both internal imports and exports. Generally speaking, shares in import and export does not vary that much except for the major exemption of Russia (larger import share), and Poland (export share) among the bigger, and Estonia and Lithuania among the smaller economies (Cornett 1999b).

The importance of proximity for trade relations has often been proved. As quoted in the introduction other than economic factors are significant regarding the creation of a system of "integration areas" or, perhaps more ambitious, a regional sy-

[4] In many respects, Finland is a special case due to the close economic links to the Soviet Union prior to the transition process.

stem of production. Networks theory and network research is of major importance in the analysis of spatial aspects of regional integration but linking the network perspective to the political and in particular the economic aspects of integration is always a difficult task. Social and political attitudes are usually related to political actors and social groups, not necessarily to a spatial system of links and flows. The same goes for economic flows. These are mainly reported as flow or stock-data for countries or groups of countries as a whole, and can only rarely be related to specific locations.

In economic analysis including the spatial dimension, the problem of disperse location of economic activity is often solved in a rather pragmatic way, using the national capital as location of all external trade exchange. To small countries this does not matter that much. For larger countries, and in particular when the models are applied on a regional level, the issue can become a considerable problem.

Most countries analysed in this article have stronger external than internal links with regard to te Baltic Rim region. *Figure 2* illuminates the fact that for most of the Baltic Rim states external ties are stronger than intra regional flows. The only exception to this pattern are Estonia with regard to trade and received FDI and Lithuania, Latvia and Denmark concerning received FDI in 1997.

Figure 2: Trade and FDI of the Baltic Rim countries according to origin 1997, Baltic Rim share as percentage of total imports and FDI received

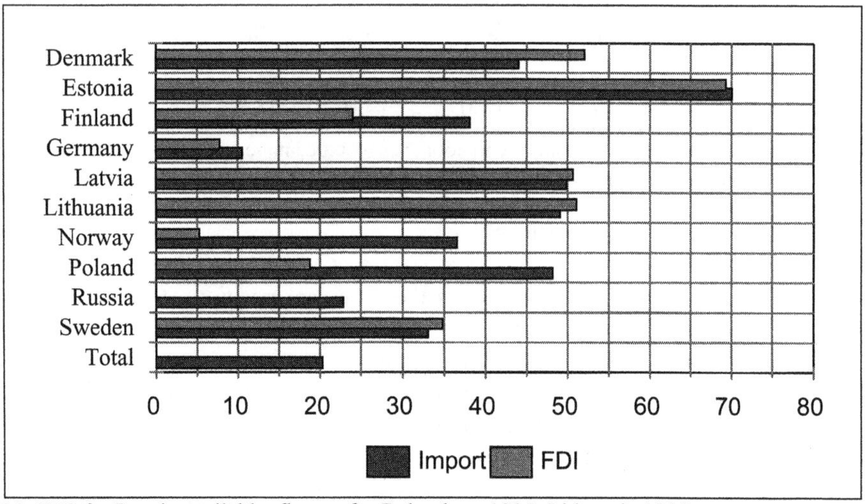

No FDI for Russia available, figures for Poland are 1995, Lithuania 1996.
Source: IMF (1998) and Table 2.

Due to the summarizing nature of the pattern reported in *Figure 2*, one must stress that the sketched picture has to be interpreted carefully, because Germany, Russia and Poland, in particular, are all part of the analyzed region with only a minor part of their economy.

The investigation in the remaining part of this Section will concentrate on economic indicators of regional integration and development. One implication of this approach is that we are not operating within the context of a real network of nodes and links in a traditional sense (Törnqvist 1990). The economic units are the nodes (countries) and the links are trade and capital/investment relations, measured by imports and exports and foreign direct investment (FDI).

Foreign direct investment is used as an indicator of a more formalized international integration of the economic systems. *Table 2* provides an overview of FDI patterns within the region. Figures must be used very carefully due to lack of data and the methodological problems involved in the process of data collection and the periodization of the flows. Nevertheless, the Baltic Rim economies' importance for FDI in the three Baltic states is evident. This can be considered to be at least a slight indication of increased participation in the regional system of divisions of production.

Table 2: Share of intra-regional FDI as percentage of total FDI Baltic Rim countries (receiving countries) since 1992

	1992	1993	1994	1995	1996	1997
Denmark	119.0	60.6	37.7	30.2	-2000.0	51.9
Estonia	-	-	59.0	63.5	61.6	69.0
Finland	44.0	42.9	70.6	10.1	14.9	23.8
Germany	-	1.6	-1.4	2.1	2.2	7.5
Latvia	28.9	40.9	50.1	60.8	56.0	50.4
Lithuania	-	-	-	35.8	50.8	-
Norway	-	-	6.6	52.7	15.2	5.1
Poland	-	20.1	25.7	18.6	-	-
Russia	-	-	-	-	-	-
Sweden	-	28.8	4.5	14.9	61.2	34.7

Figures for Western European countries include only FDI from western countries. Sweden includes some figures for Russia, Finland includes Russia but exclusive reinvested earnings. All figures reported in national currencies and are based on net-flow, which can cause major disturbances in some years. Figures for Denmark in 1996 are effected by heavy net outflow to the Netherlands in this particular year. German figures for 1994 are effected by huge net outflows to Denmark and Sweden. German figures do not include the Baltic states. Source: Hedegaard, Lindstrøm (1999), Deutsche Bundesbank (1993–1999).

Also with regard to FDI, the strong position of the German economy and in particular the non Baltic Rim part has to be taken into account. Based on GDP, the Baltic Rim part of Germany counts only for 8.3 % of the German GDP in 1996[5].

[5] Another figure can illuminate the point. Export as percentage of total turnover in the German manufacturing sector was 29.7 % in 1996. Looking at the Baltic Rim part of Germany, the figures were 11.9 % for Hamburg, 26.0 % for Schleswig-Holstein and 10.6 % for Mecklenburg-West Pommerania (IdDW 1997, Table 4).

The analysis of trade and FDI has proved that the transition economies of the Baltic Rim have been integrated into the regional economic system, simultaneously with disintegration of the old state-trade links. This is only the first step in a long catch-up process, indicated by the huge intra-regional difference in GDP per capita within the region. The last step in the three-tier concept of this article is a brief examination of intra-industry trade in the region.

Table 3: Intra-industry trade of Baltic Rim OECD members 1988 -1996

	1988	1989	1990	1991	1992	1993	1994	1995	1996
DK: World	68	68	69	70	69	70	69	70	72
DK:Baltic Rim	67	70	71	71	70	70	69	70	72
DK:Baltic East	14	21	26	28	26	31	27	28	31
D: World	68	68	72	75	75	73	74	74	73
D: Baltic Rim	49	50	52	57	53	49	49	49	48
D: Baltic East	27	29	33	38	30	27	28	31	31
FIN: World	52	54	57	57	61	59	61	62	61
FIN: Baltic Rim	59	59	61	67	69	65	65	68	70
FIN: Baltic East	15	17	18	58	29	21	26	28	30
S: World	69	70	69	68	68	67	69	69	68
S: Baltic Rim	71	70	71	73	73	75	75	73	74
S: Baltic East	26	38	41	44	28	35	33	36	39
N: World	41	40	40	40	37	38	38	38	37
N: Baltic Rim	46	51	46	46	44	44	46	46	47
N: Baltic East	37	37	32	33	34	33	35	36	35
PL: World	...	...	...	...	54	49	50	53	52
PL: Baltic Rim	...	...	...	...	45	42	43	45	46
PL: Baltic East	...	...	...	...	20	10	11	13	13

Data according to Harmonized System Rev.1 1988-1997, Grubel Lloyd index estimated on 2 digit level 100 (100 commodities). Source: OECD, ITCS 1998.

Table 3 provides a brief overview of the level of intra-industry trade of the six OECD member countries in the region. Apart from Germany, the level of intra-industry trade for the old market economies in the Baltic Rim area as a whole is higher than for their total trade. With regard to east-west trade intra-trade is significantly lower, but generally increasing during the period reported. The latter can be seen as an indicator of increasing integration of the transition economies into the regional system of production and specialization. An examination of non-agricultural trade confirms the pattern reported in *Table 3*, generally with slightly higher scores on the Grubel Lloyd index[6].

---

[6] For details see Cornett (2000). For a technical discussion of the Grubel-Lloyd index see Lüthje (1996).

5. Final Remarks

The concept of European regions became popular in the aftermath of the Maastricht Treaty (TEU), and today it is an integrated part of the European political landscape (Commission 1994). In this system, the Baltic Rim area constitutes a distinct region bridging the old gap between East and West and the former Western European division of the Nordic countries with regard to economic and political affiliation.

The analysis of economic flows has proved that the region develops towards a comprehensive economic area. The three Baltic states tend to move towards a trade pattern similar to Nordic countries, despite of the huge economic differences prevailing. The low level of intra-industry trade between the old market economies and the former state trade countries indicates that the road towards an integrated functional system of production is still long and full of obstacles. Compared to regions in Western Europe the Baltic Rim region is still far away from forming a functional region. The experience of Nordic Cooperation and the economic orientation of most Nordic countries towards Central Europe and the world as a whole may indicate that the Baltic Rim as well as the Nordic group of countries has to be seen as a subsystem embedded in a broader European economic system rather than as a system of it's own.

Nevertheless, the question put in the title of this contribution: *Regional Economic Integration in the Baltic Rim: Towards a European Region after 10 Years of Transition?* has to be answered affirmative.

References

Balassa B (1963/1973) The Theory of Economic Integration. Unwin University Books, London

Baldwin RE (1995) Regional Economic Integration. In: Grossmann G, Rogoff K (eds) Handbook of International Economics, Vol III. Elsevier Science B.V., pp 1597-1644

The Baltic Institute (1994) Vision and Strategies Around the Baltic Sea 2010. The Baltic Institute, Karlskrona

Brada JC, Méndez JA (1985) Economic Integration Among Developed, Developing and Centrally Planned Economies: A Comparative Analysis. The Review of Economics and Statistics 67: 549-556

Chryssochoou DN (1997) New Challenges to the Study of European Integration: Implications for Theory Building. Journal of Common Market Studies 35: 521-542

Cornett AP (2000) (forthcoming) Economic Links in the Baltic Rim. Working Paper. USUN-project, Sonderborg

Cornett AP (1999a) The Problem of Transition and Reintegration of East and Central Europe – Conceptual Remarks and Empirical Problems. In: Fischer MM, Nijkamp P (eds) Spatial Dynamics of European Integration Regional and Policy Issues at the Turn of the Century. Springer, Berlin, Heidelberg, New York, pp 255-279

Cornett AP (1999b) Regional Integration and Regional Development? Concepts and Empirical Relevance. Paper presented at 38th Congress of the European Regional Science Association, Dublin, August 1999 (CD-rom procedings)

Cornett AP (ed) (1996) Økonomiernes Internationalisering – Fra Regional til Global Orientering (red). The Internationalization of Economies – From Regional to Global Orientation. DJØF-Publishers, Copenhagen

Cornett AP, Iversen SP (1993) Commercial Relations in the Baltic Rim Region in an Integration/Network Perspective. In: Lundqvist L, Persson LO (eds), Visions and Strategies in European Integration. A North European Perspective. Springer, Berlin, Heidelberg, New York, pp 107-130

Cornett AP, Iversen SP (1997) The Baltic Rim in the European Trade System. In: Owsinski JW, Stepniak A (eds), The Nordic-Baltic Europe: Integration Risks, Barriers & Opportunities. The Interfaces Institute, Warsaw-Sopot, pp 131-164

Deutsche Bundesbank (1993–1999) Statistische Beihefte zu den Monatsberichten der Deutschen Bundesbank, Zahlungsbilanzstatistik, Frankfurt

European Commission (1994) Europe 2000+ Cooperation for Territorial Development. Luxembourg

European Economy (1994) The Economic Interpenetration Between the European Union and Eastern Europe. Reports and Studies No 6. Luxembourg

Fischer MM, Nijkamp P (eds) (1999) Spatial Dynamics of European Integration Regional and Policy Issues at the Turn of the Century. Springer, Berlin, Heidelberg, New York

Gidlund J (1990) Den Oförklarede Integrationen – Statsventenskapen inför Europas Omvandling. In: Karlqvist A (ed), Nätverk Teorier och Begrepp i Samällsvetenskaben. Gidlunds Bokförlag, Värnamo, pp 119-151

Hedegaard L, Lindström B (eds) (1999), The NEBI Yearbook 1999 – North European and Baltic Sea Integration. Springer, Berlin, Heidelberg, New York

IdDW Institut der Deutschen Wirtschaft (1997) Zahlen zur wirtschaftlichen Entwicklung der Bundesrepublik Deutschland 1997. Köln

Illeris S (1998) Outsourcing of Textile and Clothing Industry from Denmark to Baltic Transition Countries. Paper prepared for the 5th Nordic-Baltic Conference in Regional Science, Pärnu (Estonia), October 1-4, 1998 (Published in CD-proceedings). Pärnu

IMF International Monetary Fund (1998) Direction of Trade Statistics Yearbook. Washington D.C.

Karlqvist A (1990) Nätverk Teorier och Begrepp i Samällsvetenskaben. Gidlunds Bokförlag, Värnamo

Laaser CF, Schrader K (1992) Zur Reintegration der Baltischen Staaten in die Weltwirtschaft. Die Weltwirtschaft 92: 189-211

Lundqvist L, Persson LO (eds) (1993) Visions and Strategies in European Integration. A North European Perspective. Springer, Berlin, Heidelberg, New York

Lüthje T (1996) Den Danske Intra-Industrielle Handel. In: Cornett AP (ed), Økonomiernes Internationalisering – fra Regional til Global Orientering. The Internationalization of Economies – from Regional to Global Orientation. DJØF-Publishers, Copenhagen pp 127-153

OECD, ITCS (1998) International Trade by Commodities Statistics Edition 1998. Paris

Owsinski JW, Stepniak A (eds) (1997) The Nordic-Baltic Europe: Integration Risks, Barriers & Opportunities. Warsaw-Sopot

Panild TN (1989) Det Indre Marked og Integrationsteori. Politica (Aarhus) 21: 441-455

Pentland C (1973) International Theory and European Integration. Faber&Faber, London

Peschel K (1993) Perspectives of Regional Economic Development around the Baltic. In: Lundqvist L, Persson LO (eds), Visions and Strategies in European Integration. A North European Perspective. Springer, Berlin, Heidelberg, New York, pp 19-31

Robson P (1987) The Economics of International Integration. Allan & Unwin, London

Tichy G (1998) Geography Lost and Found in Economics (?) Key note presentation at 38th European Congress 1998, August 28-September 1, 1998, Vienna. CD-Rom proceedings, Vienna

Törnqvist G (1990) Det Upplösta Rummet – Begrepp och Teoretiska Ansatser inom Geografin. In: Karlqvist A (ed) Nätverk Teorier och Begrepp i Samällsvetenskaben. Gidlunds Bokförlag, Värnamo, pp 119-151

Viner J (1950) The Customs Union Issue. New York, London

World Trade Organization (1995) Regionalism and the World Trading System. Geneva

From Vision to Action: Spatial Development in Europe and Around the Baltic Sea

Hans-Peter Gatzweiler, Wilfried Görmar

Bundesamt für Bauwesen und Raumordnung (BBR)

Federal Office for Building and Regional Planning

Bonn, Germany

1. European Integration Process Challenges Spatial Planning

Salient features of contemporary spatial planning are a growing transnational and a more action- and project-oriented approach. The first tendency is caused by European integration. This integration, strengthened through the Economic and Monetary Union leads to more intensive relationships and inter-dependencies between European cities and regions. Internal borders of the European Union are increasingly losing their separating character. At the interest of a common European prosperity, more attention has to be paid to impacts of regional development projects which go beyond national borders: Motorways, ports, power stations, factory outlet and holiday centres etc. Transnational spatial impacts and conflicts of development projects represent a challenge for spatial planning which stops very often at national borders. However, in order to strengthen complementary effects and spatial cohesion on the EU territory, spatial planning efforts of different member states should be co-ordinated and projects should be orientated to common objectives for spatial development.

The preparation and implementation of the ESDP goes in that direction. It promotes a common understanding on development problems, potentials and possible solutions on EU territory. The ESDP defines common objectives and policy options for a sustainable development of the EU territory and serves as a framework for sectoral policy measures (ESDP 1999). This idea is now being further developed for the wider European territory.[1] Similar concepts have been established for smaller transnational action areas and larger European regions. For the Baltic Sea region, the elaboration of "Visions and Strategies around the Baltic Sea – VASAB 2010" represents the respective activity (VASAB 2010, 1994).

---

[1] European Conference of Ministers responsible for Regional Planning, Guiding Principles for Sustainable Spatial Development of the European Continent. Draft September 1999.

Another challenge is however, to actively support the implementation of visions and policy options through concrete actions and projects. A more project-oriented approach is already very common on regional and national level. It does there not replace but accompany the often more restrictive traditional instruments of spatial planning – land use and regional plans and programmes, regional impact assessment procedures. Beside other new features like moderating of decision-making, co-ordinating through informing, participatory planning, also project-orientation forms a new innovative element of spatial planning. On transnational level, this means to promote pilot actions and projects in order to help realising objectives for spatial development.

2. Visions for Spatial Development of the EU Territory and of the Baltic Sea Region

The preparation and implementation of the (ESDP) has considerably influenced the working out of similar concepts and their application on lower regional levels, among them transnational co-operation areas like the Baltic Sea region and vice versa (see *Figure 1*).

The way to transnational co-operation was paved by the EU-member states together with the European Commission with documents like "Europe 2000" (European Commission 1991), "Europe 2000+" (European Commission 1995) and "Principles for a European Spatial Development Policy" (BMBAU 1995: the "Leipzig Paper"). The latter explicitly stressed the necessity for transnational co-operation in larger territories based on common visions, strategies and development concepts. The "Leipzig Paper" was further developed to form the ESDP.

The ESDP evaluates the cultural variety, concentrated in the relatively small EU territory as one of the most important development factors. At the same time, it analyses serious economic imbalances which hamper a regionally balanced sustainable development. Although differences in economic power between "prosperous" and "poor" regions are declining on EU level there are even growing disparities within most of the member states. Economic power concentrates in a core area between the cities London, Paris, Milan, Munich and Hamburg. Despite all efforts of national and European regional and structural policy, it was not possible in many regions, to transform economic power into adequate quality of life and job creation. At the same time, growing transport volumes, land consumption through settlements, insufficient management of water resources etc. cause massive pressure on nature. The ESDP however, analyses considerable development potential in larger cities and regions outside the core areas which can be better used for overall European development.

Based on these analyses, *the ESDP develops policy aims and options* in particular on how

- to achieve a polycentric and balanced settlement structure,
- to reach equal access to infrastructure and knowledge, and

- to wisely manage the natural and cultural heritage.

An application programme forms an integral part of the ESDP, setting out main activities to be taken on the levels of the Community and of the member states as well as through transnational, cross-border and interregional co-operation. In particular, the new Community Initiative INTERREG II C on transnational co-operation for spatial development was intended to support ESDP implementation. Consequently, the formation of large transnational co-operation areas was promoted, among them transnational co-operation around the Baltic Sea.

Figure 1: Spatial development in Europe and in the Baltic Sea region

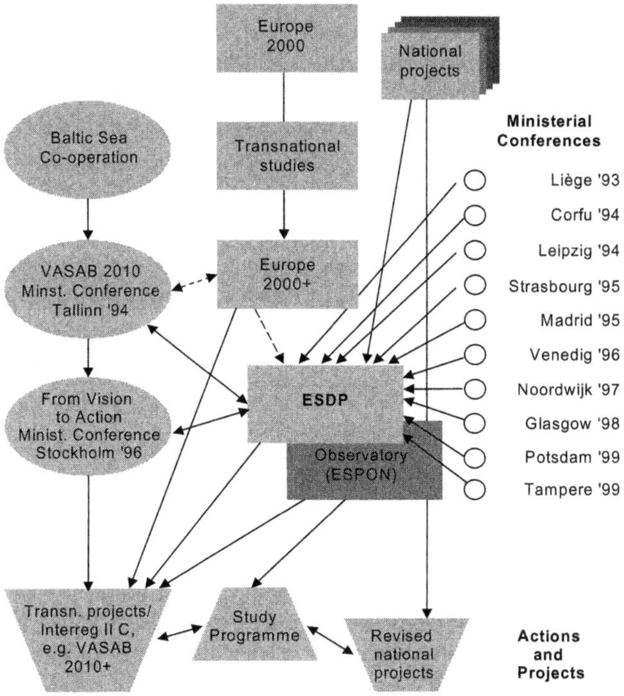

In a parallel process to ESDP preparation, similar concepts have been prepared for the Baltic Sea region. Thus, the basic document for further spatial development in the Baltic Sea region (Vision and Strategies around the Baltic Sea 2010 – Towards a Framework for Spatial Development in the Baltic Sea Region) was adopted in 1994. It was worked out through spatial planning experts of eleven countries, organised in the Committee on Spatial Development of the Baltic Sea Region (CSD/BSR). Thus, Belarus, Denmark, Estonia, Finland, Germany, Latvia, Lithuania, Norway, Poland, Russia and Sweden participated in the preparation process. Later on the label and the logo VASAB 2010 became somewhat a trade mark and contributed to the emergence of regional identity in that area. The close inter-relations between ESDP and VASAB were guaranteed also by persons taking part in both processes.

On the other hand, differences between the functions of the two documents have to be considered: the ESDP was intended to provide a guiding framework for structural and sectoral policies of the EU. The VASAB-document had a different background. While the ESDP supported the deepening of existing co-operation, VASAB had to overcome separation. It was intended to facilitate the process of growing together between the Baltic Sea states, to stress the sense of community within this region and to support the transition process in Central and Eastern European countries (Görmar 1997). Several analyses revealed a potential for more intensive economic co-operation between the Baltic Sea states.[2] To a large extent however , the Baltic Sea represents also a barrier for co-operation. Compared to the ESDP, the VASAB documents pay therefore more attention to sea and air transport and forms of combined transport in order to diminish obstacles. They also deal more intensively with coastal zones and islands and with specific structures of non-EU states, in particular Central and Eastern European states. In addition, tourism as a regional development factor, has got a higher priority.

VASAB evaluates in particular deficits in the urban system and enormous regional disparities in settlement structures. It also analyses imbalances in the transport system and missing links. On the other hand, potentials of the rich natural and cultural heritage, of high education level and of experienced and qualified labour force are stated. The very different tradition, structures and experience of spatial planning could serve as modules for improved planning systems.

Based on these analyses, VASAB addresses four main issues:

- promoting competitive networks of cities, urban-rural partnerships and balanced settlement structures;
- supporting effective communication links and environmentally friendly energy solutions;
- making use of potentials of border areas, coastal zones, islands and other specific areas and promoting sustainable development;
- improving efficiency and transnational co-operation of spatial planning.

For the Baltic Sea region, the VASAB activities related to these issues comprise also fields of implementation of the ESDP. In that context, the Baltic Sea region was a forerunner in elaborating common visions and strategies as well as defining common projects and actions in order to help realising the visions. The move from visions to concrete measures and actions was already accentuated in the basic document of 1994. It was further underlined with the "Stockholm Declaration on Sustainable Spatial Development Policy for the Baltic Sea Region" and the adoption of the document "From Vision to Action" at the Fourth Conference of Minis-

[2] Peschel (1993), Peschel (1998), Toczyski et al. (1997), Orlowski (1997).

ters responsible for Spatial Planning in 1996 (VASAB 2010, 1996). The participating countries agreed on the following project fields:

- setting up a programme on sustainable settlement and urban networks development ("pearls");
- combining the promotion of a European transport network with sustainable regional development concerning specific development corridors ("strings");
- establishing a set of pilot projects to manage sustainable development of specific areas ("patches"), i.e., cross-border areas, islands, lakelands, cultural landscapes, rural and forest areas, coastal zones, nature protection areas;
- creating a network of marinas, taking account of criteria of regional and environmental impact;
- elaborating a maritime transport programme with port hinterland connections and focusing on multimodal transport centres;
- building up a monitoring system of spatial development for the BSR;
- organising regional conferences for the presentation of key projects and a permanent project management for the implementation of VASAB 2010.

Representatives of all participating countries were fully aware that it was necessary to supplement the preparation process of a spatial vision through a similar process of preparing and implementing concrete actions and projects. This process started in the framework of VASAB, using national funds or through bilateral and multi-country projects. However, not at least missing instruments hampered the process of implementation. Also in that respect, the new Community Initiative INTERREG II C concerning transnational co-operation on spatial planning was seen as a means to overcome certain weaknesses of the VASAB process in order to implement spatial development projects.

3. From Vision to Transnational Action – the Role of the New Community Initiative INTERREG II C

On the European scale, seven larger INTERREG II C co-operation areas – among them BSR – have been identified in order to carry out common spatial development projects (see *Figure 2*).

For project management, Operational Programmes (OP) have been worked out on each area. The existence of analyses, of common visions and of organisational structures, provided through VASAB, were important advantages for elaborating a common BSR Operational Programme for INTERREG II C. Other inputs were given in particular from analytical work of the Nordic countries. In general, spatial planners of the respective ministries together with experts of Ministries responsible for the Structural Funds and external experts took part in the direct preparation of the OP but a broader "Baltic audience" was consulted on the respective drafts.

Figure 2: Interreg II C transnational co-operation programmes

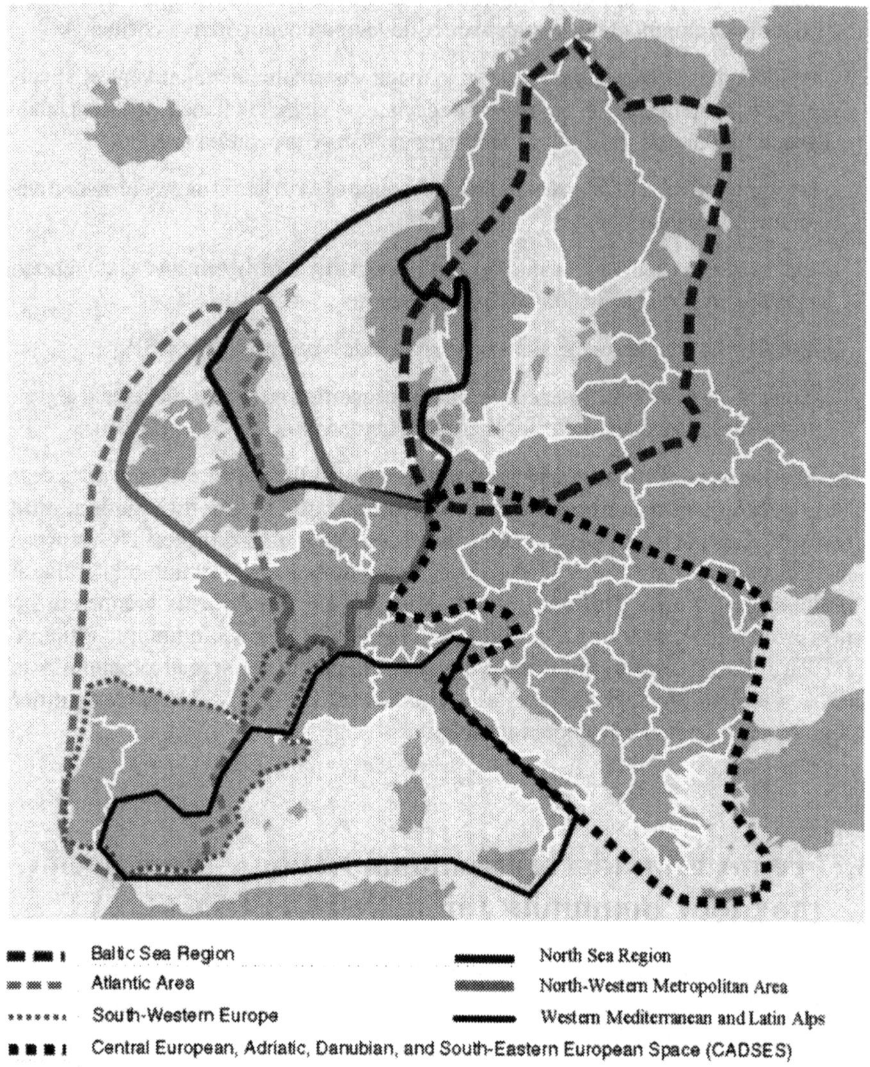

Already the preparation of the OP was therefore an intensive co-operation process. Thanks to the VASAB structures, not only EU members but also all the other Baltic Sea states took part in this process. Moreover, use could be made of results of years of co-operation within VASAB and on European level. Thus the VASAB and the ESDP concepts form the "red line" of the BSR Operational Programme for INTERREG II C.[3] The OP provides a platform for implementing both concepts in a concrete area of action. For this purpose, transnational management and finance structures have been established. This kind of co-operation has an innovative character as it contains working together of public authorities in transnational management and finance structures, decision-making on common funds in multinational bodies which did not happen so far in Europe. It supports new forms of vertical and horizontal co-ordination and mutual understanding of different national administration, legislation and approaches to spatial planning. It might also be innovative in a way of defining regional development measures from a transnational context. It is at the same time no general working together and exchange of experience but action-oriented co-operation, aimed at concrete common project development and implementation.

The process of carrying out common projects started successfully with a broad participation of regional and local authorities from all eleven states which participate in the Operational Programme (see *Figure 3*).

Figure 3: Participation of Baltic Sea states in projects of the Community Initiative INTERREG II C

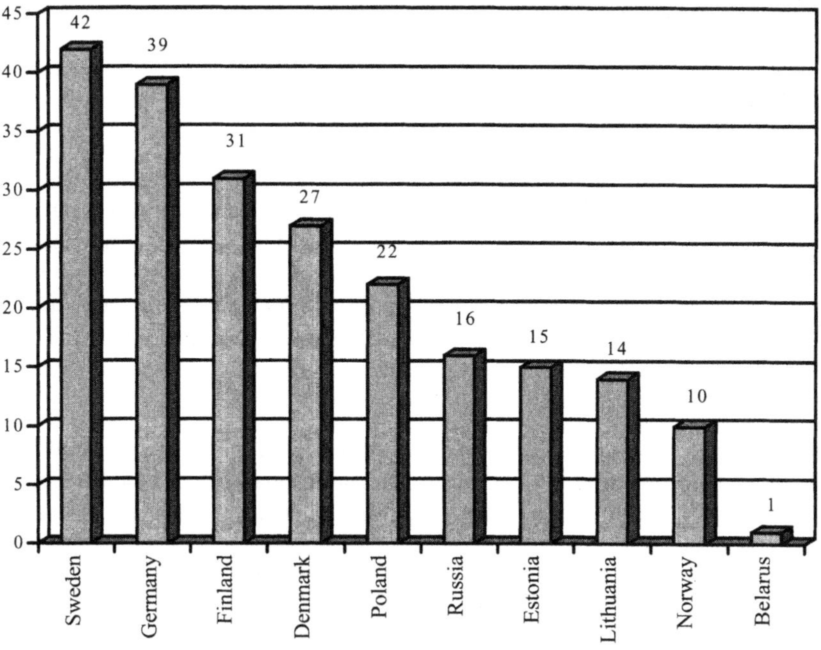

[3] Operational Programme "INTERREG II C Baltic Sea Region", approved by the EU-Commission, December 1997. European Commission (1997).

4. Projects for Baltic Sea Region Development

As mentioned above, the main project ideas of VASAB became an integrated part of the OP and the 45 projects approved under INTERREG II C, cover all relevant fields of VASAB and many policy options of the ESDP:

Projects on *urban networks* try to solve major problems of cities and their relations to surrounding areas in networks of city regions (uncontrolled urban growth spreading into the countryside, social and spatial segregation, traffic congestion, environmental pollution, using up of natural resources like water, non-sufficient recycling, lack of open spaces and untapped landscapes). These projects will not only propose strategies but also concrete practical guidelines for handling problems and preparing investment. Other projects on urban networks deal with city functions towards waterways and towards the coast. The background is overcoming the political division of the Baltic Sea region. There is a great challenge but also a chance that cities can regain their functionality for the Baltic Sea region and strengthen their overall international competitiveness. Specific features of such projects are use of derelict land, conversion of old harbour areas, strengthening attractiveness of the waterfronts of towns by means of urban building and planning. Cities and towns of EU and Non-EU states will be restructured in that way. Another project has its starting point in existing sport boat harbours. Based on spatial planning principles, the creation of a network of such harbours around the Baltic coast will be supported, taking into account economic, environmental and spatial criteria. In addition the strengthening of the attractiveness of ports cities through urban development measures will be prepared.

Several projects pay attention to *transnational (trans-European) corridors* (see *Figure 4*). The question is here to combine transport development with sustainable regional development, to find suitable forms of combining modes of transport, to pay attention to the development of settlements and their transport connections, to use and to develop potential for tourism, to use and maintain natural and cultural heritage and to prepare the ground for concrete investment. Some of these projects deal with transport corridors between EU and non-EU states, supporting the process of growing together for the whole area.

A series of projects is dedicated to *coastal zone planning and management.* Via those projects the operability of "Common Recommendations for Spatial Planning of the Coastal Zone in the Baltic Sea Region", prepared by VASAB (CSD/BSR) will be examined.[4]

Interesting projects are also prepared on using and maintaining *Baltic natural and cultural heritage* and on specific areas ("patches"). An example is co-operation between Swedish, Polish, Latvian and German regions which are characterised by

---

[4] VASAB 2010 (1996): "Common Recommendations for Spatial Planning of the Coastal Zone in the Baltic Sea Region".

large nature protection areas. Here, ways and means will be examined and implemented on how economic development can be combined with nature protection. The project will also deal with alternatives to and inside agriculture as development factors for rural areas.

Figure 4: Baltic projects of transportation development zones

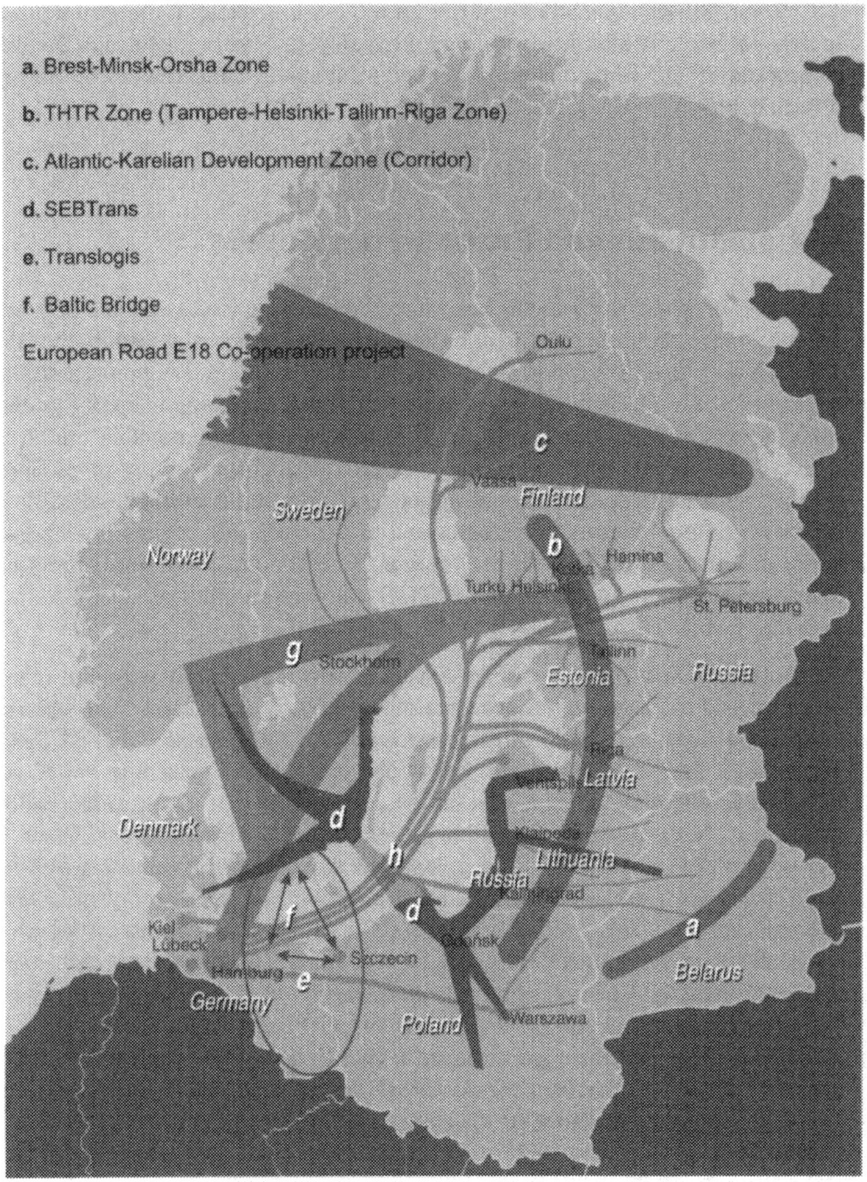

Some projects work out *transnational development concepts* and promote pilot projects for smaller action areas inside the Baltic Sea region, e.g., for the South Western Baltic Sea area, the Bothnian Arc.

Another project family deals with *spatial planning systems* itself. The respective projects develop and apply new innovative planning methods and instruments and try to make use of strong points of the different systems. In that context, the project "VASAB 2010 Plus" further develops the existing strategy for spatial development in BSR. It also tries to define key projects, to be implemented in the framework of the forthcoming Community Initiative INTERREG III between 2000 and 2006.

5. Conclusions and Further Perspectives

The *ESDP* itself and the broad debate on spatial planning issues was and still is an important input to further practical transnational co-operation and to the revision of the existing spatial development perspective for the Baltic Sea region. The Baltic activities will on the other hand facilitate the implementation of ESDP policy options. For *ESDP implementation*, a major task consists of promoting useful, innovative and ambitious transnational, interregional and cross-border projects and exchange on "best practise". Those projects should also be stronger linked to investment and pre-investment measures and to the creation of public-private partnerships. Another issue is to further develop the ESDP-strategy towards wider European co-operation (in preparing the CEMAT-Conference during EXPO in Hanover in October 2000).

In the framework of *VASAB 2010*, the national levels played an important role in defining visions for spatial development and translating these visions into concrete priorities and fields of action in the framework of the Operational INTERREG programme. At the same time, a broad debate on spatial planning issues was launched with regional and local authorities, some sectors and also with scientific institutes and consulting firms and the "bottom up approach" was strengthened. As a result, 75 % of all project financing is provided by regional and local authorities, the rest through national and international institutions, universities, private firms and associations. All main fields of BSR INTERREG II C OP and subsequently VASAB 2010 strategy and ESDP have been covered. This outcome is in line with the principle of subsidiarity. For the *implementation of VASAB 2010* strategy and the working out of the project VASAB 2010 Plus, it is necessary to concentrate on key issues of transnational importance, to take part more actively in generating projects for the new Community Initiative INTERREG III and to intensify discussion with regional authorities in that context. For Germany, it is also important to promote better integration of New German Länder (Berlin, Brandenburg, Mecklenburg-West Pommerania) into Baltic Sea co-operation.

In co-operation between EU and non-EU countries of BSR, progress has been reached on matching the financing instruments of INTERREG, PHARE and TACIS. All countries took part in the programme preparation and have equal rights to decide on projects. However, only some partners in one third of all projects will receive finances from the EU support programmes PHARE and TACIS for Eastern European countries. In many cases only regional authorities of one or two non-EU countries managed to get approval whereas regions of other countries did not succeed to get finances for the same common project. *For the next programming period* (2000–2006) therefore, harmonising of instruments towards project development "from one source" remains an urgent task.

Sectoral and inter-regional co-operation is widely developed in the Baltic Sea region and transnational organisations exist in several fields. It proved however often difficult to reach a common approach to spatial development measures. So far, co-operation with several sectors and on such issues as elaboration of Baltic Agenda 21 was realised (Baltic 21 1998a, 1998b). There is also a constructive co-operation with such transnational organisations as the Union of the Baltic Cities and the Baltic Sea States Sub-Regional Conference. It seems that the implementation of the OP has strengthened a common understanding on spatial development issues. *For the next INTERREG programme* (INTERREG III B), spatial planning should intensify efforts to invite sectoral policies to carrying out common projects on sustainable spatial development.

References

Baltic 21 (1998a) Spatial Planning for Sustainable Development in the Baltic Sea Region. A VASAB contribution to Baltic 21. The Committee for Spatial Development in the Baltic Sea Region (CSD/BSR), April 1998. In: Baltic 21 Series No 9

Baltic 21 (1998b) An Agenda 21 for the Baltic Sea Region–Baltic 21. Adopted at the 7th Ministerial Session of the Council of the Baltic Sea States, Nyborg, June 22-23, 1998. In: Baltic 21 Series No 1

European Commission (1991) Europe 2000: Outlook for the Development of the Community's Territory. Luxembourg: Office for Official Publications of the European Communities

European Commission (1995) Europe 2000+ Cooperation for European Territorial Development. Luxembourg: Office for Official Publications of the European Communities

European Commission (1997) INTERREG II C – Community Initiative Concerning Transnational Co-operation on Spatial Planning. Operational Programme Baltic Sea Region 1997–1999. Approved by the Commission on December 11

European Conference of Ministers Responsible for Regional Planning (1999), Guiding Principles for Sustainable Spatial Development of the European Continent. Draft September 1999

BMBAU Bundesministerium für Raumordnung, Bauwesen und Städtebau (1995) Principles for a European Spatial Development Policy. Published by Bundesforschungsanstalt für Landeskunde und Raumordnung, Bonn

Görmar W (1997) Erfahrungen und Perspektiven der transnationalen Kooperation zur Raumordnung in der Ostseeregion. Information zur Raumentwicklung 6: 405-418

Orlowski WM (1997) The Baltic Economy: Did it Exist? Does it Exist? Will it Exist? In: Kuklinski A (ed) European Space, Baltic Space, Polish Space, Part One. Warsaw, pp 71-87

Peschel K (1993) Perspectives of Regional Economic Development Around the Baltic. In: Lundqvist L, Persson LO (eds) Visions and Strategies in European Integration. Springer, Berlin, Heidelberg, New York, pp 19-31

Peschel K (1998) Perspectives of Regional Development Around the Baltic Sea. Annals of Regional Science 32: 299-320

Toczyski W, Zaucha J, Szmytkowska M, Szydarowski W (1997) Competition and Cooperation in the Baltic Sea Region. In: Kuklinski A (ed) European Space, Baltic Space, Polish Space, Part Two. Warsaw, pp 157-176

VASAB 2010 (1994) Vision and Strategies Around the Baltic Sea 2010, Towards a Framework for Spatial Development in the Baltic Sea Region. Third Conference of Ministers for Spatial Planning and Development. Tallinn, December 7-8

VASAB 2010 (1996) Vision and Strategies Around the Baltic Sea 2010, From Vision to Action. Forth Conference of Ministers for Spatial Planning and Development of the Baltic Sea States. Stockholm, October 22

Potential Labour Mobility between the Baltic States and Sweden

Lars Olof Persson

KTH – Royal Institute of Technology

Department of Infrastructure and Planning

Stockholm, Sweden

1. Introduction

After the long period of high unemployment in the 1990s, the Swedish labour market is now recovering quite rapidly. Since 1998, there is an increasing shortage not only of certain types of highly skilled labour but also within social services and the building and construction industry. This concerns particularly the larger Swedish city regions. Together with the ageing population, which reduces the relative supply of domestic labour force, there is an emerging debate on the need for immigrating labour to the Swedish labour market. In this debate, it is stated that the potential immigration to metropolitan regions is quite large in a future situation with free mobility of labour and entrepreneurs between the Baltic states and the other EU-countries. Initially, the major driving push factor is expected to be the lower income level and the prospects of much higher income and material welfare. The strength of this factor is to a large extent decided by the economic growth and how welfare will be distributed among candidate countries. If both large professional groups and people living on transfers expect a continuing improvement of their and their families living conditions at home, this reduces the potential emigration.

A counteractive factor, hampering the realisation of the large potential for emigration, is expected to be the economic and institutional situation in Sweden. Another hampering factor is the trade unions, which favour a regulated labour market. The labour market policy, however, is currently shifting in favour of more flexibility. These and other counteractive forces are estimated to be so strong that they will prevent any mass migration to Sweden.

2. Current Immigration to Sweden

In 1998, residence permits in Sweden were granted to approximately 36,000 adults and children belonging to a number of categories: refugees, relatives, labour market immigrants, adopted children, EEA-nationals (Swedish Institute 2000: www.si.se). In the same year, almost 14,000 foreign nationals left Sweden.

At the end of 1997, about 522,000 foreign nationals were living in Sweden. The proportion of European immigrants is greater than that of non-Europeans, the main reason being the conflicts in former Yugoslavia. In addition, about 690,500 immigrants had become naturalized Swedish citizens. Not less than 50 % of all foreign nationals in Sweden were from the other Nordic countries.

Citizens of EU member states and EEA states can enter Sweden and work without any permit for a period of up to three months. After that he or she must apply for a residence permit. Citizens of all other countries are, in principle, granted residence permits for labour market reasons only if the need for labour cannot be met in Sweden.

In a discussion on the future immigration, it is relevant to explore the experiences of the free Nordic labour market since the mid 1950s (Johansson, Persson 2000; Lundh, Ohlsson 1994; Lundborg 1991). Immigration from Denmark has remained surprisingly stable at a low level since the decision on the common Nordic labour market was made. It is recognized that the level of benefits to unemployed in Denmark influences immigration to Sweden. Immigration was low during the last part of the 1970s and the 1980s in spite of high unemployment in Denmark and high frequency of vacancies in Sweden. Increasing benefits in Denmark had clear negative incentives for the unemployed to migrate.

Immigration from Norway to Sweden has by large been stable – also at a low level – in the post-war period. The end of the 1980s experienced, however, a strong increase. This mobility has a strong connection with rising unemployment in Norway in combination with an overheated labour market in Sweden.

The most apparent result of the common Nordic labour market was an outflow of labour from Finland to Sweden, which reached its peak in 1969-1970 that resulted in a large return migration some years later. During these two years, 80,000 people moved from Finland to Sweden. The Finnish authorities introduced restrictions against labour migration, which however probably were unnecessary because the demand for unskilled labour in the Swedish industry had already slowed down. Unskilled industrial workers were just the kind of labour that Finland supplied. From that time the factors behind migration are less pronounced and do not follow the pattern from the 1960s.

3. Development of Immigration Policy

Since the mid-1960s, a large number of reforms have been carried out to improve immigrants' conditions in Sweden (Swedish Institute 2000). A programme of free Swedish language instruction was started in 1965; a government-subsidized newspaper for immigrants began publication in 1967; a bill providing for special tuition in Swedish and other subjects for immigrant school children was adopted by Parliament in 1968.

To move away from a situation in which immigrants tended to be viewed as a group and to help implement more general measures in the social policy field, the Government set up the new National Integration Office in 1998. The main tasks are:

- monitoring and evaluating trends in Swedish society from an integration standpoint,
- promoting equal rights and opportunities for everyone, regardless of ethnic and cultural background,
- preventing and combating xenofobia, racism and discrimination.

In order to increase immigrants' opportunities for making themselves heard in public life, government grants to national immigrant organizations were introduced. A special effort has also been made to support cultural activities among immigrants. The government subsidizes literature in various minority languages and funds are available for public libraries to purchase foreign literature. The ethnic press is entitled to the same kind of subsidies as the Swedish press. The Swedish Broadcasting Corporation broadcast radio and television programmes in several immigrant languages.

Newly arrived immigrants, who do not have Swedish, Danish or Norwegian as their mother tongue, are entitled to an introduction to Swedish society and tuition in Swedish. The municipalities receive government compensation for their expenditure during the introduction period.

Since 1986 there has been an Ombudsman Against Ethnic Discrimination whose task is to counteract ethnic discrimination both at work and within other areas of community life.

A policy reform adopted in 1975 gives all aliens, who have been resident in Sweden for at least three years, the right to vote and run for office in local and regional elections is of great significance in this respect.

It should be noticed that Sweden pursues a very restrictive policy as regards the immigration of labour from countries outside the EEA. Consultation with the National Labour Market Board and the trade unions is required in the case of work permit applications.

Those granted a permanent residence permit in Sweden (today mainly refugees and relatives of those already settled in Sweden) do not require a special work permit to seek employment. During fiscal year 1998, Sweden had a maximum quota of 1,800 persons for refugees needing relocation in another country. However, a much greater number of refugees come to Sweden on their own and seek asylum at the border or after a certain period in the country. In 1996 the Parliament decided that remigration is to be an element of the country's migration policy. In various ways the Government now promotes a more active remigration policy.

In conclusion, the Swedish immigration policy can be seen as relatively favourable to immigrants, because of the ambition to integrate new immigrants in the Swedish society. However, there are few if any policy measures oriented towards the stimulation of immigration to Sweden, definitively not from non-EAE countries and hardly not from EAE-countries. It is still an open question whether the changing labour marker with increasing shortage of labour in some sectors will be reflected in changes of the immigration policy.

4. Assessing Future Migration

4.1 Migration Around the Baltic Sea During the 1990s

Despite the large discrepancies in incomes between the transition countries in the Baltic Sea region and the Western countries, official emigration from the former countries has decreased since the beginning of the 1990s. In Estonia, the peak was reached in 1993 with a 2.4 % outflow of the population. In both Latvia and Lithuania, the corresponding peaks were already reached in 1992: 2.0 % and 0.8 % respectively. The exception is Poland, where the highest emigration intensity was reached in 1995 when 0.7 % of the population migrated. These outflows of people have not been counter-balanced by a corresponding immigration.

In the middle of the 1990s, there were almost 16,000 persons from Poland who worked in Sweden and around 3,000 from Estonia. From Latvia, the corresponding figure was a little more than 500, and from Lithuania the numbers were very small. For every country, the numbers had decreased since the beginning of the 1990s.

4.2 Towards a Scenario

In this section, we launch a set of assumptions on preconditions for migration that will develop as a response to the differences in living conditions in Baltic states, the economic and institutional development in Sweden. The period we overview reaches to the years 2010–2015. A central precondition is that any future migration will encompass several categories of migrants. This is based on observations of migration patterns in other parts of the world. Immigrants to any country differ in terms of educational backgrounds, professional background, in terms of formal and informal networks in the new country and partly in motives for immigration.

The future scenarios that we outline build upon that labour mobility will rather increase than stagnate during the next ten years. This builds on four assumptions –

economic growth, social stability, no environmental disasters, and full membership in the EU – on the development in Estonia, Latvia, Lithuania, and Poland.

Economic growth will continue at a high annual level, but in spite of that, GDP per capita will remain at a level well below the Nordic countries for 10–15 years. This implies that in material living conditions Estonia, Latvia, and Lithuania will hardly reach much above 25 % of the Finnish and Swedish figures and in Poland not over 50 %. With respect to the potential future emigration from these countries, we expect that there will be strong private income incentives to move.

The political development in these countries is also expected to be characterised by social stability. The democratisation process continues and the citizenship and land ownership issues are settled in a legislatively and administratively efficient way. The welfare distributive system develops towards a situation with reasonable cohesion. Hence, we do not count on a scenario with mass refugee emigration.

We do not expect any surprising and devastative things to happen to change environmental conditions negatively – no environmental disasters of a size that it will change the living conditions in the transition countries. This however presupposes that both international and national resources continue to improve nuclear security and reduce pollution. This is why we do not calculate a scenario with ecological disaster with pressure on mass out migration. Rather, with an eventual improvement of the environment in the Baltic states very few people are expected to consider emigration for ecological reasons.

A future common labour market around the Baltic Sea will, thus, stimulate labour mobility as the obstacles for free migratory movements have disappeared. Besides problems with language, culture and education, a potential labour market mismatch between the countries in the Baltic Sea region will not stimulate extensive labour mobility. We know also from migration within the EU that unskilled unemployed workers have a very low propensity to move. The catching-up process will stimulate migration and labour mobility in both directions as a consequence of increased similarities in economic structure on both sides. Some lessons with regard to the future migration around the Baltic Sea can be drawn from the migratory movements between Sweden and Finland since the free Nordic labour market was established in the 1950s. When the income gap was closed, migration between the two countries slowed down very sharply and return-migration increased.

The free mobility of labour within Europe has not meant that immigration to the Nordic countries has increased. It is against this background we will discuss the economic, institutional, and social future conditions that will influence the composition and size of labour migration from Baltic states to the Nordic countries.

Economic growth will continue but at a slower rate than in the Baltic states. The industry's international competitiveness will develop such a way that market shares will be maintained. Many Swedish corporations will continue to expand abroad and with the consequences that future jobs in the "Swedish" manufacturing industries will continue to a large part be created abroad.

Economic policy in Sweden is based on the idea that competitiveness is based on knowledge intensive branches and comparatively high wage structure. Education policy has an important role with strong support to both higher education and lifelong learning. Large resources will be put into secondary education for recent immigrants and dropouts.

Labour market institutions have considerable effects on labour migration. A more flexible wage structure means that more professions will be relying on individual contracts. For labour – immigrants or domestic – this will mean that there will be more possibilities to underbid each other. More and more jobs will be offered in terms of project employment, part-time basis. In total, we expect that recruitment frequency and mobility between branches and workplaces will increase and hence reduce long term unemployment. For potential immigrants this signal will be interpreted as stimuli for immigration.

Tax pressure will remain high with small possibilities also for more affluent households to purchase labour intensive services. However, small firms with temporary labour and low costs will market such services, especially in metropolitan regions with relatively high concentration of affluent households. Many such firms are – and even will be in the future – managed by immigrants. Self-employed foreigners are and will be relatively high in the "lower" segment of the private service sector.

The basic welfare systems will remain largely as today. This means that unemployment and other social benefits will remain at current levels. This means also that comparatively large social transfers are made to immigrants from other countries. The Swedish welfare system may stimulate immigration from other countries around the Baltic Sea especially if there will be large discrepancies with respect to the social welfare systems between the countries.

4.3 Categories of Potential Immigrants

The propensity to emigrate for the highly educated has in addition to the economic incentives a connection to the bilateral alliances that most universities establish. Many universities are expanding the co-operation with corresponding institutes in the Baltic Sea region. Co-operation is gradually established along the full range go university activities – graduate courses, master programmes, doctoral courses, and research. This group of immigrants get contact through formal co-operation programmes. In practise, this leads to an increasing flow of students, teachers, and researcher paying shorter or longer visits to Sweden. It is likely that a number of them will consider staying more permanently.

Another group of immigrants consists of professionals with specialised education, work experience, and multiple languages. They reach contact with the Nordic countries through international big firms' and organisations' active recruitment missions. Increasingly, firms like Ericsson and ABB headhunt people for work initially in their home country. With the international network and the labour mobility characterising such firms, it is likely that a number of these will stay for longer period also in Sweden.

Labour to professions with bottleneck problems is a group of immigrants, who through formal or informal employment agencies look for a job in the Swedish regions that are in short supply for the moment. It is certainly difficult if not impossible to point out which jobs will be in short supply after five or ten years. The education system in Sweden is generally planning in order to avoid such a situation. In spite of that, for periods during the last decade there has been a shortage in supply of nurses, teachers, technicians etc. It is likely that the future European cross-border programmes for the Baltic region will facilitate this kind of labour migration. The networks between organisations, institutes, enterprises, communes, and cities will be used in this purpose. It will also be facilitated by improvement of the communication systems, both between the old and the new member states, but also within the new member states.

Low educated in informal networks is a group of people with short formal education and limited foreign language knowledge, looking for sources of income especially in the metropolitan areas without previous contacts. The propensity for this group to emigrate is obviously expectations of a better life. From other studies, we know that low educated people's migration often has a ground in informal networks – relatives or friends that have previously migrated. These social networks often have importance to potential immigrant entrepreneurs in retailing, services to households and handicraft. Many of these immigrants are going to be self-employed in the "grey" or even the "black" sector.

It is obvious that this class of migrants could result in extensive search unemployment for periods in Nordic metropolitan regions and result in a further concentration of immigrants to certain housing areas.

Immigrant entrepreneurs within handicraft and service sectors with price competition as a business strategy may become common especially in the metropolitan regions. There are several niches that are still to be explored. It could be agencies for firms with pre-fabricated goods from Baltic states, such as in textiles and food industry. It should be remembered that for Estonia and Latvia, Stockholm is the largest closest metropolitan region in the European Union.

5. Concluding Remarks

The aim of this chapter is to discuss future migration across the Baltic Sea to Sweden. The assessment is based on experiences taken from the history of the free Nordic labour market since the 1950s, on assumptions on future push and pull conditions in the expected new member states and moderating factors in the Nordic countries, particularly within the institutional framework. However, the factors discussed are economic, institutional and cultural.

The aggregate migration flows are likely to reach a peak quite soon after the introduction of the single labour market. This expectation is based on experiences of the history if the free Nordic labour market. This is also the background to the assessment that this peak will rapidly be reduced and even reversed.

Our two major conclusions concern the categories of potential migrants and the volume of migration. Future migration is expected to be divers in terms of categories of labour expected to move. The following categories are likely to dominate in the first round: skilled and highly educated people, intra-firm recruiting, small entrepreneurs, and low educated people in the informal sector. In the long-run, migration flows are expected to stabilise at a low level. Against this background, instead of a restrictive migration and labour market policy in Sweden, we expect that an active policy in order to stimulate labour migration will emerge. This development is expected to be driven by the increasing shortage of labour in Sweden, as a consequence of both economic recovery and ageing of the population.

References

Hedegaard L, Lindström B (eds) (2000) The NEBI Yearbook 2000: North European and Baltic Sea Integration. Springer, Berlin, Heidelberg, New York (forthcoming)

Johansson M, Persson LO (2000) Approaching a Single Labour Market Emerging Migration Patterns in the Baltic Sea Area. In: Hedegaard L, Lindström B (eds) The NEBI Yearbook 2000: North European and Baltic Sea Integration. Springer, Berlin, Heidelberg, New York (forthcoming)

Lundborg P (1991) Determinants of Migration in the Nordic Labour Market. Scandinavian Journal of Economics 3: 363-375

Lundh C, Ohlsson R (1994) Immigration and Economic Change. In: Bengtsson T (ed) Population, Economy and Welfare in Sweden. Springer, Berlin, Heidelberg, New York

Economic Integration and Transport Infrastructure in the Baltic Sea Area[1]

Johannes Bröcker, Frank Richter

Technische Universität Dresden

Institut für Wirtschaft und Verkehr

Dresden, Germany

1. Introduction

Until the recent wave of theoretical economic geography, the mainstream foreign trade theory – and the theory of economic integration in particular – did not care about space. Neither the internal spatial structure of integrating national economies nor their respective geographical location had any importance for potential gains and losses of different forms and institutional arrangements of economic integration. Besides this mainstream there is a special German tradition disseminated by Lösch (1962) and Predöhl (1949) putting international trade and economic integration into a spatial perspective. Predöhl was convinced that integration areas can not be formed ad libidum by political decisions, but that there is a spontaneous spatial process at work forming natural integration areas with their respective "centres of gravity". One can reap the gains from integration if policy supports this spontaneous process, while integration policy is bound to fail if it tries to form non-natural blocks. As Predöhl's student in Münster, Karin Peschel became "obsessed" by this idea of looking at the world economy as a spatial system. "Economically high integrated areas" or "economic spaces", for short, became a leitmotiv of her research.

One branch of her research is to identify these spaces by trade data (Haass, Peschel 1982). A remarkable observation brought to the fore by this research is that the formation of these spaces in market economies has first and foremost to do with distance, just with the simple distance as the crow flies. Geographically neighbouring countries form clusters because spatial interaction is declining with distance, ceteris paribus. This is the gravity law of spatial interaction, one of the most stable empirical regularities in social sciences, and at the same time one of

[1] Financial support by the Deutsche Forschungsgemeinschaft for the project "Wie wirken sich neue Verkehrstechnologien und die Entwicklung Transeuropäischer Netze auf die Europäische Standortverteilung aus?" is gratefully acknowledged.

the most ignored one by mainstream economics. A closer look reveals, of course, that distance can be measured in a more sophisticated way rather than just as the crow flies. Measuring distance – transport distance, cultural distance, linguistic distance – therefore became another central theme of Karin Peschel's work (Herrmann et al. 1993). Starting from her ideas about forms of distance and formation of economic spaces, she more recently speculated about the present and future potential degree of economic integration of the countries around the Baltic sea (Peschel 1998, 1999): are they likely to form a common economic space after the cold war barriers of spatial interaction have been removed? What are the gains from such an integration process, and how can it be reinforced?

This short paper is not aiming at an answer to such broad questions, but it just adds a few small pieces of evidence helping to keep these speculations alive. The empirical results come in two parts: the first (Section 3) shows estimates for the present level of international trade impediments between the countries of "Regio Baltica". As countries of this region (RB-countries, for short) we count Germany, the Scandinavian countries Norway, Denmark, Sweden and Finland, the three Baltic states, Russia and Poland. We subdivide this group into two subsets, the members of the European Economic Area (EEA) on the one hand (Germany and the Scandinavian countries) and non-EEA countries (transformation countries) on the other.

As expected, it turns out that the impediments between the EEA members are much smaller than those between the transformation countries as well as those between transformation countries and EEA members. From this observation we draw the conclusion that there is still a high potential for economic integration, even though tariffs have already been abolished. Some impediments result from different norms and standards and will be removed when these countries enter the EU. Other obstacles are not institutional in nature, but result from a lack of specialisation and adjustment required to compete in the European market, and they will therefore decline only gradually during the continuing transformation process. In the end, impediments are likely to come down to levels observed between present EU or EEA countries. Comparative static simulations in Section 3 evaluate the spatial implications of this integration process by looking what would have happened, if in 1995 the high impediments of the transformation countries would have jumped down to the low EU levels over night, and the economy would have adjusted over night, given regional factor stocks and levels of productivity.

The second part of the paper (Section 4) studies another type of integration, namely the integration brought about by new transport links around the Baltic. Since the Maastricht treaty, activities of the commission of the EU to promote the provision of new transport links play a prominent role as an instrument in cohesion policy. Article 154 (former 129b) of the EU treaty (EU 1997a), newly introduced in Maastricht, assigned the obligation to the union bodies to contribute to the establishment of trans-European networks in transport, telecommunication and energy. On this basis a master-plan for a trans-European transport network has been set up, with a priority list of projects for the EU itself and a list of transport corridors in central and eastern Europe (EU 1997b). It contains a series of projects surrounding the Baltic Sea. Building these links will also reduce transaction costs and thereby further enhance the integration process in northern Europe, even though the impact is much smaller than that of the trade impediment reductions to be studied in Section 3.

Before presenting the empirical results, Section 2 gives a short overview of the methodology, a detailed description of which is to be found elsewhere (Bröcker 1998, 2000).

2. A General Equilibrium Model of Interregional Trade

The empirical results to follow are obtained by calibrating a computable multiregional static general equilibrium model for a system of regions covering the whole world, with Europe (from Atlantic to Ural) subdivided into 800 regions. In each region there is a representative household receiving his income from selling factor services to regional firms and spending this income for consumption and investment. Regional firms produce two types of goods, non-tradable local goods and tradables. Tradables are differentiated and are supplied under Chamberlinean monopolistic competition; the other markets (local goods and factor service) are perfectly competitive. Households buy both types of goods, local goods and a diversified bundle of tradables stemming from all regions in the world. Firms use both types of goods plus factor service as inputs. Preferences and technologies are nested CD-CES.

Most important in the context of this paper is that trading goods causes transaction costs of two types, namely (1) transaction costs depending on transport distance, and (2) transaction costs due to all kinds of impediments to international trade. Transport distance is calculated as the shortest travel time along roads of a European road network with 3,600 links and 6,300 non-directed arcs. Roads are distinguished by average speed classes; ferry connections with expected shipping and waiting times and sea links with the rest of the world are also included. Other modes of transport are not yet included in the model. Even though pure transport costs are of minor importance today, travel costs are still relevant due to the necessity of exchanging information by face-to-face contact. In spite of electronic communication technology this "means that the distance sensitivity of communication costs increases as trade flows become more software intense" (Peschel 1999, p 298). The first type of transaction costs is meant to cover not only pure transport costs, but also distance sensitive costs of communication which are connected with trade flows. The second type of transaction costs covers any costs emerging from selling or buying goods to or from a foreign country, may they result from different institutional settings, product norms and standards, or different languages or cultures. As we measure these costs indirectly, by a catch-all dummy, we do not need to specify them more precisely.

Formally, we model transaction costs as a mark-up on price. If p_r is the mill price for tradables in region r, then $p_r\tau_{rs}$ is the local price in region s including all transaction costs, with

(1) $\tau_{rs} = \exp\left(\zeta g_{rs}{}^{\omega}\right)\delta_{kl}$.

g_{rs} is road travel time along the shortest route from r to s, ζ and ω are parameters. The parameter ω, which is expected to be positive and less than one, allows for reproducing the observation that the percentage price increase per unit of distance is decreasing in distance. $\delta_{kl}-1$ is the share of costs due to international impediments in the value of traded goods, if goods are valued inclusive of distance related transaction costs. We call $\delta_{kl}-1$ the *Implied Trade Barrier* (ITB) for exports from k to l. ITBs are our measure of disintegration between countries, to be presented in Section 3.

ITBs are an outcome of the model calibration. In the calibration procedure the ITBs are determined such that international trade flows between any pair of countries are exactly reproduced by the model flows in equilibrium. It can be shown, however, that individual ITBs are not uniquely determined by this rule. Hence, we assume symmetry of ITBs as an additional restriction rendering the ITBs uniquely identified. Symmetry means that, for a pair of countries, ITBs between the two countries for trade in both directions are the same. Under the symmetry restriction, ITBs are calibrated such that, for each pair of countries, trade in both directions in the model and in the data adds up to the same number.

After identifying ITBs for the RB-countries in Section 3, we simulate economic integration by reducing the high impediments observed for foreign trade of non-EEA countries. By a similar approach, welfare effects of new road links are estimated in Section 4. Starting from the calibrated benchmark for 1995, new road links are introduced in a comparative static experiment. A new equilibrium with reduced transaction costs is calculated, and welfare changes are measured in monetary terms by Hicksian variations.

3. Trade Barriers and the Integration Potential

The calibrated ITBs for the 10 RB-countries are shown in *Table 1*. It has a clear structure, largely corresponding to prior expectations. The impediments between the five EEA members in the group are much smaller than the others, but they are significantly positive and remarkably close to one another; the average[2] amount is 16.7 % (16.5 %). This is slightly more than the average for the four Scandinavian

[2] Unweighted average, averages weighted by trade flows in parenthesis.

members of the group alone, which is 16.2 % (15.9 %), and less than the average for all EEA countries, which is 19.0 % (16.9 %). The smallest impediments are observed between Germany and Finland. Particularly in this case one should keep in mind that the calibration controls for distance. Next comes the relation Sweden –Finland. The five non-EEA countries have ITBs of 30.8 % (26.4 %) among each other, on average. Particularly high impediments are observed for flows between Poland and the three Baltic states. ITBs between EEA members and non-members within the group of RB-countries are somewhat smaller than those between non-EEA countries, namely 26.3 % (22.2 %). Among these ITBs, those between Germany and Russia, between Sweden on the one hand and Estonia and Latvia on the other and between Finland and Estonia are relatively small.

Table 1: Implied trade impediments, percent of trade value

	Ger	Den	Nor	Swe	Fin	Rus	Est	Lat	Lit	Pol
Germany	0	20	18	16	13	17	25	26	28	23
Denmark	20	0	17	16	16	25	23	28	27	30
Norway	18	17	0	16	18	29	31	27	35	32
Sweden	16	16	16	0	15	29	19	19	29	28
Finland	13	16	18	15	0	23	19	29	33	26
Russia	17	25	29	29	23	0	25	26	23	27
Estonia	25	23	31	19	19	25	0	26	27	44
Latvia	26	28	27	19	29	26	26	0	28	44
Lithuania	28	27	35	29	33	23	27	28	0	40
Poland	23	30	32	28	26	27	44	44	40	0

Now let us see what happens if potentials for integration are exploited by reducing the high barriers to exports and imports of non-EEA countries down to EEA levels. In the experiment we integrate the ten candidate countries for EU membership in Central and Eastern Europe with the EEA by reducing the barriers for their external trade by 16 percentage points. This is the average difference between the calibrated level of these barriers in 1995 and the calibrated intra-EEA level of barriers. *Figure 1* shows regional welfare changes, measured by the Hicksian relative equivalent variation. This is the hypothetical percentage increase in regional income which would have been necessary before integration in order to generate the same welfare change as the integration. *Figure 1*, which is zoomed for the Regio Baltica in *Figure 2*, shows three clear results:

1. The gains are highest in the new member countries and – in relative terms – small in present EEA-countries.

2. Within new member countries, gains are particularly high in border regions, as predicted by Giersch (1949) half a century ago.

3. Welfare gains show a gravity pattern with higher gains close to the new members and virtually no effects far away. As a consequence, the gains within the EEA are comparatively high in the Regio Baltica.

Figure 1: Integration of ten Central and Eastern European countries – annual welfare gains, equivalent variation, percent of regional GDP

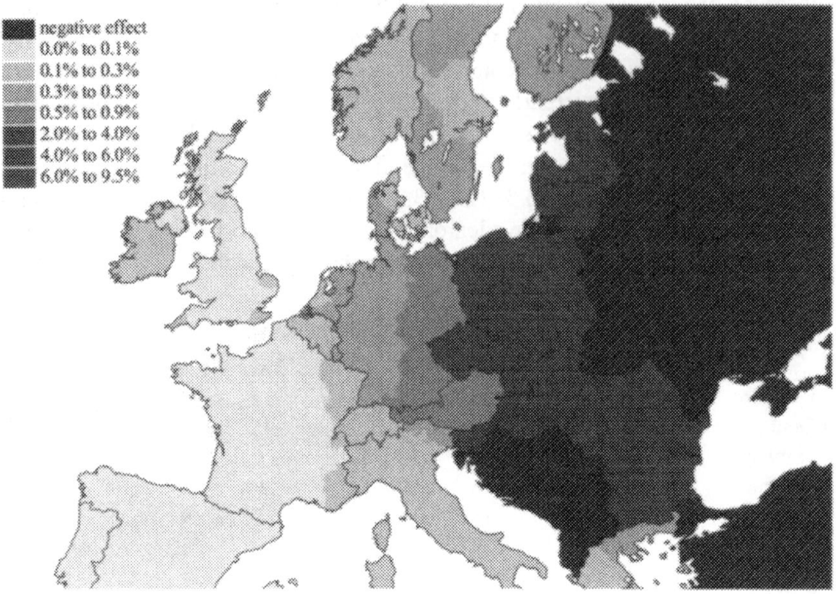

Figure 2: Integration of ten Central and Eastern European countries – annual welfare gains

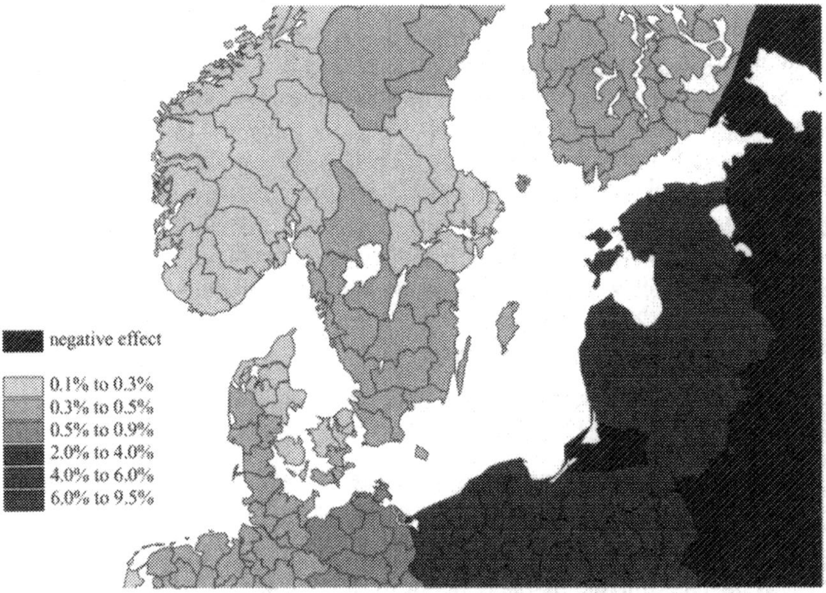

4. Spatial Effects of New Roads

We study the following seven road building projects around the Baltic sea, all belonging to the project list of the TEN-T master plan, either as a first or second priority project in the list of the Christophersen-group or as part of the Helsinki-corridors (EU 1997b):

(1) Öresund bridge (Ös),
(2) Completion of motorway Oslo–Göteborg (O–G),
(3) Completion of motorway Oslo–Stockholm (O–S),
(4) Completion of motorway Malmö–Stockholm (M–S),
(5) Completion of motorway Helsinki–St. Petersburg (H–SP),
(6) Fehmarnbelt link (Fb),
(1) Motorway Tallinn–Gdańsk (T–G).

Roads serve many purposes; passengers use them for commuting (work, shopping, education), for consumption purposes (leisure, tourism, etc.) or for business trips, and roads are used for transporting goods. We consider the utility generated by these types of use only partly: our analysis is confined to costs related to commodity trade, under which we do not only count pure transport costs, but also costs of business trips related to interregional trade. Hence, for a total cost-benefit analysis we would have to add utilities generated for the other types of users. Roads are the only mode of transport considered (plus ferries and sea links between Europe and the rest of the world).

New roads generate welfare gains in regions improving their accessibility to markets in other regions. Better market access allows them to improve their terms of trade and to increase product diversity. Households and firms substitute cheaper tradables from better accessible regions for other tradables and local goods. Regions may also suffer from new roads, however, if they lose markets to those competitors having obtained an advantage by the new links, or if they must pay higher prices for tradables from regions coming closer to their sales markets. Only by a general equilibrium model can these complex repercussions be modelled appropriately. Furthermore, new links generate welfare losses, because they produce more traffic, and more traffic produces more negative externalities. This would also have to be considered in a full cost-benefit analysis (even though it is not in cost-benefit analysis according to the official German assessment manual, BMV 1993), but we do not consider it here. Hence, reading the quantitative results, the reader should keep these limitations as compared to a full general equilibrium cost-benefit analysis in mind.

Compared to the effects of market integration the effects of new roads are tiny. For example, the network model generates an estimated time saving along the Fehmarnbelt link of roughly 100 minutes. Given the calibrated transaction cost function this causes a cost saving in the order of 1 % of the trade value, varying with the distance of the respective trade flow. This is less than the integration effect studied before by a factor of more than 10.

Table 2 summarises the most important results. Regarding the TEN projects on the Scandinavian side of the Baltic Sea, Sweden is the obvious winner. Southern Sweden is the only region (except Bornholm), where the sum of the effects exceeds 1% of GDP (see *Figure 3*). Bornholm is a special case. It gains strongly from the Öresund fixed link, because intra-national trade between Bornholm and the main part of Denmark flows along this link. Intra-national flows are much larger than international flows, as shown in the forgoing section; hence, the cost savings are comparatively large. Interesting observations can be made for the Fehmarnbelt link (see *Figure 4*). The strongest effects are in Sweden and Eastern Denmark, while there is a loss (though only a small one) in Jutland. Schleswig-Holstein gains very little, the north of Schleswig-Holstein gains nothing.

Table 2: Annual welfare effects of new roads, relation to GDP, basic points (100 basic points are 1 %)

	Ös	O–G	O–S	M–S	Fb	H-SP	T–G	Σ	7 P
Germany	0	0	0	0	1	0	0	2	2
Schleswig-Holstein	1	0	0	1	3	0	0	5	5
Central	1	0	0	1	4	0	0	6	6
North	1	0	0	1	0	0	0	2	3
South-West	1	0	0	0	3	0	0	5	5
East	1	0	0	1	4	0	0	6	7
South	1	0	0	0	3	0	0	5	5
Hamburg	1	0	0	0	3	0	0	5	5
Niedersachsen	1	0	0	0	2	0	0	3	4
Bremen	1	0	0	0	2	0	0	4	4
Meckl.-Vorpommern	1	0	0	1	0	0	0	2	2
Rest of Germany	0	0	0	0	1	0	0	2	2
Denmark	4	1	0	1	10	0	0	17	17
Sjælland, Lolland	7	1	0	2	26	0	0	36	36
Bornholm	110	2	0	2	18	1	0	133	139
Fyn	3	1	0	1	–5	0	0	1	1
Jylland (north)	1	1	0	1	–1	0	0	2	2
Jylland (south)	0	1	0	0	–4	0	0	–3	–3
Sweden	14	1	7	15	19	0	0	56	58
Southern Sweden	45	2	–2	18	29	0	0	93	101
Western Sweden	12	4	3	4	25	0	0	48	47
Småland	17	2	–2	17	23	0	0	59	61
Rest of Sweden	7	–1	12	16	14	0	0	49	50
Norway	6	13	6	0	13	0	0	38	40
Finland	5	0	1	7	10	10	3	35	35
Poland	0	0	0	0	0	0	0	1	1
Russia	0	0	0	0	0	1	1	2	2
St.Peterburg region	0	0	0	0	1	9	15	25	23
Kaliningrad region	0	0	0	0	0	–1	75	74	74
Lithuania	0	0	0	0	0	0	4	4	4
Latvia	0	0	0	0	–1	0	34	33	33
Estonia	0	0	0	0	–1	0	42	41	40
Rest of Europe	0	0	0	0	1	0	0	1	1
Europe	1	0	0	0	1	0	0	3	3

Figure 3: Annual welfare effects of new roads, percent of regional GDP (equal class width)

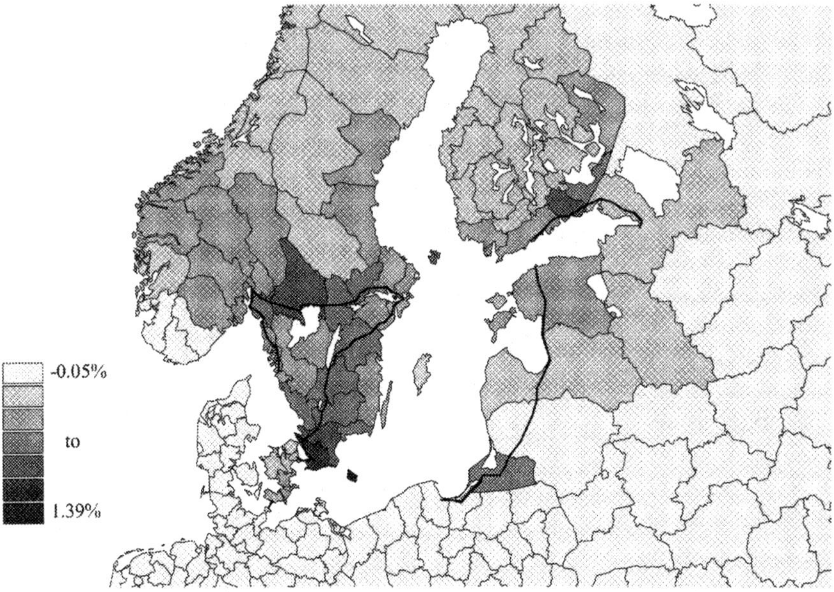

Figure 4: Annual welfare effects of the Fehmarnbelt link, percent of regional GDP (equal class width)

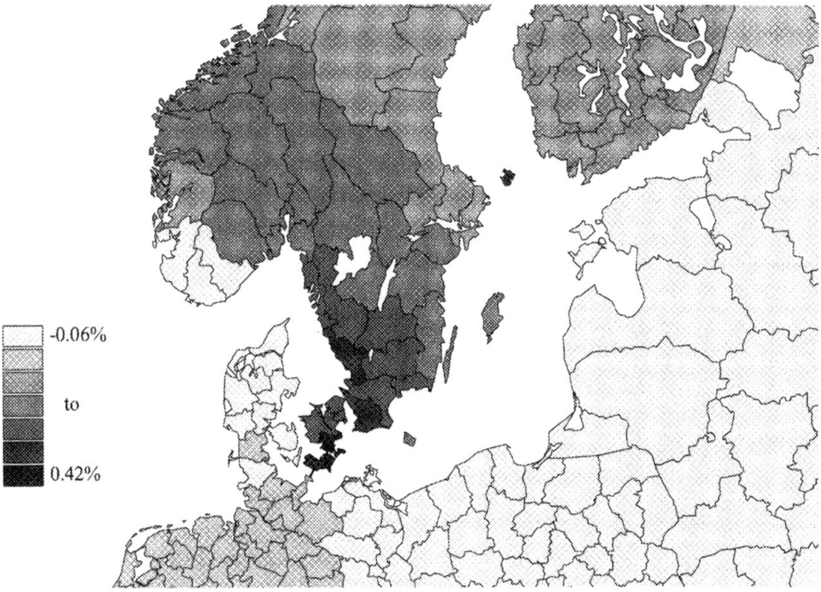

Table 3 shows the share of the regions in the overall welfare gain generated by the respective road projects. Again Sweden appears as the main winner of the Scandinavian projects. Denmark obtains only a little share because it is to a large extent "off the road". Germany's gains are modest as well. It might be disappointing that Schleswig-Holstein is going to reap not more than 1.4 % of the gains generated by the Fehmarnbelt link, even a bit less than Hamburg. The Helsinki–St.Peterburg motorway mainly favours Finland and Russia, as expected, and even harms the Baltic states. The Tallinn–Gdańsk connection mainly favours Russia. Surprisingly, the gains are small in Lithuania and Poland. Interestingly, Germany reaps a higher share than any of the Baltic states or Poland in this project.

Table 3: Annual welfare gains of new roads, relation to total effect, percent

	Ös	O–G	O–S	M–S	Fb	H-SP	T–G	Σ	7 P
Germany	11.8	8.4	–2.3	8.8	14.9	0.6	13.9	11.1	11.2
Schleswig-Holstein	0.9	0.6	–0.1	0.6	1.4	0.3	0.4	0.9	0.9
Hamburg	1.0	0.6	–0.1	0.6	1.7	0.3	0.6	1.0	1.1
Denmark	8.5	6.2	–0.9	3.3	10.2	0.7	0.7	6.6	6.4
Sweden	39.1	7.1	71.4	56.9	27.9	3.4	1.3	31.3	31.8
Norway	10.5	61.2	34.3	–0.3	10.8	1.9	0.2	12.4	12.6
Finland	8.0	–0.4	5.4	16.2	8.5	58.3	11.4	12.0	11.5
Poland	0.2	0.4	–0.2	0.2	0.0	–0.1	4.0	0.4	0.4
Russia	0.0	–0.1	1.0	0.1	0.1	25.5	30.9	4.4	4.1
Lithuania	0.0	0.0	0.0	0.0	0.0	0.0	2.4	0.2	0.2
Latvia	0.0	0.0	0.2	–0.1	0.0	0.0	10.6	0.9	0.9
Estonia	0.0	0.0	0.2	0.0	–0.1	–0.1	0.9	0.8	0.7
Rest of Europe	23.8	19.3	–6.4	17.0	30.9	1.1	19.2	21.8	22.0

A final and important observation regards additivity of welfare gains of different road projects. It has often been speculated that adding the welfare gains of a series of new links might be seriously misleading. The effect of the changed network as a whole might be significantly larger (super-additivity) or smaller than the sum of the individual effects. In this study (and others which we have done) there is no such non-additivity or "network-effect". This is evident from the last two columns of *Tables 2* and *3*, showing the sum of individual links and the effect of the entire network improvement, respectively. There is virtually no difference!

5. Conclusion

In Regio Baltica the degree of integration between transformation countries among each other as well as between these countries and the developed market economies of the EEA is still considerably lower than within the EEA. Hence, there is a potential for further progress in reducing trade impediments and deepening integration in the area. Eastern expansion will favour the EEA members in Regio Baltica more than other countries (except Greece and Austria) because of geographical proximity to the prospective new member countries. New transport links will enhance the integration, but not all countries involved will reap the benefits to the same degree. Sweden gains most from the TEN projects in the area.

References

BMV Bundesminister für Verkehr (1993) Gesamtwirtschaftliche Bewertung von Verkehrswegeinvestitionen. Schriftenreihe des BMV, Heft 72, Bonn

Bröcker J (1998) How would an EU-Membership of the Visegrád Countries Affect Europe's Economic Geography? Annals of Regional Science 32: 91–114

Bröcker J (2000) Spatial Effects of Transport Infrastructure: The Role of Market Structure. In: Roy JR, Schulz W (eds), Theory of Regional Competition. Nomos, Baden-Baden

EU (1997a) Treaty Establishing the European Community, Official Journal of the European Communities C 340, November 10

EU (1997b) Kommission der Europäischen Gemeinschaften, Generaldirektion Verkehr, Auf dem Wege zu einer Gemeinsamen Kooperativen Gesamteuropäischen Verkehrsnetzpolitik. Amt für Amtliche Veröffentlichungen der Europäischen Gemeinschaft, Luxembourg

Giersch H (1949) Economic Union Between Nations and the Location of Industries. Review of Economic Studies 17: 87–97

Haass J, Peschel K (1982) Räumliche Strukturen im internationalen Handel: Eine Analyse der Außenhandelsverflechtung westeuropäischer und nordamerikanischer Länder 1900–1977. Florentz, Munich

Herrmann H, Schmidtke WD, Bröcker J, Peschel K (1993) Kommunikationskosten und internationaler Handel. Florentz, Munich

Lösch A (1962) Die räumliche Ordnung der Wirtschaft, 3rd ed. Gustav Fischer, Stuttgart

Peschel K (1998) Perspectives of Regional Development Around the Baltic Sea. Annals of Regional Science 32: 299–320

Peschel K (1999) The Baltic Sea Region: An Economically Highly Integrated Area in Future? In: Domański R (ed) The Competitiveness of Regions in the Polish and European Perspective. Polish Academy of Sciences, Committee for Space Economy and Regional Planning, Warsaw, pp 295–313

Predöhl A (1949) Außenwirtschaft: Weltwirtschaft, Handelspolitik und Währungspolitik. Vandenhoeck & Ruprecht, Göttingen

Infrastructure and Mobility in the Baltic Sea Region

Siamak Baradaran, Lars Lundqvist

KTH – Royal Institute of Technology

Department of Infrastructure and Planning

Stockholm, Sweden

1. Introduction

The Baltic Sea region (BSR) has been the scene of many drastic changes during the last decade. The dismantling of the "iron curtain" between east and west from 1989 led to unification of Germany and transition to market economies in Eastern Europe. Later developments included the extension of the single European market to the EFTA countries in 1993, the entrance of Sweden and Finland into the European Union in 1995 and negotiations on further enlargement of the European Union with east European countries from 1998.

All these changes have reduced the political and economical barriers between the various parts of the BSR. With increasing interactions, the infrastructure networks have been upgraded, first in terms of air connections and ferry routes. Trade patterns have been characterised by drastic re-orientations and rapid growth. Tourism and cultural exchanges have expanded. Hence, the BSR has developed into a very dynamic region with many more or less simultaneous socio-economic factors triggering rapid changes. However, there are big differences in accessibility and interaction intensities within the region: the accessibilities of Eastern Baltic regions are very low at the outset and the growth in cross Baltic trade between eastern and western economies occurs from very low levels.

The region can be seen as a full-scale laboratory offering unique challenges for theoretical and empirical research. Building a comprehensive geographical information system (GIS) of the BSR would open up a wide potential for monitoring and analyses of spatial interaction, accessibility, urban and regional development and interdependencies between spatial transitions and infrastructural changes.

This paper presents ongoing work on studying infrastructure and mobility patterns in the BSR within a GIS environment. The project is supported by the National Swedish Road Administration as part of its work on future scenarios for the Swedish road transportation system. Earlier work, inspired by Peschel (1993) and the series of Baltic regional science meetings that she initiated, has focused on infrastructure and accessibility (Lundqvist 1995), dynamics of trade and mobility (Persson, Lundqvist, Berglund 1997) and on current trends in economic integration (Lundqvist, Persson 1998). These studies have been of an aggregate character with trade between countries, number of direct air connections between major airports, number of ferry passengers etc. Within the GIS environment outlined in this paper and further developed in the project, integrated analyses of more detailed and complete mobility patterns on the one hand and more disaggregate infrastructure networks will become possible and feasible. The aim and research strategy is further elaborated in Sections 2 and 3.

In Section 4 the completed road system is described as an example of a full-fledged set of infrastructure networks to be developed within the project. Section 5 presents some early examples of accessibility case studies performed on the road and air networks of the Baltic Sea region. In Section 6 we present the available data sources for estimating mobility patterns of goods and people. The dynamics of trade and mobility is illustrated with available aggregate data and some projections of future trade growth are reported. Finally, in Section 7 we summarise the future work on synthesising networks and mobility patterns in the beginning of the 1990s, on modelling these patterns and on using the system for analyses of the implications of future mobility patterns for the Swedish transport system.

2. Aim and Research Strategy

The main aim of this project is to monitor the changes in infrastructure and mobility within the BSR and analyse their linkages to the rapid and superimposed change processes mentioned above. This is achieved by building a high quality knowledge base that can be used for analyses and judgements on how future socio-economic scenarios and infrastructure developments will affect the mobility of goods and people. The analysis should handle both supply driven (e.g., infrastructure investments, TENs (Trans-European Networks) and demand driven change processes (e.g., economic development, trade re-orientations and growth of tourism). A system view of economic development, infrastructure and transport patterns in northern Europe is adopted and seen as a necessary component of the research strategy.

Many research and development projects have focused on spatial planning issues (e.g., VASAB 2010, 1994) or infrastructure developments and Northern European integration (Hedegaard, Lindström 1998). However, to our knowledge no earlier attempts have been made to compile a detailed and coherent information system as a resource for analysing spatial planning and infrastructure development issues. In order to create maximum possible flexibility for studies on various levels of aggregation and to benefit from our investment in establishing databases for future studies, an early decision was taken to compile maximally disaggregate data on infrastructure and mobility within a geographical information system (GIS). Use of a

GIS also increases the flexibility in our work since different national and regional databases can be geo-coded and an integrated knowledge base for multidisciplinary enquiries can be created. Since infrastructure and mobility are the focal points of the project, a transportation oriented GIS with some analytical capabilities was selected as the main tool: TransCAD. Other GIS systems are used as well.

The first stage of the project consisted of collecting and building databases of regions (population, socio-economic data), infrastructure networks (road, rail, ferries) and available mobility patterns (trade, travel surveys). A major challenge is to estimate complete mobility patterns of goods and people on a disaggregate level. The infrastructure networks and population data have been used for various preliminary investigations of accessibility, see Section 5.

3. A Geographic Information System for the Baltic Sea Region

Within the first stage of this project, extensive amounts of data have been collected for the following countries defining our conception of the BSR: Sweden, Finland, western parts of Russia, Estonia, Latvia, Lithuania, Poland, Germany, Denmark and Norway. The databases are from different national and regional sources, with inherent diversities concerning the levels of aggregation, geographical projections and dates. The harmonisation work on these databases was a great challenge and required comprehensive work. Our Baltic Sea region geographical information system is basically an assembly of five sub-databases interrelated by their different unique attributes:

- several polygon layers representing the political boundaries in accordance with NUTS1, NUTS2 and NUTS3[1] regional aggregation levels and a few polygon layers on the municipality level for some of the individual countries,
- several point layers representing the location of populated places in BSR,
- four line layers representing the road, railroad, waterways and air networks within BSR arranged with certain attributes as length, speed and other necessary variables required for the network assignment procedure,
- several socio-economic databases (e.g., REGIO[2], national statistics databases and trip surveys) expressing characteristics of the populated locations within the BSR and the travellers, and
- mobility pattern matrices corresponding to person trips and commodity flows.

---

[1] NUTS: nomenclature defined by EUROSTAT for administrative and statistical regions within the European Union.

[2] REGIO: a socio-economic database on the member states of the European Union, with regional breakdown (Source: EUROSTAT).

Figure 1 represents a map of BSR based on the NUTS3 regional aggregation level together with around 1,700 populated locations. Different combinations of the data sources described above can be used depending on the enquiry in focus.

Figure 1: Major cities in the Baltic Sea region

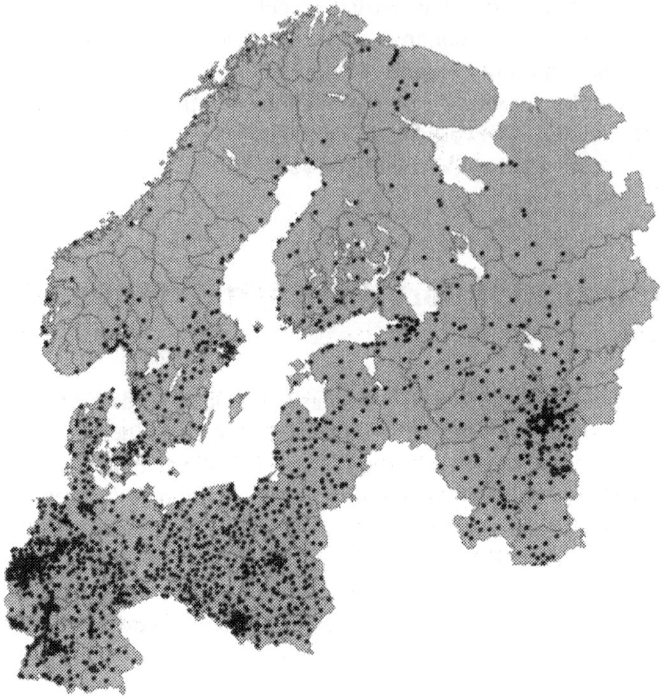

4. Example of Infrastructure Network: System of Roads

The road network constructed for this project is generally based on the road network from IRPUD[3]. The IRPUD network is however modified by replacement of the Swedish and Finnish roads with their corresponding national networks. This substitution has increased the density of links in the two countries which is important since the future use of the Swedish road system is of particular interest to the National Swedish Road Administration.

[3] IRPUD road network is a digitised road network developed by the Institute of Spatial Planning in Dortmund, Germany.

Some of the issues connected to the structure of the road network and the zoning system are frequently discussed in terms of the modifiable areal unit problem. Depending on the projected resolution of the studied area, different results can be obtained, e.g., expressed as the optimal paths chosen within the network assignment operation and the related link loads. Different network assignment methods can also result in diverse link flows. *Figure 2* is the result of a network assignment operation using the user equilibrium algorithm[4] on origin-destination matrices for commodities based on the NUTS2 regional division. In this case no congestion is taken into account and hence the assignment is reflecting shortest paths.

Figure 2: Flow of commodities in the Baltic Sea region

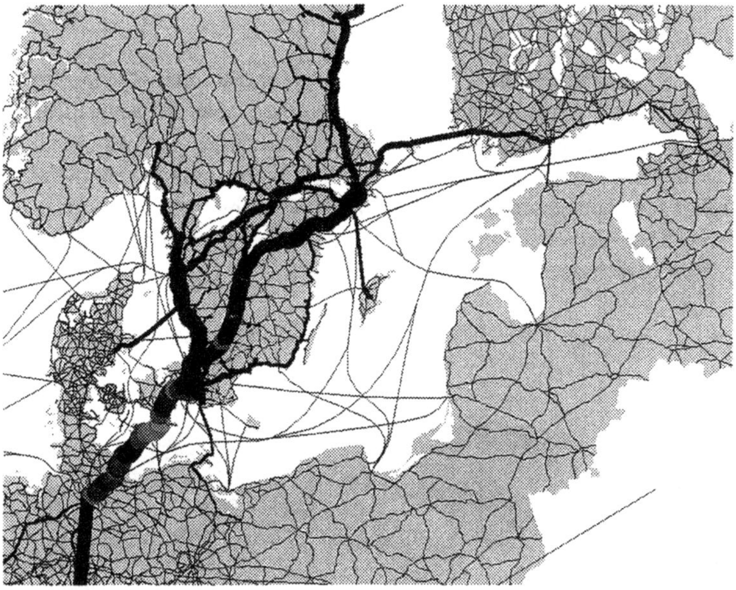

Other compelling questions as effects of time or money penalties on cross-border passages, effects of other spatial barriers and effects on accessibilities exerted by the introduction of new international links (e.g., improvements of TEN or introduction of the Öresund bridge) are also subject to closer analysis in this project.

5. Sample Case Studies of Accessibility

In the field of transportation and regional and urban economics, especially in the case of trip generation, trip distribution and location analysis, the concept of ac-

---

[4] User equilibrium is a network assignment algorithm. Oppenheim (1994).

cessibility is well known (e.g., Bruinsma, Rietveld 1998). As an instrument for evaluation of infrastructure investments, accessibility models are strong candidates and frequently employed (e.g., Lundqvist 1978). Although there is no universally acknowledged definition of accessibility, various indicators with different theoretical backgrounds and complexity have been proposed and implemented in empirical investigations. This variation can also be observed in several excellent European studies[5]. One of the earliest attempts to formulate a structural and operational indicator for accessibility is provided by Hansen (1959), who defines the accessibility as "potential of opportunities for interaction" or literally "a generalisation of the population over distance relationship" that can be defined by:

$$(1) \quad A_i = \sum_{j=1}^{n} \frac{W_j}{e^{\beta c_{ij}}},$$

where A_i is the accessibility of location i, W_j is the amount of opportunities available at location j and βc_{ij} is the weighted cost of travel between location i and j. *Figure 3* represents an accessibility map of the BSR, assuming population of the cities as a proxy for W_j. c_{ij} is the travel time by car in minutes[6] and $\beta = 0.00329$ is a constant travel time sensitivity. In the absence of an appropriately estimated parameter value for β on BSR data, the value above was borrowed from a Swedish study of long distance trips (Baradaran 1999).

Figure 3: Hansen-type accessibility map of the Baltic Sea region

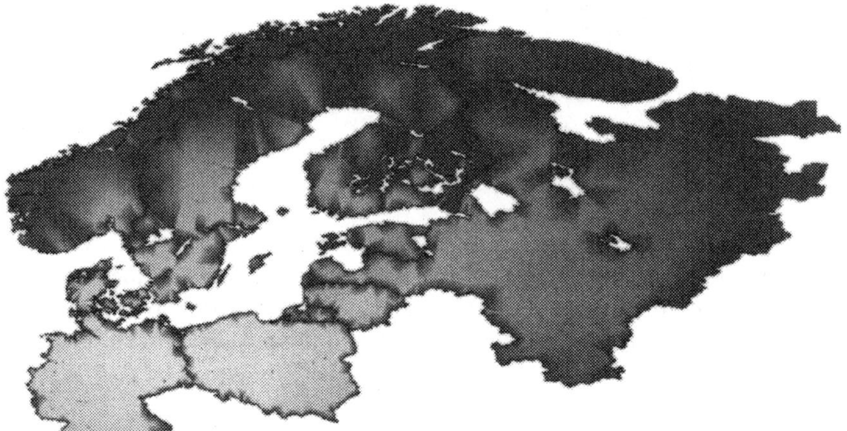

[5] See accessibility studies by Datar (1989), Cattan (1992), Healey, Baker (1994) and Spiekermann, Wegener (1996).

[6] Travel times are calculated using a shortest path algorithm.

The isochronal surfaces are obtained by creation of TIN data structures (Triangulated Irregular Network) in the GIS. The rank of each city is used as the z-value, which differentiates the isochrones. The bright colours represent highly ranked areas, while the dark areas have less accessibility ranks.

The assumption of a single and constant travel time sensitivity (weighting parameter) for the deterrence function could however be dubious. Often we have not enough information about the functional form of the friction variable. Having the traveller's preferences in mind, intuitively there should be differences between the travel time sensitivity for short distance and long distance trips. However, in the accessibility model above we assigned the same weighting coefficient for all trips, regardless of their length.

One solution to that problem is to split the trips depending on the trip lengths and assign different coefficients to them (a so called piecewise linear travel time function). Another solution to this problem is to transform the spatial separation variable. A Box-Cox transformation[7] of the travel time variable of the Hansen type model explained above will result in the following model ($\theta = 0.545$, $\beta = 0.07014$) (Baradaran 1999):

$$(2) \quad A_i = \sum_{j=1}^{n} \frac{W_j}{e^{\beta\left(\frac{t_{ij}^{\theta}-1}{\theta}\right)}}.$$

Figure 4: Accessibility map with a Box-Cox transformed deterrence variable.

---

[7] Box-Cox transformation implies: $y = \dfrac{x^{\theta}-1}{\theta}$.

Figure 4 is the accessibility map resulting from the model with Box-Cox transformed travel times. We can see that the distribution of accessibilities has changed within the BSR. The most accessible locations are still highly ranked while accessibilities in the peripheral regions have decreased.

One particular kind of accessibility measure can be generated by only focusing on the spatial separation variable (Allen et al. 1993):

$$(3)\quad A_i = \sum_{j=1}^{n} \frac{1}{e^{\beta t_{ij}}}, \qquad \text{where } j \neq i \text{ and } i = 1,2,\ldots,n.$$

Figure 5: Air accessibility in the Baltic Sea region

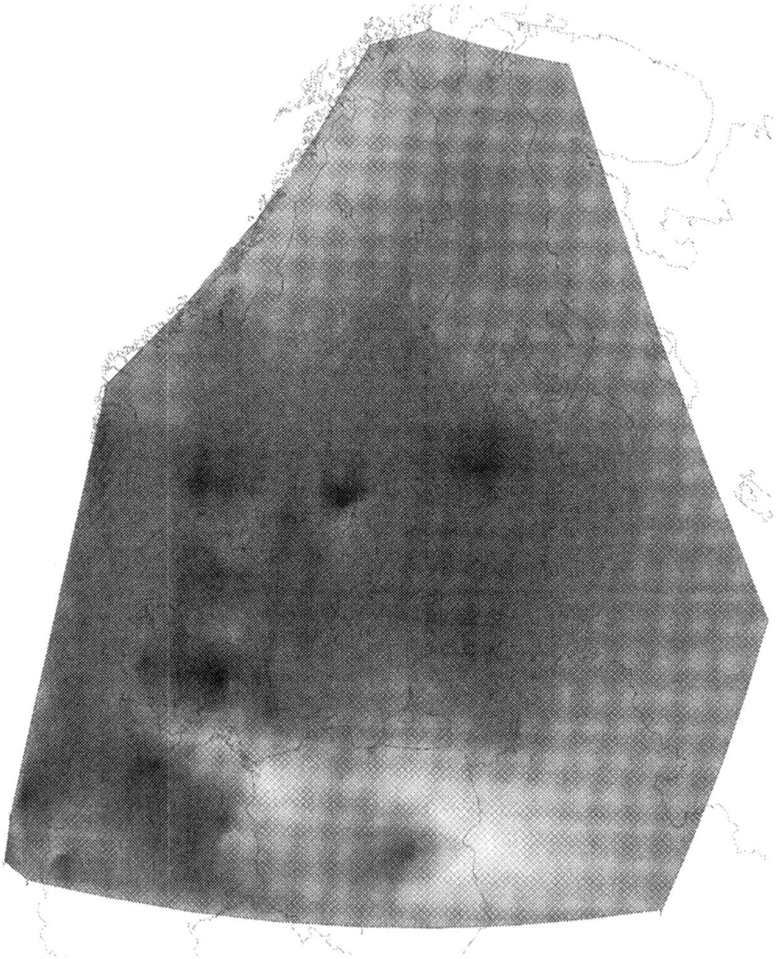

Figure 5 is an illustration of accessibility by the air network in accordance with the model specified above. The travel time variable (m_{ij}) is the sum of in-flight, waiting and interchange times (in minutes), $t_{ij}= \ln m_{ij}$ and β is given a value of 1. This leads to the accessibility measure

$$(4) \qquad A_i = \sum_{j \neq i} 1/m_{ij} \, ,$$

used by Bruinsma, Rietveld (1998) (the source for the air network data and travel times is Mkmetric GmbH in Karlsruhe, Germany).

6. Transport Patterns for Goods and People

For the estimation of origin-destination (OD) matrices of goods and people, data on intra-national transport patterns in the beginning of the 1990s have been collected. In the Swedish case also interactions between Swedish regions and aggregate European regions are available. The following data have been acquired.

- An OD-matrix for person trips in Sweden by the car mode and three OD-matrices for freight transports in Sweden and between Swedish regions and aggregate European regions (the total freight flows have been divided into three different categories of goods). The number of regions is 668 for person trips and 284 for freight. The ongoing National Travel Survey and Tourist and Travel Survey will provide additional data on interregional and international trip patterns with origins and destinations in Sweden.
- For transport patterns within Finland, there are five person trip matrices available (divided into car, bus, train, bicycle and pedestrian modes) and fifteen freight matrices for different categories of goods. The number of regions is 489.
- For Norway, there are five matrices for person trips (divided into car, train, bus, air and ferry modes) and four matrices for freight transport divided into different categories of goods. The number of regions is 20.
- For Denmark, there is one matrix for person trips and three matrices for freight transport divided into different categories of goods. The number of regions is 603.

Obviously, the variation in categories of goods, modes and regional subdivisions of the national matrices will require some harmonising efforts before these OD matrices may be used for estimation purposes. The row and column sums of the intra-national OD matrices for goods may be taken as proxies for the location of production activities. Such proxies may be employed for regional disaggregation of international trade data. Another alternative is to use regional employment data. This method is likely to be pursued for international trade between regions in non-Nordic countries. For interregional trade within these countries, data are completely missing. This means that the level of congestion within these countries will be underestimated if observations or projections of link flow counts in these countries can not be acquired.

Figure 6: Major trade flows in the Baltic Sea region 1997 (million US$, both directions)

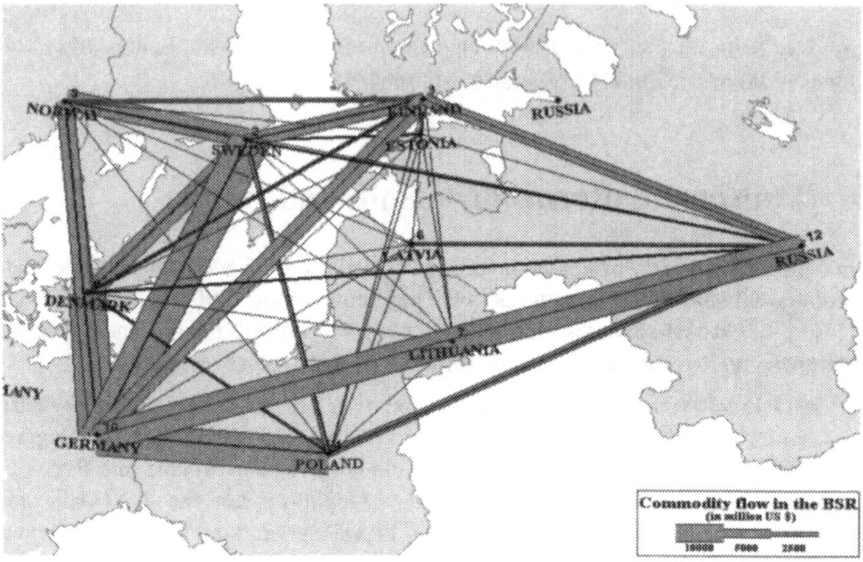

Source: IMF Direction of Trade Statistics, 1998.

From earlier research (Lundqvist, Persson 1998) we know that Germany has by far the strongest position in intra-Baltic trade. The next strongest position is held by Sweden and the strongest single links (both directions) are between Germany–Sweden, Germany–Poland and Germany–Denmark, see *Figure 6.*

The full matrices of trade flows in 1992 and 1997 show that the volume of exports from the Baltic republics and Poland to BSR countries has more than doubled in five years. Also exports from Finland and Russia to Baltic region countries have expanded faster than the average five year growth of about 45 % (corresponding to an annual growth rate of 7.7 %). The trade matrix of 1995 has been used to estimate a gravity type trade model, where the trade flows are explained by the GDP of the exporting and importing countries, the distance between the countries and some dummy variables for free trade association or economic union memberships and sea-borne transport (Strömqvist, Åberg 1998). The estimated parameters of the model have then been used in projections of future trade scenarios. Annual growth rates of about 5 to 6 % between 1995 and 2015 are foreseen. Other estimates show somewhat lower growth rates of about 3.5 % (Callsen 1998). We plan to develop our own model of Baltic trade at a later stage of the project.

Figure 7: Frequencies of direct air connections, February 1998, number of weekly return flights

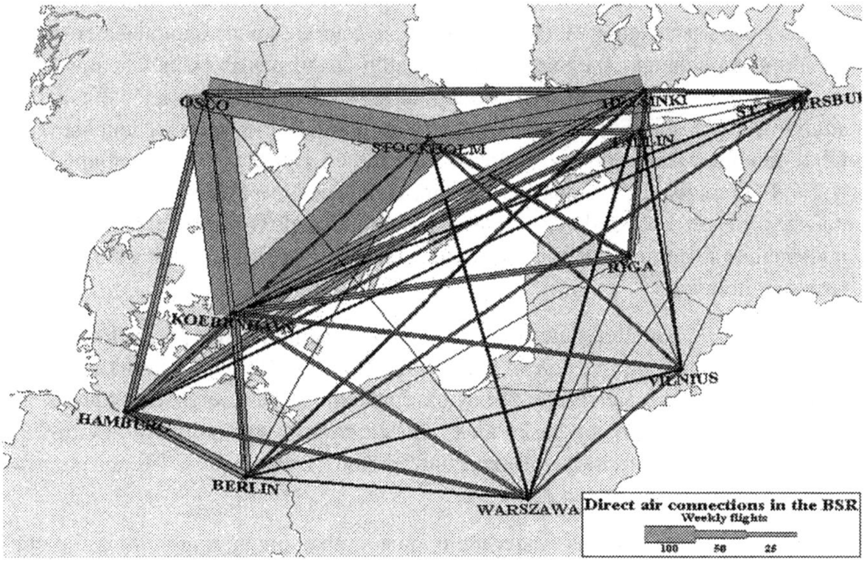

Source: OAG World Airways Guide, February 1998.

The pattern of direct air connections in the Baltic Sea region in 1998 is displayed in *Figure 7*. The pattern shows some similarities with the pattern of trade links: the interactions are strong among the Nordic countries and between the Nordic countries and Germany (to some extent via Copenhagen). The total frequency from the Baltic republics is increasing rapidly from low levels. The absolute growth is, however, greater in the western part. Between 1994 and 1998 the total number of direct flights from the Nordic countries to the BSR have increased by about 300 (30 %). The corresponding figures from Eastern Baltic countries and Southern Baltic countries are 85 (49 %) and minus 32 (minus 8 %) respectively.

The passenger traffic by sea to/from Sweden is about 4 to 5 times higher than the total international air traffic. Passenger traffic by sea with Denmark is dominating but has been loosing shares of the total market to interactions with Finland and (to a lesser extent) with Germany since the 1970s.

7. Plan for Future Work

The railway networks for the individual countries have been collected and a network for the whole region has been constructed. An air network has recently been included (see Section 5). We aim to complement the road, railway and air networks by short-sea shipping as well. This will extend and improve the analysing potential of our GIS database and modelling system for studies of infrastructure and mobility of the Baltic Sea region.

Another long-term goal of this project is to construct a multimodal network for freight and passenger transports. We are studying the possibilities to convert the constructed networks into a so called multimodal super-network. We are also studying the possibility to synthesise the multimodal network by using the NODUS computer programme developed within the Group on "Transport and Mobility"(GTM)[8] in Mons, Belgium (Jourquin, Beuthe 1996). Based on the multimodal network we plan to study the potential for intermodality and decisions on combined mode and route choice alternatives and the resulting loading on the infrastructure networks.

On the basis of completed networks and estimated interaction patterns in terms of trade and personal mobility during the first half of the 1990s, we plan to model the relations between infrastructure provision and mobility. More disaggregate trade models could be estimated based on a rich description of transport conditions. Models of personal international (and interregional) travel by different transport modes may similarly be developed.

A specific research issue is to study the impact of spatial aggregation on the model results. By varying the level of regional aggregation, we hope to be able to study the robustness of model parameters. This would give us an idea about the suitable level of spatial aggregation in this project or similar research contexts.

The ultimate aim of the project is to provide analyses of future scenarios for mobility within the Baltic Sea region and their consequences for the Swedish transport system. In particular, the impacts of future scenarios in terms of link loads in the Swedish national road system will be of interest.

References

Allen WB, Liu D, Singer S (1993) Accessibility Measures of U.S. Metropolitan Areas. Transportation Research 27B: 439-449

Baradaran S (1999) The Influence of Spatial Heterogeneity of Locations on Large Scale Accessibility Models. Working Paper. Division of Transport and Location Analysis, Royal Institute of Technology, Stockholm

Bruinsma FR, Rietveld P (1998) Is Transport Infrastructure Effective: Transport Infrastructure and Accessibility Impacts on the Space Economy. Springer, Berlin, Heidelberg, New York

---

[8] The GTM group has developed a multimodal trans-European freight transport network which is used within the European programmes EUNET, COST 328 and TERMINET.

Callsen S (1998) Trade Potentials in Northern Europe and Consequences for Traffic Flows. In: Hedegaard L, Lindström B (eds) The NEBI Yearbook 1998 – North European and Baltic Sea Integration. Springer, Berlin, Heidelberg, New York, pp 73-86

Cattan N (1992) Air and Rail Accessibility and Attractivities of European Metropolis. In: Bonnafous A (ed) Selected Proceedings of the 6th World Conference on Transport Research, Vol. 1. LET Université Lumière Lyon, Lyon

DATAR Délégation à l' Aménagement du Territoire et à l' Action Région (1989) Les Villes Européenness, Maison de la Geographie, Montpellier

Hansen WG (1959) How Accessibility Shapes Land-use. Journal of the American Institute of Planners 25: 73-76

Healey & Baker (1994) European Real Estate Monitor. Healey & Baker, London

Hedegaard L, Lindström B (eds) (1998) The NEBI Yearbook 1998 - North European and Baltic Sea Integration. Springer, Berlin, Heidelberg, New York

Jourquin B, Beuthe M (1996) Transportation Policy Analysis with a Geographic Information System: The Virtual Network of Freight Transportation in Europe. Transportation Research 4C: 359-371

Lundqvist L (1978) Planning for Freedom of Action. In: Karlqvist A, Lundqvist L, Snickars F, Weibull JW (eds) Spatial Interaction Theory and Planning Models. North-Holland, Amsterdam

Lundqvist L (1995) Transportation Infrastructure and Accessibility in the Baltic Rim Area. In: Lundqvist L, Persson LO (eds) Baltic Regions and Baltic Links. The Nordic Institute of Regional Policy Research 1995:2, pp 132-148

Lundqvist L, Persson LO (1998) Current Trends in Economic Integration. In Hedegaard L, Lindström B (eds) The NEBI Yearbook 1998 – North European and Baltic Sea Integration. Springer, Berlin, Heidelberg, New York, pp 55-71

Oppenheim N (1994) Urban Travel Demand Modelling: From Individual Choices to General Equilibrium. John Wiley & Sons, New York

Persson LO, Lundqvist L, Berglund S (1997) Dynamics of Trade and Mobility in the Baltic Region. In: Owsinski JW, Stepniak A (eds) The Nordic-Baltic Europe: Integration Risks, Barriers & Opportunities. The Interfaces Institute, Warsaw, pp 97-130

Peschel K (1993) Perspectives of Regional Economic Development Around the Baltic. In: Lundqvist L, Persson LO (eds) Visions and Strategies in European Integration – A North European Perspective. Springer, Berlin, Heidelberg, New York, pp 19-31

Spiekermann K, Wegener M (1996) Trans-European Networks and Unequal Accessibility in Europe. European Journal of Regional Development 4: 35-42

Strömquist U, Åberg P (1998) Trade and Modal Change in the Baltic Region: Scenarios to 2015. Working Paper, TRITA-IP AR 98-61. Division of Regional Planning, Royal Institute of Technology, Stockholm

VASAB 2010 (1994) Vision and Strategies Around the Baltic Sea 2010: Towards a Framework for Spatial Development in the Baltic Sea Region. Third Conference of Ministers for Spatial Planning and Development, Tallinn

Sweden and the Baltic Sea Region: Transaction Costs and Trade Intensities

Scott Hacker, Börje Johansson

Jönköping International Business School

Jönköping, Sweden

1. Introduction

In her research, Karin Peschel has demonstrated that the friction of interaction between regions and between countries has a strong influence on location and trade (e.g., Peschel 1982, 1984). A particular feature of her findings is that the pertinent friction is affected by many other factors than just geographic distance. In this paper, we adopt this focus and show that geographic transaction costs can be identified indirectly for pair-wise trade links between countries in the Baltic Sea region, and that such costs strongly affect the distribution of trade flows.[1]

Peschel (1998) distinguishes four sources of geographic transaction costs: (i) costs related to distance, (ii) differences in language and culture, (iii) social and political differences, and (iv) political strategies leading to barriers between states. In the current study we further discuss the elements of geographic transaction costs. The econometric analysis concentrates on the first three factors and does provide support to Peschel's theoretical framework. Proxy variables are used to reflect the combined effect of factor (ii) and (iii) above.

In this study, we distinguish between various groups of countries, each of which we expect to have lower geographic transaction costs for trade within the group than outside it, all else equal. One such trade-region distinction is the emerging Baltic (E-Baltic) countries: Russia, Estonia, Latvia, Lithuania and Poland. Another is the Nordic area (Finland, Sweden, Denmark, Norway and Iceland), and a third is the mature-economy countries (M-countries) in Europe, i.e., the developed part of Europe. Our analysis has indicated that the delineation of regions has to be even finer to capture affinity areas with relatively low inter-country transaction costs. We focus on those delineations dealing with countries around the Baltic.

Peschel (1998) states that "a Scandinavian-Baltic economic space could come into being" with improvements in the transformation of the Latvian and Lithuanian

[1] Funding from the EU's INTERREG IIC Programme through SEBTrans is acknowledged. We appreciate the fine research assistance provided by Henrik Einarsson.

economies. She notes that among E-Baltic countries, Estonia has made the greatest inroads in integrating with the Scandinavian economic space. She also suggests that Germany and Poland are not likely to be a core part of an economic space around the Baltic. These remarks correspond to her previous (Peschel, 1993) statement that "It cannot be doubted that the Baltic Republics [Estonia, Latvia and Lithuania] will be attracted to Scandinavia..." Our findings bring further insights into her forecasts. They also show that the relevant space is that among Nordic-Baltic countries (Denmark, Sweden and Norway) and Estonia, Latvia and Lithuania (ELL countries).

Our short presentation is organised as follows. Section 2 introduces the concept of geographic transaction costs and discusses how they vary over region or country borders. Section 3 is focused on aggregate export flows between countries in Europe. We specify and estimate a gravity model for our analysis, including variables that are assumed to reflect transaction-cost differentials across trade links. Using the estimated parameters, we analyse the trade in the Baltic Sea region. In this way we are able to reveal trade affinities between exporting and importing countries, where a high affinity corresponds to low transaction costs. Section 4 examines in detail a small subset of products exported from Sweden to the E-Baltic. This subset consists of products with a high share of the export value and fast export growth. Section 5 provides some tentative conclusions.

2. Geographic Transaction Costs and Trade Links

All transport and transaction costs that vary with distances in geographical networks are denoted by the specific term "geographic transaction costs". Within a functional region, the costs of nearby (face-to-face) interactions are much lower than the same type of transactions and other direct contacts with actors outside the region. In a similar way one may assume that transaction costs vary in size across interaction links for pairs of countries as well as pairs of regions.

With a general formulation, transaction costs comprise resource consumption when property rights are transferred between two agents (from buyer to seller). These costs include search costs, communication costs, negotiations about product attributes and prices, contract costs and other adjustment costs associated with the transfer. In our definition, transport costs are included when physical goods are displaced. In addition, when seller and buyer interaction takes place, travel costs become a component of the transaction costs.

When certain transactions are repeated frequently it becomes feasible for the agents involved to standardise transaction procedures, which provides a way to reduce the transaction cost for each separate delivery. This can happen in two ways. The first may be illustrated by a situation when one particular supplier delivers frequently to a particular customer. The second way to standardise transaction procedures can be represented by the stylised case in which a supplying firm that has many customers (e.g., households) designs a system for arranging the transaction and sales by applying the same procedure for all customers. A typical household product usually is delivered in chains involving both these solutions. The steps of the chain can have the following form: (i) a producer delivers to a wholesale organisation (which may be an individual firm or a subsidiary of the producer), (ii) the wholesaler delivers to a retailer, and (iii) the latter sells to a large set of customers. The first two steps in such chains can be organised on the basis of long-term contracts with very standardised procedures for each delivery link, whereas the standardisation in the latter case is based on equal procedure for all customers.

Based on these examples, we may think of two extreme types of transactions – one with very standardised procedures and low associated costs and one with non-standardised high-cost procedures. In the latter case, we may assume that the interaction between the supplier and the customer is contact intensive, requiring many direct person-contacts (face-to-face). Products that are sold and delivered under this regime will also be distance sensitive.

Among the distance-sensitive products we expect to find investment goods, especially products that embody new technology. For the latter, a high contact intensity (with no standardised transaction procedures) may be combined with high product value. In the final assessment of Swedish export to the E-Baltic countries, we will pay special attention to such products.

In this paper, we investigate to what extent it is possible to arrange countries in and around the Baltic Sea region according to rising transaction cost levels, as illustrated in *Figure 1*. In general, the type of transaction with the lowest geographic transaction costs is that which is between agents who are close to each other. This is due to the fact that, in comparison to transactions over longer distances, such trade generally involves lower transportation costs and a greater likelihood of common characteristics of the traders. The curve for geographic transaction costs is not displayed as being smooth in *Figure 1*. These costs abruptly rise at various points (two are shown in the Figure) due to transaction barriers that generally arise at borders. Trade with an agent on one side of a border can have a significantly different cost than that with an agent on the other side of that border. This arises due to the abrupt differences in language, culture, taxes, laws, etc. between the two sides of the border. The greater the differences are, the greater the rise in cost.

Figure 1: A sequence of transaction barriers in trade over various distances

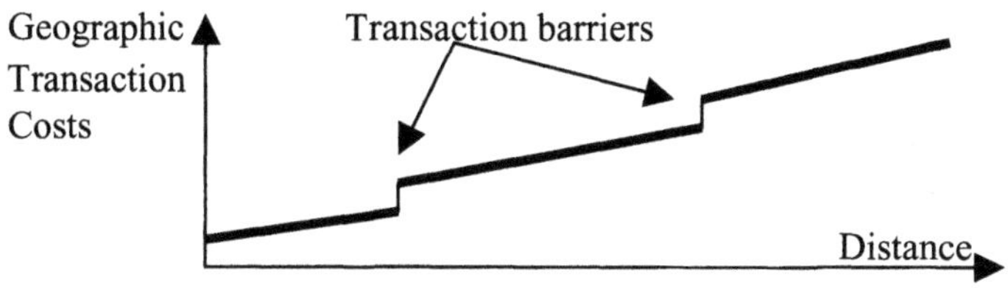

3. Aggregate Trade Intensities – Emerging and Mature Market Economies

3.1 Gravity Modelling in Trade Analysis

To analyze the effect of transaction barriers between various countries, we utilize a gravity model. The typical form of a gravity model for trade analysis is

$$(1)\quad x_{rs} = Y_r^{\alpha} Y_s^{\beta} F_{rs} \,,$$

where x_{rs} is the value of exports from country r to country s, Y_r is aggregate income in country r, Y_s is aggregate income in country s, F_{rs} is the friction effect, and α and β are constants. As friction decreases (transaction costs decrease), the F_{rs} term increases, lifting the value of trade between countries. The α and β terms are hypothesized to be positive. A higher value for Y_r represents a greater supply potential for the exporting country, and a higher for Y_s represents a greater market potential for the importing country. Under either circumstance, the value of exports from country r to country s is expected to be higher.

The notion of market potential was introduced as a standard tool for spatial flows in the 1960s (e.g., Lakshmanan, Hansen, 1965). Already in Stiglitz (1951), this concept plays an important role for analysing industries with scale economies. Gravity models represent one approach to capture the influence from market potentials (e.g., Isard, Bramhall 1960). Fujita, Krugman, Venables (1999) have recently demonstrated this concept's importance for trade analysis.

Gravity models have had a long and rich history in empirical trade research. The earliest estimates of trade gravity models were by Tinbergen (1962) and Pöyhöynen (1963). Even though gravity models have long enjoyed empirical success, they suffered from a lack of solid microeconomic theoretical foundations for many years. Such foundations were ultimately found, however. Gravity models were first shown to be consistent with trade models including product differentiation (see Anderson 1979, Bergstrand, 1985, 1989, 1990). Later, gravity models were shown to be also consistent with the Heckscher-Ohlin theory (Deardorff 1995) and with reciprocal dumping theory (Feenstra, Markusen, Rose 1998).

3.2 An Empirical Model of Export Flows in Europe

Based on the general gravity model (*Equation 1*), a regression equation can be formulated to include factors that affect the size of the geographic transaction costs, as reflected in the friction-effect term, F_{rs}. We develop a regression equation that focuses on trade frictions facing E-Baltic countries especially. The equation to be estimated is

$$(2)\quad \ln x_{rs} = h + \alpha \ln Y_r + \beta \ln Y_s + \lambda d_{rs} + \gamma C_{rs} + \xi M_{rs} + \psi P_{rs} + \mu N_{rs} + \eta E_{rs} + \varphi B_{rs} + \varepsilon_{rs} \,,$$

where h and ε_{rs} respectively signify the intercept and error term. Otherwise, each of the variables and some of the data sources are described below. For the dependent variable, $\ln x_{rs}$, we use 1993–1996 constant-dollar average trade flows between each of nineteen countries – fourteen developed European countries[2] and the five E-Baltic countries. All of the trade data comes from the IMF's *Direction of Trade Statistics.* Y_r and Y_s respectively are the GDPs of the exporting and importing country, measured as the average over 1993-1996 in constant dollar terms. Most of the GDP data come from the IMF's *International Financial Statistics.* Some GDP data, especially those dealing with the E-Baltic countries, are from OECD or UN sources. The variable d_{rs} is the air distance in thousands of kilometres between the capital cities of the exporting country r and the importing country s. C_{rs} is a dummy variable dealing with whether countries r and s have a common border (1 if they do, 0 otherwise). The other five explanatory variables are dummy variables on trade flows between or within specific sets of countries.

$$(3)\quad M_{rs} = \begin{cases} 1 \text{ if both } r \text{ and } s \text{ are mature market economies } (M\text{ - countries}) \\ 0 \text{ otherwise} \end{cases}$$

$$(4)\quad P_{rs} = \begin{cases} 1 \text{ if one of the countries is Poland and the other is an } M\text{ - country} \\ 0 \text{ otherwise} \end{cases}$$

$$(5)\quad N_{rs} = \begin{cases} 1 \text{ if } r \text{ and } s \text{ are both Nordic countries (inter - Nordic trade);} \\ 0 \text{ otherwise} \end{cases}$$

$$(6)\quad E_{rs} = \begin{cases} 1 \text{ if } r \text{ and } s \text{ are both E - Baltic countries (inter E - Baltic trade)} \\ 0 \text{ otherwise} \end{cases}$$

$$(7)\quad B_{rs} = \begin{cases} 1 \text{ if one of } (r,s) \text{ is Baltic - Nordic (Denmark, Sweden, Finland) and} \\ \quad \text{the other is one of the ELL countries (Estonia, Latvia, Lithuania)} \\ 0 \text{ otherwise} \end{cases}$$

The variables M_{rs}, N_{rs}, E_{rs}, and B_{rs} are assumed to pick up affinities related to linguistic, cultural, social, and political similarities between pairs of countries. The variable P_{rs} is included to reflect Poland's rapid development in ties with the M-countries that the other E-Baltic countries have not achieved. The mature market economies are the fourteen developed countries in the sample, and all five of the Nordic countries are among these. Therefore, trade flows between Nordic coun-

---

[2] Austria, Belgium/Luxembourg, Denmark, France, Finland, Germany, Iceland, Italy, The Netherlands, Norway, Spain, Sweden, Switzerland and the United Kingdom

tries encounter both the mature market economy effect and the inter-Nordic effect (M_{rs} and N_{rs} are both set to one).

Based on previous studies, we should expect α and β to be positive and slightly smaller than unity. Our assumptions about the nature of transaction costs imply that $\lambda < 0$, and that γ, ξ, ψ, μ, η, φ, are all positive. The latter six parameters refer to factors that reduce transaction costs and thereby lower the friction factor, F_{rs}, in the gravity formula. In contrast, greater distance increases F_{rs} through higher transaction costs. Our results presented in *Table 1* show that the coefficient estimates have the expected signs and that they are all statistically significant.

Table 1: Estimated aggregate trade-flow model

Variable	Parameter	Parameter estimate	t-statistic
ln GDP, exporter (ln Y_r)	α	0.83	34.2
ln GDP, importer (ln Y_s)	β	0.74	30.5
Distance (d_{rs})	λ	-0.87	-14.3
Common border (C_{rs})	γ	0.38	3.3
Inter M-countries (M_{rs})	ξ	1.46	16.0
Poland – M-country (P_{rs})	ψ	1.37	10.0
Inter Nordic (N_{rs})	μ	0.61	3.8
Inter E-Baltic (E_{rs})	η	1.47	7.8
Baltic-Nordic – ELL (B_{rs})	φ	0.97	5.4
Intercept	h	-20.87	-19.6

Adjusted $R^2 = 0.94$. Number of observations = 342.

From *Table 1* we may now ask: do the E-Baltic countries display the same affinity in their relation with Sweden as Sweden has vis-à-vis a Nordic neighbour? In fact, the Nordic effect comes out as not larger than the B_{rs} effect, which in this case reflects the affinity between Sweden and an ELL country.

As regards the small ELL countries, they currently lack the mature transactions effect, M_{rs}, which is present in, e.g., Sweden's trade with Germany. However, as the modernisation continues, one should expect that the M_{rs} variable gradually would start to apply also for the ELL countries. Apparently, such application already exists today for Poland given the similarity of the estimates for ξ and ψ. More broadly it may be noted that the estimates for ξ, ψ, and η are very similar. That implies that, all else equal, there are no significant differences in trade among E-Baltic countries, trade among mature countries, and trade between Poland and mature countries.

3.3 Interpreting Residuals as Additional Affinity Differentials

In the preceding subsection we discussed that E-Baltic countries tend to have trade affinities with each other and that ELL countries also seem to have an affinity with

Baltic-Nordic countries. How do the observed affinities in the trade relations vary between the individual E-Baltic countries, and how do these patterns of reduced transaction costs look if we instead investigate the affinities of individual E-Baltic countries with individual mature Baltic countries? To consider these questions we examine the residuals (actual minus predicted log trade flows) from the regression presented in *Table 1*.

These residuals for trade flows among emerging Baltic countries and between these countries and other Baltic countries are displayed in *Table 2*. When reading these residuals, one should keep in mind that all the impacts from the affinity dummies shown in *Table 1* are already taken into account. The residuals can indicate higher or lower affinity effects on various trade flows than what the affinity dummies suggest.

What stands out from these residuals is that Estonia, Latvia, and Lithuania all have positive residuals in trade among themselves. This is in stark contrast to the residuals on trade flows involving any of the emerging countries with Poland or Russia, which are all negative. These negative residuals are nevertheless less in magnitude than the positive coefficient estimate for the inter E-Baltic dummy (1.47). Apparently, even trade flows involving any of the emerging countries with Poland or Russia are lifted by some trade affinities. Overall, it seems that there are trade affinities among all the emerging Baltic countries, but the strongest are those for trade flows between Estonia, Latvia, and Lithuania.

Table 2: Selected residuals from Table 1 regression (actual minus predicted log trade flows)

Importer Exporter	Estonia	Latvia	Lithuania	Poland	Russia	Sweden	Denmark	Finland	Germany
Estonia	---	1.56	1.50	-1.03	-0.66	0.51	0.05	1.25	0.08
Latvia	0.31	---	0.67	-0.92	-0.58	-0.23	-0.89	-0.74	0.01
Lithuania	1.14	1.64	---	-0.31	-0.21	-0.63	-0.19	-1.19	0.54
Poland	-0.84	-0.34	-0.07	---	-0.39	-0.14	0.28	-0.13	0.35
Russia	-0.93	-0.20	-0.06	-0.28	---	-0.32	-0.59	0.33	0.68
Sweden	0.39	-0.01	-0.44	0.17	-0.63				
Denmark	-0.05	-0.23	0.10	0.22	-0.25				
Finland	1.77	0.48	0.06	0.37	-0.10				
Germany	0.24	-0.06	0.53	0.05	0.55				

We see that on all but one of the trade flows between ELL countries and Nordic Baltic countries, the residual is either negative of lower magnitude than the coefficient estimate for the Baltic-Nordic-ELL dummy (0.97) or positive. The exception is on the exports from Lithuania to Finland.

Other interesting information may be gathered from these residuals, which again must be considered in light of the affinity variables already included in the model.

Sweden shows stronger-than-predicted trade flows with Estonia and lower-than-predicted ones with Latvia and Lithuania. Finland has larger-than-predicted exports to the E-Baltic countries (excluding Russia), but lower-than-predicted imports from most of these countries. Germany exhibits larger-than-predicted trade flows on a majority of its displayed trade links. It is also interesting to note that there is often a lack of symmetry in the table's pair-wise residuals (residuals between the same pair of countries).

4. Trade Flows and Modernisation of the Emerging Market Economies: Products with a Large Share of Sweden's Export to E-Baltic Countries

To complement our finding of an apparent special trade affinity between Nordic Baltic countries and E-Baltic countries, we examine the composition of the export flow of one of these Nordic-Baltic countries, Sweden, to the E-Baltic. Between 1993 and 1998, the value of Sweden's exports to E-Baltic countries increased in real terms annually by about 22 % on average (the constant continuous growth equivalent). One question to consider is whether this export flow is oriented towards products that are especially associated with investment and modernisation of the E-Baltic economies. Another issue has to do with to what extent Swedish firms export to these economies products with a high price. Moreover, are these products based on advanced technology, do they embody advanced technique standards, and is their production in Sweden knowledge intensive?

To carry out this analysis, we have used 5-digit level export data from Statistics Sweden for the years 1993–1998. First, we have selected the products with the highest value share of the export to the E-Baltic over the 1997–1998 period. We find that as few as 48 products out of 2,886 generated almost 49 % of the total value of the export flow to the E-Baltic. Second, we selected among these products those with export growth to the E-Baltic between 1993/1994 and 1997/1998 higher than Sweden's average to these countries (120.8 % in real terms), leaving us with 43 product groups. Third, we divided these 43 products into groups based on whether they demonstrated high value (top 49 %) or fast growth (above average) in Swedish exports to the other mature Baltic economies (M-Baltic: Germany, Denmark, Finland). *Table 3* characterises these groups.

What are our main conclusions? First, high value products for the E-Baltic tend to be high value products also for the M-Baltic (17.9 % + 16.2 % = 34.1 % of export value compared to the 43.9 % group total). Second, the price level of E-Baltic imports is generally very high for those products with high value and fast growth rate in export to M-Baltic countries. Third, the growth rate is generally much higher for the E-Baltic than the M-Baltic flows. Can a catching-up growth process among the E-Baltic countries explain this? Do they concentrate their imports from

Sweden on products that are used in modernising the economies to standards of the M-Baltic countries? The information in *Table 4* sheds some light on this question by examining the products in group (I) of *Table 3*.

Table 3: Groups of products with a high value share and a fast growth in the export flow to the E-Baltic region

	1997/1998 Average SEK price per kg of exports to E-Baltic	1993/1994-1997/1998 Export growth in real terms (%) to E-Baltic	to M-Baltic	1997/1998 Share of total Swedish export value to E-Baltic (%)
(I) High value & fast growth in M-Baltic	892	667*	87	17.9
(II) Low value & fast growth in M-Baltic	541	530	107	5.6
(III) High value & slow growth in M-Baltic	92	222	3	16.2
(IV) Low value & slow growth in M-Baltic	89	465	-8	4.2
Groups (I), (II), (III) and (IV)	474	388	40	43.9

* Note that this implies a 68 % annual growth rate on average (constant continuous growth equivalent).

Table 4: Products in export flows of group (I) from Table 3 (Price levels are those on 1997/1998 exports to E-Baltic)

Very high price (924-2471 SEK/kg)	High price (92-295 SEK/kg)	Medium high price (22-58 SEK/kg)	Low price (0.2-16 SEK/kg)
•Telephone switchboards •Radio transmitters •Radio transmission equipment	•Pharmaceutical products •Medical and surgical instruments •Electrical transformer and motors for aircraft •Motor vehicles for freight	•Plastic products •Rubber tires •Floor covering of plastic materials •Parquet floor materials	•Prefab buildings •Basic iron and steel prod. •High quality paper for printing •Iron ore

All products in *Table 4* are intermediary deliveries, although some are mixed final/intermediary products. A large share consists of investment goods for sectors such as construction, transport, communication and health care. The supply comes from industries with a strong specialisation in the Swedish production and trade, with scale economies that require a large market potential.

5. Conclusions

This paper has demonstrated the existence of strong trade affinities among various groups of countries in Europe. These affinities are not fully symmetric, which means the friction of trade in one direction sometimes differs significantly from that in the opposite direction. There appear to be strong trade affinities among the

Nordic countries and also among the Baltic-Nordic countries and the small Baltic states (Estonia, Latvia and Lithuania). An examination of detailed industrial data indicates that investment goods have played an important role in Sweden's rapidly expanding exports to the emerging Baltic countries.

References

Anderson J (1979) A Theoretical Foundation for the Gravity Equation. American Economic Review 69: 106-116

Bergstrand J (1985) The Gravity Equation in International Trade: Some Microeconomic Foundations and Empirical Evidence. Review of Economics and Statistics 67: 474-481

Bergstrand J (1989) The Generalized Gravity Equation, Monopolistic Competition, and the Factor-Proportions Theory in International Trade. Review of Economics and Statistics 71: 143-153

Bergstrand J (1990) The Heckscher-Ohlin-Samuelson Model, the Linder Hypothesis and the Determinants of Bilateral Intra-Industry Trade. Economic Journal 100: 1216-1229

Deardorff A (1995) Determinants of Bilateral Trade: Does Gravity Work in a Neoclassical World? National Bureau of Economic Research (NBER) Working Paper No. 5377, Cambridge (Massachusetts)

Feenstra R, Markusen J, Rose A (1998) Understanding the Home Market Effect and the Gravity Equation: the Role of Differentiating Goods. National Bureau of Economic Research (NBER) Working Paper no. 6804, Cambridge (Massachusetts)

Fujita M Krugman P, Venables AJ (1999) The Spatial Economy – Cities, Regions and International Trade. The MIT Press, Cambridge (Massachusetts)

Isard W, Bramhall DF (1960) Gravity, Potential and Spatial Interaction Models. In Isard W (ed), Methods of Regional Analysis. MIT Press, Cambridge (Massachusetts)

Lakshmanan TR, Hansen WG (1965) A Retail Market Potential Model. Journal of the American Institute of Planners 31: 134-143

Peschel K (1982) International Trade, Integration and Industrial Location: the Case of Germany. Regional Science and Urban Economics 12: 247-269

Peschel K (1984) International versus National versus Regional Impacts on Regional Development. In: Institut for Graenseregionsforskning, Aabenraa, Institut für Regionalforschung, der Universität Kiel (eds) Regional Research in an International Perspective. Florentz, Munich, pp 7-28

Peschel K (1993) Perspectives of Regional Economic Development Around the Baltic. In: Lundqvist L, Persson LO (eds), Visions and Strategies in European Integration. A North European Perspective. Springer, Berlin, Heidelberg, New York, pp 19-31

Peschel K (1998) Perspectives of Regional Development Around the Baltic Sea. Annals of Regional Science 32: 299-320

Pöyhönen P (1963) A Tentative Model for the Volume of Trade Between Countries. Weltwirtschaftliches Archiv 90: 93-99

Stiglitz G (1951) The Division of Labour is Limited by the Extent of the Market. Journal of Political Economy 59: 185-193

Tinbergen J (1962) Shaping the World Economy: Suggestions for an International Economic Policy. The Twentieth Century Fund, New York

Part II

Infrastructure and the Regions

Public Research Institutions in Regional Innovations Systems: Assessment and Outline of a Research Agenda

Michael Fritsch

Technical University Bergakademie Freiberg

Faculty of Economics and Business Administration

Chair for Economic Policy and Research Unit Innovation Economics

Freiberg (Saxonia), Germany

1. Introduction

As a scientist but maybe even more as the political person that she is, Karin Peschel has always been very aware of the contribution universities and other publicly funded research institutions make to technological and economic development.[1] Indeed, recent research has clearly demonstrated that this contribution tends to be rather significant. This result should be not at all surprising, because to generate such positive effects for innovation and growth constitutes an essential part of the mission these institutions have. In sharp contrast to the considerable importance of public research institutions for development, our state of knowledge about their role in innovation systems is extremely poor. This deficiency not only limits our understanding of innovation processes, but also constitutes a severe bottleneck for the design of growth policy, particularly for a policy that aims at improving or securing the effectiveness of public research institutions and their contribution to economic development.

In this contribution, I will give an overview on the state of knowledge about the role that public research institutions may play for economic development (Section 3). Based on this survey, I will outline an agenda for further research with regard to this important element of the innovation system (Section 4). Starting point of the discussion is a brief characterization of the basic concept of an innovation system that constitutes the analytical framework for the discussion (Section 2).

---

[1] The term "publicly funded research institutions" encompasses all research institutions that are financed by the state to a considerable degree. In Germany, this includes all universities and *Fachhochschulen* (universities with focus on applied studies in engineering, business and other subjects areas) as well as non-university research institutes like those of the Max-Planck- or the Fraunhofer Society which are not part of the higher education system.

2. Regional Innovation Systems as a Concept of Analysis

It has become widely recognized in recent years that innovation processes are characterized by an intensive division of labor between firms or organizations. Such a division of innovative labor involves private sector firms as well as the publicly funded research institutions and may encompass relationships among or between these two groups of actors. Because the different institutions may make considerable contributions to innovation processes, it would be inaccurate or misleading to restrict the analysis to innovation activities of a single innovator. Instead one should attempt to account for the contributions of other firms or of public research institutions and investigate the division of innovative labor in more detail. The analysis of the division of innovative labor represents the basic idea behind the concept of (national, regional or sectoral) "innovation systems" that has been introduced to the analysis of innovation processes only a little more than a decade ago.[2] The innovation system-approach is explicit in accounting for the specific purposes and contributions of different types of organizations such as universities, public research facilities, and entrepreneurial R&D departments to individual innovation activities.[3]

With regard to the spatial delineation of an innovation system, many authors deal with whole nations, thereby implicitly or explicitly assuming that the similarities of institutions, language and culture form a "natural" geographical boundary (Lundvall 1992). However, there is no need to limit the innovation-system approach to nations and there are many topics that can be analyzed in a more appropriate way by applying other geographical boundaries of the innovation system. For some topics (e.g., markets in global technological competition) it may be more suitable to choose a higher level of aggregation and to investigate the international division of innovative labor (Lundvall 1992). Other questions may be analyzed more appropriately on a lower aggregation level, e.g., regions within nations. Regional innovation systems may constitute an appropriate geographical framework of analysis, particularly when the local environment proves to be important and short-distance interaction in the division of labor plays a significant role like in so-called industrial districts (Cooke, Uranga, Etxebarria 1997; Cooke 1998). Obviously, there is no single fitting spatial framework of an innovation systems but the

---

[2] For an outline of the concept see Lundvall (1992) and Edquist (1997).

[3] "A... system of innovation is that set of distinct institutions which jointly and individually contributes to the development and diffusion of new technologies and which provides the framework within which governments form and implement policies to influence the innovation process. As such it is a system of interconnected institutions to create, store and transfer the knowledge, skills and artifacts which define new technologies" (Metcalfe 1995, p 462-463).

appropriate delineation of an innovation system depends on the topic of the analysis and the related questions.

3. What Do We Know About the Role of Public Research Institutions in Regional Innovation Systems?

In the realm of economic theory, a treatment of public research institutions has been nearly exclusively limited to the issue of possible market failure with regard to certain types of research and higher education. Approaches to growth theory, however, have largely neglected the role of public research institutions for a long time (Nelson 1998). Only recently, the introduction of the concept of knowledge spillovers into so-called new growth theory has opened a door for explicitly including the contribution that public research institutions make to economic development. With the concept of knowledge spillovers also the issue of space and economic distance started to play a role in theories of economic growth because it is commonly assumed that such spillovers tend to be concentrated in the direct neighborhood of the respective source.

A basic issue with regard to the public research institutions is why they are public and not purely profit-oriented private enterprises? This involves the main questions why public funding of research and of higher education is necessary and in how far a pure market solution to the provision of these goods would lead to unsatisfactory results? Another basic question relevant in his regard is in how far research and higher education should be carried out in the same institutions (e.g., research universities)? With regard to public assistance of research, the conventional answer states that activities in the field of basic research are likely to generate positive technological external effects with the consequence that the amount of basic research conducted in the economy will be "too small" (see Fritsch 1994 for an exposition of this standard approach). According to this standard view, applied research that leads to results that may be patented and for which a commercial application is foreseeable, should be left to the market.

The case for public support of higher education is far less clear. In his survey of university education in the USA, Winston (1999) shows that all of the leading universities there are non-profit organizations, be it in public of private ownership. In contrast to that, all of the pure for-profit universities are in the lowest ten percent when ranked according to the quality of education provided. Moreover, tuition fees cover only a fraction of the respective costs with this proportion being lowest among the top universities and highest at the lower end of the hierarchy. No doubt that the US system of higher education is characterized by a high degree of competition between the different suppliers, but no doubt that it is very different from a regular commercial market. That in none of the developed countries the sector of higher education is left completely to private markets clearly indicates a pronounced tendency of governments to mistrust a pure market solution here and that other solutions may lead to superior results.

The contribution of public research institutions to innovation processes has been analyzed empirically in a number of case studies that concentrated on prominent high-tech regions like the Silicon Valley, Route 128 near Boston, the Austin/San Antonio Corridor, the Phoenix Area or the Cambridge region in the UK (Dorfman 1988; Saxenian 1994; Segal 1988; Smilor, Kozmetsky, Gibson 1988; Wigand 1988). These case studies have led to some important insights, particularly, to a better understanding of the division of innovative labor between public research institutions and private sector firms. In a number of cases, the public research institutions have acted as the nucleus for the emergence of fast growing high-technology clusters (e.g., Stanford University for the Silicon Valley or the MIT for the Route 128 district). One general conclusion that may be drawn from these results is that a high level of interaction, particularly R&D co-operation, between the institutions or individuals is conducive to the performance of the respective regional innovation system (see Fritsch, Lukas 1999 for an overview). However, because these regional case studies are limited to either one or only some few regions, it is quite unclear to what extent the findings may be generalized.

Several econometric studies for the U.S. have sought to overcome this problem of generalization by using data that cover a larger number of regions or all the individual states. In one of the first studies of this kind, Jaffe (1989) found evidence that at the state level the number of patents generated by private firms is stimulated not only by the amount of industry R&D but also by the R&D expenditures of the universities. A whole set of subsequent empirical investigations of the impact of university R&D on innovation processes in the private sector used a data base that provided detailed information on product innovation (Acs, Audretsch, Feldman 1992; Anselin, Varga, Acs 1997; Audretsch, Feldman 1996; Feldman 1994). Overall, these studies support Jaffe's evidence. Anselin, Varga and Acs took the smaller Metropolitan Statistical Areas (MSA) as their regional framework rather than the states. They find that the spillover effects generated by R&D activities in public research institutions tend to be concentrated within a radius of about 50 miles around the location of the research. While such positive effects of R&D in public research institutions for private sector innovation activities has been found in a number of studies, there is no evidence for positive spillovers in the opposite direction, i.e., that university R&D benefits from spillovers generated by private innovation activities conducted inside or outside the region.

However, by analyzing aggregate data on the total number of innovations or total R&D expenditures in a region, the concrete channels or ways by which public research institutions may contribute to private sector innovation activities remain unclear. A better understanding of how exactly regional innovation systems work and what the most relevant linkages are between the various participants, by contrast, requires empirical investigation on a micro level. Micro level analysis may allow to identify and distinguish the different ways by which knowledge is transmitted between the different types of organization. Up to now, however, such micro studies tend to be rather rare.

In one of such micro level-analyses, Audretsch, Stephan (1996) found for biotechnology enterprises in the USA that geographic proximity between academic researchers and biotechnology firms is positively related to the collaboration of these two groups, but they conclude that the evidence is not overwhelming. Furthermore, they detected that the importance of the spatial dimension depends on the role that academic scientists play within the company. Academic founders or chairmen of the scientific advisory boards are more likely to be located close to universities than are other affiliated academic scientists. Inspecting different types of academic founders of new biotechnology firms according to their career patterns, Audretsch, Stephan (1999) conclude that the incentive structure associated with the institutional environment relevant for a certain scientist has a significant effect on the ways he or she may try to transform knowledge or reputation into private returns, for example, by seeking affiliation with a commercial venture or starting a firm on his or her own. Zucker, Darby, Armstrong (1998) find that the success of California biotechnology firms is closely linked to an affiliation of star scientists of nearby research universities with these firms. Compared to the effect of such direct relationships, the impact of generalized knowledge spillovers from universities to private sector firms is not significant in this study. Zucker, Darby, Armstrong (1998, p81) conclude that "university policies which limit professor's ability to contract freely with and to establish ownership positions in firms may protect norms of disinterested science at the cost of limiting technology transfer and local development".

Mansfield (1995) and Mansfield, Lee (1996) investigated the co-operation between large U.S. corporations and university scientists. Apart from its size and quality, a university's proximity positively influences its chance of being chosen as a collaborator. This indicates a trade-off between the quality and the spatial proximity of a potential partner. Interestingly, in the case of basic research, enterprises seem to value a university's quality more than in the case of applied sciences.

Until now, relatively few micro-level studies have been carried out for countries other than the United States. Van Dierdonck, Debackere, Engelen (1990) conducted a survey among 300 Belgian university scientists. A large majority responded with the assertion that they co-operate with industrial companies. In most cases, this collaboration was initiated by the academic scientists themselves, while explicit technology transfer mechanisms were of only minor importance. Faulkner, Senker (1994) conclude from a rather small sample of 60 R&D personnel in British and American enterprises that the co-operation with universities in many cases was based on personal contacts. These contacts, in turn, often derived from scientific publications.

Some recent studies carried out in Germany found that co-operative relationships between public research institutions and private sector firms constitute a widespread phenomenon (Fritsch, Lukas 1999 and 2000; Fritsch, Schwirten 1999). Obviously, the research institutions are quite active in this respect and make a significant contribution to innovation activities in the private sector. This contribution of public research institutions to private sector innovation is primarily related to the early stages of the innovation process, such as the generation and the development of new ideas; support in realizing already existing ideas is far less important. The private sector firms that maintain co-operative relationships with pubic research institutions tend to be located in close proximity (see Beise, Stahl 1998). However, for co-operative relationships with other public research institutions distance seems to be much less important because these contacts are geographically much more widespread (Fritsch, Schwirten 1999 and 2000). Based on these spatial patterns, Fritsch, Schwirten (1999) conclude that public research institutions take on the role of an "areal" by absorbing knowledge from research institutions and firms in other regions and making it available to innovation processes in their region. If public research institutions are – as our results suggest – key players in the regional innovation system, this may make them an instrument for a policy aiming at stimulating regional development. Critical issues with regard to this contribution of public research institutions to regional development are the amount of resources available to them, the quality of their research or education as well as the intensity and quality of their interrelation with other research institutions and firms inside and outside the region. However, we still have an only incomplete understanding of the factors that determine the impact of public research institutions on the regional innovation system. Particularly, nearly nothing is known about the most important ways by which knowledge spillovers come about. Research on spillover processes is still at its very beginning.

4. An Agenda for Further Research

The recognition that publicly funded research institutions may make a quite significant contribution to innovation processes in a region qualifies them as a subject of policy measures that are aiming at stimulating innovation activities and regional economic development. However, in contrast to the high impact that public research institutions obviously have, their role in innovation systems has remained largely unexplored. As a direct consequence, our knowledge base for policy directed to these institutions is rather incomplete. In this Section, I will outline some of these deficits that should be addressed by future research.

If, and this conclusion constitutes a broad consent in the literature, basic research and higher education should not be entirely left to the market, the question arises how this sector can be appropriately organized and in which way the state should take an active role here. From an economic point of view, the different solutions should be judged by their consequences for static allocation (market failure problem) as well as with regard to the performance of the (regional or national) innovation system. However, our current state of understanding of these issues is very incomplete. The deficiencies begin with the concrete definition of the types of research and higher education for which market allocation will probably lead to only unsatisfactorily results. Is a market failure to be expected in other fields of research than pure basic research (e.g., so-called applied basic research)? In how far will the quality of basic research be improved if the respective personnel of institution is also involved in applied research? Which types of higher education benefit from an involvement of faculty in research? What are the (dis-)advantages of different ways to link education and research?

Still, only very little is known about the principles and incentives that govern the activities of public research institutions in both fields, research and education. We particularly need a better understanding of the impact that a certain institutional framework has on the activities of the members of public research institutions. Is it, just to give one of the related questions as an example, conducive to research activities that researchers become tenured at some point of their career (Carmichael 1988; McPherson, Shapiro 1999) or that they become civil servants, as is the case in Germany? In how far, to give another example, is commercialization of R&D results of universities compatible with their main mission? The discussion concerning the Bayh-Dole Act that allows American universities to enter into far reaching agreements with private firms with regard to the commercialization of their research results strongly suggests that there are certain limits to such forms of technology transfer (Henderson, Jaffe, Trajtenberg 1998). Furthermore, to name a third issue, what are the effects of tuition fees on both sides of this market, the students and the universities? What are the advantages and disadvantages of different kinds of tuition fee systems with regard to the allocation of higher education? How can deterrence or discrimination of the poor in such a system be avoided?

With regard to the growth effects of public research institutions, the transfer of research results into further application, particularly into commercial products, constitutes a main issue for their contribution to the (regional, national or world wide) innovation system. Not only that the relevant knowledge should be documented and transferred into further use more or less completely; it is of even greater importance that this transfer takes place rapidly, because time plays an important role for a successful commercialization of new knowledge. Therefore, the question arises what are the main ways of commercialization and what institutional framework of rules may be conducive to a speedy commercial application of research results in order to stimulate competitiveness and growth. A main issue here is that a considerable part of the respective knowledge is "tacit" in character, i.e., it can not be codified completely. Because such tacit knowledge is attached to the bearer of this knowledge, a transfer of the respective person or, at least, some face-to-face contact is necessary to transmit this kind of knowledge.

Main channels by which the knowledge accumulated in public research institutions may be diffused and spill over to other economic actors are:

- publications and presentations by members of the public research institutions,
- the "output" of graduates that are employed outside the respective university,
- contract research for private firms or public authorities,
- formal or informal co-operative relationships with external firms or organizations including other public research institutions, as well as
- spin-offs of private firms set up by persons that still are or have formerly been affiliated with public research institutions.

We know from the results of empirical research that all these types of spillovers may play a considerable role, but the details of such diffusion processes are still in the dark. How important are different spillover channels? What is the microeconomic "anatomy" of these spillover effects, i.e., which rules or conditions govern the amount and the speed of knowledge transfers to which type of recipient? Who will be likely to benefit from such knowledge spillovers in what way? In how far do the different institutional regimes include mechanisms that lead to a coordination of research conducted in the public institutions and the needs of private firms? This also implies the question for the relationship between basic and applied research in public research institutions? Which are appropriate rules for the commercialization of research results? In how far should personnel in public research institutions be allowed to work some of their time for money in commercial firms, thereby taking private advantage of their research conducted within the framework of a public institution? Should researchers in public institutions be allowed for starting their own private firm to commercialize research results? Should they be even encouraged to do so? Also, how could and should the research institutions be compensated for their contribution to the respective knowledge without obstructing their main mission?

With regard to all such questions, location and geographic proximity may play a considerable role as is demonstrated by some empirical research in this field (see Section 3). However, we still have only rather incomplete knowledge, how such regional effects do come about and what role is played by geographic distance. Recent approaches to a theory of regional development speculate that co-operative relationships between different institutions located in a certain region may be of considerable importance for the division of innovative labor leading the relatively high effectiveness of the innovation system. Correspondingly, in a number of countries policy programs have been set up aiming at stimulating co-operation within a region in order to promote innovation activities. At least up to the present, however, empirical research has not been able to confirm a positive relationship between the level of co-operation in a region and the performance of the respective innovation system (Fritsch, Lukas 1999; Fritsch, Schwirten 1999), and one may well conclude from these studies that the role of R&D co-operation for innovation activities is highly overestimated in the respective literature. But if R&D co-operation in general does not play such a role, then the question arises if there are certain forms of R&D co-operation that prove to be important and by which channels other than co-operation knowledge spillovers come about. This leads us to the general question about the different forms of impact that public research institutions have on regional development. In how far can the regional endowment with public research institutions be understood as an effective means for innovation oriented regional policy?

It should be clear from this research agenda that a large part of the issues mentioned requires micro-level analysis. Only investigation on the micro-level of individual firms, university departments and individual persons will enable us to develop an understanding of what the relevant factors are that determine micro behaviour and the quality of an innovation system. For an empirical analysis of the impact of different institutional frameworks, it constitutes a necessary condition that the data reflect a certain variety of these framework conditions. Because the degree of such variety that can be found within a certain country will be quite limited, international comparisons may be needed in order to be able to find and account for a sufficiently large degree of heterogeneity. In the empirical research that Karin Peschel has conducted and inspired throughout her career, such international comparisons played a rather prominent role.

5. Concluding Remarks

There can be no doubt that public research institutions represent an important topic for further research, particularly in the fields of innovation economics and growth theory (Nelson 1998). That they also are an important subject or means of a policy directed to innovation and growth in a nation or region follows to a considerable part from the recognition that basic science and higher education should not be completely left in the realm of market allocation, because certain kinds of market failure are likely to occur. There are a number of alternative ways to deal with this danger of market failure, and the choice between these alternatives may have considerable implications for the contributions that public research institutions make to innovation and development. Obviously, measures responding to market failure problems and growth policy are interlinked with regard to public research institutions. It may be interesting to investigate, in how far a conflict between these two policy objectives may occur.

Measures towards public research institutions constitute a central element of growth policy and policy makers in the different fields that affect public research institutions should be well aware of their importance. Because our understanding of this key element of the innovation system is still rather limited, future research should attack this bottleneck and address considerable attention to this issue. Progress in this field could be of great benefit for the development of economic theory, particularly growth theory and theory of innovation, as well as for improvements of policy. We still know only very little about an appropriate institutional framework for public research institutions that is conducive to innovation and growth. Much further research in this field is necessary, and there is reason to assume that the return to such research in terms of welfare improvements could be immense.

References

Acs ZJ, Audretsch DB, Feldman MP (1992) The Real Effects of Academic Research: Comment. American Economic Review 82: 363-367

Anselin L, Varga A, Acs ZJ (1997) Local Geographic Spillovers Between University Research and High Technology Innovation. Journal of Urban Economics 42: 422-448

Audretsch DB, Feldman MP (1996) R&D Spillovers and the Geography of Innovation and Production. American Economic Review 86: 630-640

Audretsch DB, Stephan PE (1996) Company-Scientist Locational Links: The Case of Biotechnology. American Economic Review 86: 641-652

Audretsch DB, Stephan PE (1999) Knowledge Spillovers in Biotechnology: Sources and Incentives. Journal of Evolutionary Economics 9: 97-107

Beise M, Stahl H (1998) Public Research and Industrial Innovations in Germany. Discussion Paper No. 98-37. Zentrum für Europäische Wirtschaftsforschung, Mannheim

Carmichael HL (1988) Incentives in Academics: Why is there Tenure? Journal of Political Economy 96: 453-472

Cooke P, Uranga MG, Etxebarria G (1997), Regional Innovation Systems: Institutional and Organisational Dimensions. Research Policy 26: 475-491

Cooke P (1998) Introduction: Origins of the Concept. In: Braczyk HJ, Cooke P, Heidenreich M (ed) Regional Innovation Systems: The Role of Governance in a Globalized World. UCL Press, London, pp 2-25

Dorfman N (1988) Route 128: The Development of a Regional High Technology Economy. In: Lampe D (ed) The Massachusetts Miracle: High Tech and Economic Revitalization. MIT Press, Cambridge (Massachusetts), pp 240-274

Edquist C (1997) Systems of Innovation Approaches: Their Emergence and Characteristics. In: Edquist C (ed) Systems of Innovation: Technologies, Institutions and Organizations. Pinter, London, pp 1-40

Faulkner W, Senker J (1994) Making Sense of Diversity: Public-Private Sector Research Linkage in three Technologies. Research Policy 23: 673-695

Feldman MP (1994) The Geography of Innovation. Kluwer, Boston

Fritsch M (1994) The Market, Market-Failure, and the Evaluation of Technology-Promoting Programmes. In: Becher G, Kuhlmann S (eds) Evaluation of Technology Policy Programmes in Germany. Kluwer, Dordrecht, Boston, pp 311-329

Fritsch, M, Lukas, R (1999), Innovation, Co-operation, and the Region. In: Audretsch DB, Thurik R (eds) Innovation, Industry Evolution and Employment. Cambridge University Press, Cambridge, pp 157-181

Fritsch M, Lukas R (2000) Who Co-operates on R&D? Research Policy, 29

Fritsch M, Schwirten C (1999) Enterprise-University Co-operation and the Role of Public Research Institutions in Regional Innovation Systems. Industry and Innovation 6: 69-83

Fritsch M, Schwirten C (2000) R&D Co-operation Between Public Research Institutions: Magnitude, Motives and Spatial Dimension. In: Schätzl L (ed), Technological Change and Regional Development in Europe. Springer, Berlin, Heidelberg, New York (forthcoming)

Henderson R, Jaffe AB, Trajtenberg M (1998) Universities as a Source of Commercial Technology: A Detailed Analysis of University Patenting, 1965-1988. Review of Economics and Statistics 80: 119-127

Jaffe AB (1989) Real Effects of Academic Research. American Economic Review 79: 957-970

Lundvall BA (1992) Introduction. In: Lundvall BA (ed) National Systems of Innovation: Towards a Theory of Innovation and Interactive Learning. Pinter, London, pp 1-19

Mansfield E (1995) Academic Research Underlying Industrial Innovations: Sources, Characteristics, and Financing. Review of Economics and Statistics 77: 55-65

Mansfield E, Lee JY (1996) The Modern University: Contributor to Industrial Innovation and Recipient of Industrial R&D Support. Research Policy 25: 1047-1058

McPherson MS, Schapiro MO (1999) Tenure Issues in Higher Education. Journal of Economic Perspective, 13: 85-98

Metcalfe S (1995) The Economic Foundations of Technology Policy: Equilibrium and Evolutionary Perspectives. In: Stoneman P (ed) Handbook of the Economics of Innovation and Technological Change. Blackwell, Oxford, pp 409-512

Nelson RR (1998) The Agenda for Growth Theory: A Different Point of View. Cambridge Journal of Economics 22: 497-520

Saxenian A (1994) Regional Advantage. Harvard University Press, Cambridge, Massachusetts

Segal NS (1988) The Cambridge Phenomenon: Universities, Research, and Local Economic Development in Great Britain. In: Smilor RW, Kozmetsky G, Gibson DV (eds) Creating the Technopolis. Ballinger, Cambridge (Massachusetts), pp 81-90

Smilor RW, Kozmetsky G, Gibson DV (1988) The Austin/San Antonio Corridor: The Dynamics of a Developing Technopolis. In: Smilor RW, Kozmetsky G, Gibson DV (eds) Creating the Technopolis. Ballinger, Cambridge (Massachusetts), pp 145-184

Van Dierdonck R, Debackere K, Engelen B (1990) University-Industry Relationships: How does the Belgian Academic Community Feel about it? Research Policy 19: 551-566

Wigand RT (1988) High Technology Development in the Phoenix Area: Taming the Desert. In: Smilor RW, Kozmetsky G, Gibson DV (eds) Creating the Technopolis. Ballinger, Cambridge (Massachusetts), pp 185-202

Winston GC (1999) Subsidies, Hierarchy and Peers: The Awkward Economics of Higher Education. Journal of Economic Perspectives 13: 13-36

Zucker LG, Darby MR, Armstrong J (1998) Geographically Localized Knowledge Spillovers or Markets? Economic Inquiry 36: 65-86

Regional Innovation Networks. Some Theoretical Remarks

Joachim Genosko

Katholische Universität Eichstätt

Wirtschaftswissenschaftliche Fakultät

Ingolstadt, Germany

1. Introduction

In the context of learning economies, authors stress the importance of (regional) innovation networks in a globalizing world (e.g., Asheim 1999). The idea of such a network-approach consists in creating "strategic advantages over competitors outside the network" (Lipparini, Lorenzoni 1994: p18). From a regional policy point of view, (regional) innovation networks are the attempt to develop a policy tool which allows the strategic promotion of localised learning processes ensuring the regional and national ability to innovate and thus to compete internationally (Freeman 1995, Cooke 1995). The empirical background of for such considerations are experiences with regions like the "Third Italy" (Asheim 1999).

2. Regional Networks – an Attempt of Definition

Even in 1999, the Backhaus, Meyer (1993: p332) statement is true that the network concept is "enigmatic" and appears in many shapes and forms. It is sometimes so varied as to fall into the "whatever-you-like" category.

Generally speaking, a network consists of nodes and edges. Nodes can be persons, institutions, projects or events. Typical network nodes are universities, other R&D-facilities, educational and training systems, workers and management as well as the knowledge-production of firms (Smith 1997). Edges are the relationships between nodes. Authors advocating the network-approach see the advantage of such an approach in facilitating the capturing of social and economic relations, within which agents (i.e., "nodes") communicate and decide about their behaviour. According to this definition, regional networks are nodes and edges, which are in spatial proximity to each other. In a more concrete sense, *regional* networks can be understood as some sort of a development coalition bringing together regional governance mechanisms, universities, research institutes, technology transfer and training agencies, consultants and other firms (Asheim 1998; Asheim, Cooke 1999).

Another important feature of (regional) networks is the potential strength of their internal ties. Strong ties networks are characterised by common attitudes, judgements, education and training as well as the social status of their agents (Genosko 1999).

The systematic disadvantages of strong ties networks are their "structural holes". Because of mutualities and similarities between the participating agents it is difficult that new ideas penetrate networks. Thus, regional innovation and modernisation processes either do not get started or are discontinued too early. The decisive advantage of strong ties network is their ability to decode quickly information exchanged (Pfeifer 1997). On the other hand, weak ties networks are better suited to bring out interventions and innovations and so to avoid "structural holes". Weak ties networks are more or less informal in nature. Furthermore, a major task of regional (weak ties) networks is the "constitution of new ensembles of codified and tacit knowledge" (Lundvall, Borras 1999: p33). Rosenberg (1982: p143) considers "tacit knowledge (as) the knowledge of techniques, methods and designs that work in certain ways and with certain consequences, even when one cannot explain why". Thus, tacit knowledge is committed to personal interactions. "On this basis, we hypothesize that tacit knowledge is a very important element of the knowledge transferred through personal (or social – J.G.) networks" (Senker, Faulkner 1996: p85).

To sum up: Regional innovation networks are defined as weak ties networks, whose nodes and edges encompass more than only economic agents and economic relations and which are predominantly located within a certain spatial unit (Genosko 1997).

So that weak ties networks are better able to fulfil their task, they need so-called "gatekeepers". Gatekeepers are persons who are able to understand and to translate different codes. Thus, new ideas can be introduced to regional networks via gatekeepers. In other words, gatekeepers are "tools" to eliminate the structural disadvantages of weak ties (or informal) networks. In such a situation, direct peer contacts seem to be the most effective way to access to external professional information (Tushman, Katz 1980).

3. Why Regional Innovation Networks Emerge?

Usually, economists answer this question by pointing to the transaction cost approach. Additionally, we have to state that in reality information is incomplete and uncertainty about markets exist (Richter, Furubotn 1999; Hirshleifer, Riley 1979). Therefore, with informal (weak ties) regional innovation networks search and information costs, bargaining and decision costs, monitoring costs as well as the operating costs of the informal network system may be of importance. In addition, individual behaviour is decisive for the cost level. This means, if a "culture of confidence" prevails, i.e., if regional social capital exists, both act as substitutes for a formalized monitoring system, and hence they lower, all other things equal, the transaction costs.

What is the exact role of networks in connection with the reduction of transaction costs? First of all, networks allow "risk pooling" and "risk sharing" respectively. Consequently, in a certain way networks function as an insurance. The "insurance function" is especially important for projects with high fixed costs and with a high specifity of investment. Furthermore, even weak ties networks show stable and intensive interactions leading to better information about partners. This information tends to reduce the search and bargaining costs as well as the operating costs of the network system.

Network partnership generates interdependencies which should at least diminish opportunistic behaviour. The latter holds especially for regional networks. Indeed, if opportunistic behaviour can be reduced by networks, monitoring and bargaining costs can be lowered, too (Genosko 1999). Over and above innovation networks speed up the inter-organizational learning processes (Sydow 1992, Mody 1993).

Camagni (1993), however, points to the fact that networks not only reduce transaction costs, but also create additional ones. Hence if and only if regional networks lower the transaction costs on balance, they are a better alternative to other forms of organisation.

A game-theoretical substantiation of networks can be derived from the "prisoner's dilemma" (Luce, Raiffa 1967). The "prisoner's dilemma" shows that co-operative behaviour produce the best outcome for all players. In this context, Axelrod's (1984) "tit for tat"-strategy can also be used to explain the emergence of regional networks.

Further economic advantages of networks are seen in the mutual support by entering new markets, in the achievement of mutual specialization benefits and in the attainment of know how-advantages. In addition, networks can positively influence the so-called speed management. Networks are able to reduce the period between invention and innovation as well as to facilitate the capture of "pioneers surplus" (Backhaus, Meyer 1993). Mayntz (1993) argues that networks make it easier to internalize negative externalities.

Informal networking is another category of explanation, why networks come into existence. The informal networking approach is based on different "propensities to co-operate". As mentioned briefly above, not only innovating firms, but also innovating regions are confronted with uncertainty. Because of this uncertainty, they are hardly able to act ex ante on the basis of (economic) optimization criteria (Aoki, Dosi 1992). Rather they use "routines" derived from previous experiences and future expectations. Agents acting in this way start out from the idea that resorting to "routines" reduces the average search period for problem solutions and increases the project profitability (Nelson, Winter 1982). "Informal networks may thus be regarded as organizational routines adopted by firms under changing requirements and changing dynamic environments" (Pyka 1996: p11). Whether or not co-operations in the sense of networks takes place depends, among other things, on the degree of newness of technologies, ideas etc., since "radical" innovations are connected with a particularly high degree of uncertainty. A high degree of uncertainty seems to increase the "propensity to co-operate" of the participating agents.

In Section 3, several categories of reasons were presented, why (regional) informal networks can emerge. Yet however, there are no convincing empirical studies which rank the different attempts of explanation with respect to their relative importance.

4. Two Problems of Regional Innovation Networks

Already in the previous Section some of the problems concerned with regional innovation networks have been touched. However, currently important problems of networks are not on the research agenda. In the following, at least two problems of regional innovation networks ought to be brought up.

4.1 On the Stability of Networks

The "prisoner's dilemma" mentioned above does not only give reasons for the emerging of networks, but it also substantiates why networks offer an incentive for cheating network partners. In this context, cheating means that a network member can capture a greater profit share than he is entitled to capture at the expense of other members. In particular, cheating is especially remunerative if the other members do not notice it. However, if network participants recognize the opportunistic behaviour of their partners if they react with a corresponding strategy, co-operation becomes obsolete. Considered from an economic point of view, networks and co-operative behaviour seems to be inherently unstable. So, especially for weak ties networks, we have to study how such networks can be stabilized if necessary. Even if we assume an existing "propensity to co-operate", this means only that firms are making for a network solution, but nothing is said about the permanence of co-operation (Genosko 1999).

The permanence of co-operation and of a network respectively could be positively influenced by positive externalities in the form of reputation benefits. If someone breaks the network rules, he will be expelled from the network through which he experiences a loss of reputation. However, a rational agent will weight the benefits of cheating and the costs of reputation loss. The higher the benefits of cheating on balance, the more he makes a choice for a selfish behaviour (see Becker 1976 for a similar argument).

Hence, the central issue of networks seems to be, how binding commitments about future actions can be set. Game theory suggests that an infinite time horizon is necessary for all agents involved to produce networks (Tirole 1989). In other words, in a world with a finite time horizon game theory can neither explain nor give reasons, why selfish agents should co-operate (Holler, Illing 1991).

An infinite time horizon, however, is only a theoretical construction. In reality, the time horizon is limited. Nevertheless, we can observe real co-operation and real networks. One explanation for this observation could be "bounded rationality" (Simon 1957). According to Radner (1980, 1996), bounded rationality reveals itself in the so-called "satisficing behaviour". This form of actors' behaviour is connected with a certain inertia; agents do not intend to capture each possible benefit, especially since losses combined with satisficing behaviour become smaller and smaller in comparison with maximising behaviour, the longer the actors' time horizon. Another reason for inertia could be the complexity of the real word; this complexity, however, can be diminished by co-operation (Holler, Illing 1991).

"Reputation" can be underpinned theoretically by the new institutional economics when we assume that the creation of "reputation" needs investment. In this case, potential partners have to contribute assets to co-operation and to networks respectively. These assets can contain human capital ("social capital") and/or physical capital. Innovations networks are good examples of the considerations just made.

The binding effect of "reputation" investment can be additionally strengthened when such an investment causes "sunk costs". Gibbson (1992) suggests, a "reputation" equilibrium is only attainable, if there is "reputation" investment.

"Partner-specific" investment has a close connection to sunk costs. This sort of investment is characterized by the fact that it is more precious within than without a partnership. A so-called "lock in"-effect (Hart 1987: p752) develops. Each network member is interested in the reciprocity of "partner-specific" investment, since otherwise a one-sided "lock in"-effect is the consequence which can be used by some members of a network to exploit others; all members have to make "partner-specific" investment, so that all members are subjected to "lock in"-effects. Perhaps it is necessary that big firms do more "partner-specific" investment than small and medium ones, since the strength of "lock in"-effects seems to depend on a firm's size.

Williamson (1985) proposes that each member firm should be obliged to give "hostages" instead of making "partner-specific" investment. In this context, "hostages" are specific assets which are handed over to partners with a strongly reduced "price". If a partner cheats, his "hostages" are lost.

Mody (1993), however, rejects all these explanations. For him, the common interest of all network members to learn is the best guarantee to stabilize networks. In his opinion, transaction costs offer only supplements to the "learning model".

For several reasons, proximity seems to strengthen network stability. Proximity creates a special "culture of trust", where losses of reputation are very serious. Furthermore, regional agents can act more easily as if they have relationships with an infinite time horizon. Additionally, in regional networks members tend to have better opportunities to judge (individual) risks and to monitor investment in reputation and financial interdependencies.

4.2 On the Governance of Networks

To reduce transaction costs, "weak ties"-networks need an efficient governance mechanism. In this context, we have to take into account that there are strong interdependencies between the governance of networks on the one side and the stability as well as the emerging of networks on the other side. Moreover, (regional) innovation networks should bring small and medium-sized enterprises (SMEs) into contact with global innovation networks, since only in this way small and medium-sized enterprises have a good chance to survive in the global competition (Fritsch et al. 1998). SMEs seem to gain most from region-based innovation networks, which open up the gate-way to global markets for them.

Empirical studies show that in reality regional innovation networks function well, if "steering committees" are involved. Steering committees normally have the task of determining the network rules, monitoring the observance of these rules and coordinating the network members.

Steering committees can only fulfil their task well, if they consist of firms' representatives, who have a strong decision power. The committees' members should regularly meet each other and should have the power to punish cheating network members. Last but not least, steering committees should equitably share out the network's profit.

In the regional policy context "public private partnerships" seem to be more important than the just mentioned enterprise networks. Public private partnerships can be divided into two categories. The first category encompasses networks which serve as "providers" of a good "atmosphere". The second category contains the so-called "problem-" or "solution-oriented networks". Public private partnerships make it possible for the management and trade unions to get influence on economic policy decisions, policy makers on the other hand have the opportunity to open up "private" knowledge and information.

In order to be successful, enterprise networks as well as public private partnerships have to follow the logic of creating mutual advantages. In other words, a successful governance of networks bases on the idea of compensation (Lehmbruch 1979).

Another model of governance refers to governance by a moderator external to the network or the public private partnership. According to Huebner (1997), such a moderator has two tasks. On the one side he should moderate the rigour of the (regional) actors involved in the network, on the other side he should guide the behaviour of the actors in the direction supra-regionally intended.

5. Networks and Networking as a Regional Economic Policy Instrument

5.1 Regional Policy as Networking Policy

The supporters of regional networks start out from a renaissance of regions as policy units (Bergman, Maier, Tödtling 1991). In this context, Nijkamp (1994a: p343) writes, "The trend towards transnational co-operation will regions make alert to competition, but at the same time regions will be more dependent on international force fields... A final result of the above trends will also be the foreseeable change in the societal articulation of regional economic policy, which will likely develop in two different directions... A second shift in emphasis will be more micro-oriented, namely an identification of and support for urban areas as core units in a regional network system... In a new network society the strategic position of cities and regions will become even more pronounced." Nijkamp continues, "Another development concerns the transition of modern societies towards network societies, with a high degree of interaction between nodal centres in such networks. Such networks are not only related to physical infrastructures, but also to organizational and data/knowledge interactions...Networks are increasingly seen as vehicles par excellence in a global economy". In another paper, Nijkamp (1994b) points to the fact that in recent years regional economists are more and more interested in the dynamic influence of networks on the socio-economic conditions of their regional environment.

What could a regional policy look like, which uses networks as vehicles? First of all, let us have a look at regional networks in the frame of traditional regional theory.

In particular, in the new German states network structures are demanded to improve the implementation of regional (economic) policy. Barth, Karrasch (1995) expect from policy networks ("regional conferences") more transparence with respect to regional support priorities and principles as well as a better coordination between the different authorities which are concerned with regional policy and spatial planning. In other words, in this context regional networks are not parts of the regional policy devices per se, but in a certain way they are a premise for a successful regional (economic) policy. According to Barth and Karrasch, "regional conferences" should not be restricted to the "problem solving" process, but rather have the task to bring forward regional policy conceptions.

In his paper on research parks, Goldstein (1991) uses the "traditional" growth centre or growth pole theory to explain the development of regional networks using research parks and their hinterland. Goldstein's example makes clear that growth poles can be interpreted as networks at least in a twofold way: on the one side the growth pole per se, on the other side the forward and backward linkages to its spatial environment. Its spread effects can have a network quality, though this is not necessarily the case.

Because of various (empirical and conceptual) short-comings of the growth pole approach (Buttler, Hirschenauer 1995), another regional development strategy is based on a region's endogenous forces. Such a strategy aims at the creation of regional "synergetical" or dynamic milieux. In this context, we can observe networks in a "double function": on the one hand, networks can promote the development of these milieux, on the other hand, these milieux per se are (regional) networks. A region characterized by an innovative milieu is a spatial unit consisting of intrasectoral and intersectoral networks which further R&D and innovations as well as the region's ability to compete interregionally and internationally. The essential point is that not the firm, but rather the region as a whole is the breeding place of innovations (Aydalot 1986; Matteaccioli, Peyrache 1989).

The previous remarks, however, make clear that networking as some sort of regional policy is connected with different problems, too. Firstly, especially the endogenous strategy needs "leaders", who are typically successful business people. Secondly, even the endogenous strategy requires public infrastructural and financial incentives. Thirdly, since the emerging of networks needs time networking is a strategic, not a tactical component of regional policy. Finally, one should not omit that the success of networking as a regional policy instrument depends on "soft factors" like visionary leadership or talented negotiators.

Hence, Friedman (1972) emphasizes the social prerequisites for the economic growth of a region. Friedman points to the fact that urbanized economies are not only a subject of spatial structure, but also a product of the geographical clustering of urban attitudes, values and organizational forms (see also Kamann 1991).

Consequently, we have cautiously to conclude that governments can only create the *necessary* conditions for networking, but not the *sufficient* ones. "For policy makers this means government efforts to stimulate innovative industries by supporting autonomous growth potential, developing territorial industrial complexes, and encouraging local activities" (Kamann 1991: p35). In addition, Gaffard (1987) and Perrin (1988) demand public efforts to install centers of technological transfer and of a market- and innovation-oriented regional or local administration.

As Tabaries, Peyrache (1988) indicate the integration of SMEs into regional innovation networks seems to be difficult, since big firms try to reach economies of scale by mass production, specialisation and labour division. Principally, SMEs are not able to keep up with that development. Pedersen (1991), however, suggests that SMEs can play their own role in regional networks, if they act as niche- or highly specialised enterprises. Hence, a successful networking policy will accept SMEs as highly specialised production units, which are not rigidly pinned down to certain functions within complex networks. Rather they should have the opportunity to demonstrate their flexibility. In this way, SMEs can be the lubricant of regional innovation networks.

5.2 Policy Networks and Regional Policy

In reality, the term "policy network" encompasses very different forms of political co-operation.

In many German cities and counties, we can observe economic advisory bodies organized as so-called "round tables". The starting point of such bodies are quite often expertises ordered by regional or local authorities. In order to accompany the elaboration of these enterprises, the orderers involved install "round tables" of experts. Members of such "round tables" are typically trade unionists, entrepreneurs, worker councils, chambers of commerce, representatives of local governments, scientists and local policy makers. They are all important members in the regional decision making process. Frequently, after finishing their task as escorts of ordered (scientific) expertises, the members of "round tables" resolve themselves into an economic advisory body. The essential task of such a body should be to prepare economic decision making in a region. Experiences show that economic advisory bodies will be successful, if and only if influential promoters belong to the bodies. Nevertheless, many bodies show a lot of shortcomings. First of all, a greater part of these bodies is characterized by the "cheap talk" syndrome. This means that interest groups try to use such bodies to communicate their own interests to the decision makers. Additionally, there are communication problems between different members of an advisory body, since the members have differing social backgrounds and hence they talk with a differing vocabulary. Thus, economic advisory bodies do not frequently lead to strongly instutionalized policy networks, but rather they are ending up with a gradual decrese in the bodies' members. In front of the foil of these considerations, economic advisory bodies serve quite often only as a staffage for policy makers to justify their own policies; policy makers are not interested in controversial and productive discussions within the bodies

The picture changes considerably, if an advisory body takes on the character of a task force. Task forces are installed, if the economic base of a region is threatened seriously or if a region experiences a manifest economic crisis. In this case, economic advisory boards make suggestions to solve regional economic poblems, i.e., they actually decide. The effectiveness and efficiency of advisory boards is higher the more competence is assembled within them. In other words, the "power" of economic policy "round tables" is primarily base on their instutionalized authority, but rather it depends on the competence and personality of their members.

Another variant of regional policy networks are more or less institutionalized "regional conferences". While "round tables" emerge spontaneously, "regional conferences" are legally legitimatised. Bargaining is the general modus of "regional conferences". "Regional conferences" or regional policy networks are forced to find a consensus. Therefore, participants should be interested in common solutions to problems. In addition, the participating actors should put their own interests last in favour of collective affairs. Decreasing transaction costs and "common beliefs" (Sabatier 1988) as well as "learning effects" form the decisive binders of regional policy networks (Fürst 1994).

The main critism of regional policy networks like "regional conferences" derived from the critics of neo-corporatism (Genosko 1999). These critics refer to deficits of democracy in the "corporatistic cartel" and to the waste of ressources for (unproductive) corporatistic actions, especially for the corporatistic bargaining process. Last but not least, one can argue that a corporatistic co-operation slows down the process of decision making (Franz 1991) and that solidarity within corporatistic arrangements decreases in economically difficult times (Marko 1992). To sum up: like all corporatistic arrangements, "regional conferences" are confronted with a fundamental dilemma. On the one hand, regional policy networks should not have too many members to remain capable of acting, on the other hand, democracy and representation gaps emerge if the networks are restricted to the regions' most important actors. However, these gaps are possibly necessary so that regional corporative and corporatistic arrangements remain efficient and effective.

The comprehensive analysis of regional policy networks in the context of regional innovation networks can be justified by the fact that policy networks influence essentially the infrastructural basis of a region's research and development. Maillat (1991) underlines the importance of communication, information and transport infrastructures to strengthen the regional economic base. "In regional development this concept (of synergism - J.G.) would denote that not only the presence of specific agents and institutions within a region, but also their mutual dynamic interaction, is a prerequisite for optimising regional creativity and innovation" (Stöhr 1986: p34). Regional policy networks can be vehicles to further the mutual dynamic interaction. Simultaneously, we can observe networking between and within so-called C-regions (C for competence, culture, communication, and creativity). "These C-regions tend to be locations of R&D oriented units within the new systems-architecture-designed corporations" (Andersson 1986: p34). However, the emergence of new (innovation) networks is not only a question of technical hardware, but also a question of political "software". The C-regions-networks create a new political structure, but coincidently the regional innovation (or C-) networks need the political "net" to ensure their genesis, their existence and their permanence.

6. A Résumé

Since the late 1970s and the early 1980s, the publications on innovation policy and innovation networks are legion (e.g., Genosko 1999). Nevertheless, the literature on networks and networking show white patches on the research map. Neither an undisputed definition of networks exists nor do we have theoretically conclusive concepts about the emerging of regional innovation networks. Traditionally, economists try to explain the coming into being of networks with references to transaction cost and "new" institutional economics (Furubotn, Richter 1997). According to Williamson (1991), there are a number of reasons, like the specifity of investment or the market uncertainty connected with innovative activities, why co-operation schould be superior to the pure market mechanism.

Another white patch in network researching seems to be the questions about network stability and about "tools" to stabilize networks. Game theory concludes that co-operation brings higher benefits for all network partners, but the game-theoretical "prisoner's dilemma" shows conversally that it can be advantageous to cheat if all other partners behave co-operatively. Cheating in particular seems to be advantageous in the case of innovations, since in this case the gains connected with cheating are very high. Therefore, we need instruments which are able to hinder cheating. Theoretically, different instruments have been developed in the literature. However, empirically we have only a few studies, which explore such instruments on a theoretical basis.

Virtually the same is true for the governance problem, even if social scientists dealt comprehensively with regional policy networks. However, their empirical dealing with networks is more a description than a theoretical reasoning. From an economist's point of view, the governance issue is closely connected with transaction costs, where the simple conclusion is: choose that governance arrangement which minimises the transaction costs. In reality, however, the problem is a very complex one, since a successful governance depends less on formal structures, but more on persons and personal qualities. In a certain way *regional* innovation networks seem to be more manageable, in another way they have problems in integrating SMEs.

Finally, regional policy supports regional innovation networking in at least a two-fold way. Firstly, regional policy makers create basic conditions and prerequisites for successful networks. Secondly, policy networks and public private partnerships promote regional networking between firms as well as improve networks stability and governance. Hence, regional innovation networks and regional networking produce results in the long run; a regional policy aiming at networks and networking is strategic in nature. Today, regional innovation networks are important to strengthen a region's international competitiveness.

References

Anderson AK (1986) The Four Logistical Revolutions. Papers of the Regional Science Association 59: 1-12

Aoki M, Dosi G (1992) Corporate Organization, Finance and Innovation. In: Zamagnis V (ed) Finance and the Enterprise. Academic Press, London, pp 34-58

Asheim BT (1998) Learning Regions as Development Coalitions: Partnership as Governance in European Workfare States? Paper presented at the 2nd European Urban and Regional Studies Conference, University of Durham

Asheim BT, Cooke P (1999) Local Learning and Innovation Networks in a Global Economy. In: Malecki E, Oinäs P (eds) Making Connections. Ashgate, Aldershot

Asheim BT (1999) Innovation, Social Capital and Regional Clusters: On the Importance of Co-operation, Interactive Learning and Localized Knowledge in Learning Economics. Paper presented at 39th ERSA-Congress, Dublin

Axelrod R (1984) The Evolution of Cooperation, Basic Books, New York

Aydalot P (1986) Milieux Innovateurs en Europe, GREMI, Paris

Backhaus K, Meyer M (1993) Strategische Allianzen und Strategische Netzwerke. Wirtschaftswissenschafltiches Studium 22: 330-334

Barth U, Karrash P (1995) Wirkungen der regionalen Wirtschaftsförderung im Regierungsbezirk Leipzig. Gesellschaft für Sozialwissenschaftliche Forschung und Publizistik, Berlin

Becker GS (1976) Altruism, Egoism, and Genetic Fitness: Economics and Sociobiology. Journal of Economic Literature 4: 77-86

Bergman EM, Maier G, Tödtling F (1991) Regions Reconsidering. In: Bergman EM, Maier G, Tödtling F (eds) Regions Reconsidered: Economic Networks, Innovation and Local Development in Industrialized Countries. Mansell, London, New York, pp 283-300

Buttler F, Hirschenauer F (1995) Stichwort "Wachstumspole". In: Akademie für Raumforschung und Landesplanung (ed) Handwörterbuch der Raumordnung. Hanover, pp 1058-1063

Camagni R (1993) Inter-Firm Industrial Networks. The Costs and Benefits of Cooperative Behaviour. Journal of Industry Studies 1: 1-16

Cooke P (1995) Planet Europe: Network Approach to Regional Innovation and Technology Management. Technology Management 2: 18-33

Franz W (1991) Arbeitsmarktökonomik. Springer, Berlin, Heidelberg, New York

Freeman C (1995) The National System of Innovation in Historical Perspective. Cambridge Journal of Economics 19: 5-24

Friedman J (1972) A Generalized Theory of Polarized Development. In: Hansen NM (ed) Growth Centers in Regional Economic Development. Free Press, New York, pp 82-107

Fritsch M, Koschatzky K, Schätzl L, Sternberg R (1998) Regionale Innovationspotentiale und innovative Netzwerke. Raumforschung und Raumordnung 56: 243-252

Fürst D (1994) Regionalkonferenzen zwischen offenen Netzwerken und Institutionalisierung. Raumforschung und Raumordnung 52: 184-192

Furubotn EG, Richter R (1997) Institutions and Economic Theory: The Contribution of the New Institutional Economics. University of Michigan Press, Ann Arbor

Gaffard JL (1987) La Création de Technologie: Stratégies d'Entreprises et Politiques Publiques. Sophia-Antipolis, Nice

Genosko J (1997) Networks, Innovative Milieux and Globalization: Some Comments on a Regional Economic Discussion. European Planning Studies 5: 283-297

Genosko J (1999) Netzwerke in der Regionalpolitik. Diskussionsbeiträge der Wirtschaftswissenschaftlichen Fakultät Ingolstadt der Katholischen Universität Eichstätt 126.

Gibbson R (1992) A Primer in Game Theory. Harvester Wheatsheaf, New York

Goldstein H (1991) Growth Center versus Development Strategies: The Case of Research Parks. In: Bergman EM et al. (eds) Regions Reconsidered: Economic Networks, Innovation and Local Development in Industrialized Countries. Mansell, London, New York, pp 241-263

Hart OD (1987) Incomplete Contracts. In: Eatwell J et al. (eds) The New Palgrave: A Dictionary of Economics, Vol. 2. Macmillan, London, pp 752-759

Hirshleifer J, Riley JG (1979) The Analytics of Uncertainty and Intermediation – An Expository Study. Journal of Economic Literature 17: 1375-1421

Holler M, Illing G (1991) Einführung in die Spieltheorie. Springer, Berlin, Heidelberg, New York

Huebner M (1997) Moderation als Instrument der Kontextsteuerung im Prozeß einer kooperativen Regionalplanung. Raumforschung und Raumordnung 55: 279-287

Kamann A (1991) The Distribution of Dominance in Networks and its Spatial Implications. In: Bergman EM et al. (eds) Regions Reconsidered: Economic Networks, Innovation and Local Development in Industrialized Countries. Mansell, London, New York, pp 35-56

Lehmbruch G (1985) Sozialpartnerschaft in der vergleichenden Politikforschung. Journal für Sozialforschung 25: 285-305

Lipparini A, Lorenzoni G (1994) Strategie Sourcing and Organizational Boundaries Adjurtment: A Process-Based Perspektive. Paper presented at the EMOT-Workshop, Como

Luce R, Raiffa H (1967) Games and Decisions. Wiley, New York

Lundvall BA, Borras S (1999) The Globalising Learning Economy: Implications for Innovation Policy. Office for Official Publications of the European Community, Luxembourg

Maillat D (1991) The Innovation Process and the Role of the Milieu. In: Bergman EM et al. (eds) Regions Reconsidered: Economic Networks, Innovation, and Local Development in Industrialized Countries. Mansell, London, New York, pp 103-117

Marko J (1992) Verbände und Sozialpartnerschaft. In: Mantl W (ed) Politik in Österreich. Die Zweite Republik: Bestand und Wandel. Böhlau, Wien, pp 429-478

Matteaccioli A, Peyrache V (1989) Millieux et Réseaux Innovateurs: Synthèse sous l'Anlge de la Complexite'. Unveröffentlichtes Manuskript, Paris

Mayntz R (1993) Policy-Netzwerke und die Logik von Verhandlungssystemen. In: Héritier A (ed) Policy-Analyse. Kritik und Neuorientierung. PVS-Sonderheft 24, pp 39-56

Mody A (1993) Learning Through Alliances. Journal of Economic Behaviour and Organization 20: 151-70

Nelson R, Winter SG (1982) An Evolutionary Theory of Economic Change. University Press, Cambridge (Massachusetts)

Nijkamp P (1994a) Guest Editorial: Regional Science – A Product Life Cycle Interpretation. Papers of the Regional Science Association 73: 341-345

Nijkamp P (1994b) New Borders and Old Barriers in Spatial Development. Avebury, Aldershot

Pedersen FO (1991) A Network Approach to the Small Enterprise. In: Bergman EM et al. (eds) Regions Reconsidered: Economic Networks, Innovation and Local Development in Industrialized Countries. Mansell, London, New York, pp 79-97

Perrin JC (1988) New Technologies, Local Synergies and Regional Policies in Europe. In: Aydalot P, Keeble D (eds) High Technology Industry and Innovative Environments. The European Experience. Routledge, London, pp 87-95

Pfeifer C (1997) Eine kritische Analyse neoklassischer Ökonomik vor dem Hintergrund von Orierntierung und Kognition. Dissertation der Wirtschaftswissenschaftlichen Fakultät Ingolstadt der Katholischen Universität Eichstätt

Pyka A (1996) Informal Networking. Volkswirtschaftliche Diskussionsreihe, Institut für Volkswirtschaftslehre der Univeristät Augsburg 153

Radner R (1980) Monitoring Cooperative Agreements in a Repeated Principal-Agent Relationship. Econometrica 49: 1127-1148

Radner R (1996) Bounded Rationality Indeterminancy and the Theory of the Firm. The Economic Journal 106: 1380-1393

Richter R, Furubotn EG (1999) Neue Insitutionenökonomik, 2nd ed. Mohr Siebeck, Tübingen

Rosenberg N (1982) Perspectives on Technology. University Press, Cambridge (Massachusetts)

Sabatier P (1988) An Advocacy Coalition Frame Work of Policy-Oriented Learning Therein. Policy Sciences 21: 129-168

Senker J, Faulkner W (1996) Networks, Tacit Knowledge and Innovation. In: Commbs R et al. (eds) Technological Collaboration. The Dynamics of Cooperation in Industrial Innovation. Cheltenham Brookfield, pp 76-97

Simon HA (1957) Models of Man – Social and Rational. Wiley, New York

Smith K (1997) Economic Infrastructures and Innovation Systems. In: Edquist C (ed) Systems of Innovation. Technologies, Institutions and Organisations. Pinter London, pp 146-171

Stöhr W (1986) Territorial Innovation Complexes. Papers of the Regional Science Association 59: 29-44

Sydow J (1992) Strategische Netzwerke, Evolution und Organisation. Gabler, Wiesbaden

Tabaries M, Peyrache V (1988) L´Insertion Locate des PMI Innovatrices en Ils-de-France Sud. Colloque GREMI II, Ascona

Tirole J (1989) The Theory of Industrial Organization, 2nd edn. MIT Press, Cambridge, London

Tushman M, Katz R (1980) External Communication and Project Performance. An Investigation into the Role of Gatekeepers. Management Science 26: 1071-1085

Williamson OE (1985) The Economic Institutions of Capitalism. Free Press, New York

Williamson OE (1991) Economic Institutions: Spontaneous and Intentional Governance. The Journal of Law, Economics and Organization 7: 159-187

Urban Agglomeration and Regional Development Policies in an Enlarged Europe

Riccardo Cappellin

Università di Roma "Tor Vergata"

Department of Economics and Institutions

Rome, Italy

1. Introduction

"The decentralised history of Europe – characterised by independent nation states, many of which in turn originated relatively late from smaller regional states – has favoured the emergence of a strong polycentric urban system. A complex web of large, medium-sized and smaller cities has arisen, which in large parts of Europe forms the basis for urbanised spatial structures even in agricultural areas" (European Commission 1999).

Urban agglomeration and urban size have been traditionally explained by economies of scale and transport costs advantages both in manufacturing activities and in public utilities. While the real nature of the "new economy" is still subject to a debate, it clearly appears that cities are the core of this far-reaching sectoral transformation of the national and international economy and that the competitive advantage of cities and regions is not determined any more by lower production costs, but rather by a greater increase of productivity and a faster change of technology.

Certainly, after the massive de-industrialization of the urban economies during the 1970s and 1980s, the economic engine of cities has changed. In particular, cities have anticipated the rest of the economy in the deep changes occurred in the labour markets and in the organization of the relationships among the firms.

Secondly, the gradual enlargement of the European Union to many other countries challenges the feasibility to continue the traditional approach in European regional policy based on a strictly economic perspective. While according to a neoclassical model, the capital inflows and the expansion of production capacity would be the crucial factors in determining the growth of employment, a modern regional policy should assign a greater role to the different speed of technological change in the various regions, to an efficient organization of the territory and to the role played by cities in facilitating the immaterial flows of information and knowledge, both between and within the regional economies.

This paper first analyses the interesting insights that modern organization theory and innovation and knowledge economics may give on the factors of urban agglomeration and city size. Then, it analyses the effects of a territorial approach on a future reform of the European regional policy, which could assign a greater role to the aim of a better integration of the European territory with respect to the traditional aim of decreasing regional disparities.

2. Transactions Costs and Urban Agglomeration

The spatial distribution of economic activities indicates a bewildering variety of organizational forms. Extreme spatial organization models may consist in large metropolitan areas and in diffused rural or non-urban settlements. However, an increasing importance is played by intermediate forms, such as polycentric urban systems and networks of small and medium sized urban centres, characterised by a stronger interaction among the local actors internal to each urban centre and weaker but still important interactions among the actors of different centres.

Transaction costs (Williamson 1981) have been widely used in explaining the organization of relationships among firms, but they may be useful in the analysis of the territorial organization as well. In fact, urban agglomeration is favoured by a similar language, similar technological and development level, similar culture and socio-political institutions, and it allows a greater reciprocal knowledge and trust among local actors. Thus, transaction costs may be lower when the two parties involved in a relationship are concentrated in the same urban centre (Cappellin 1988).

As transaction costs usually decrease the lower is the distance between the two parties involved in a relationship or the higher is their spatial concentration, large urban centres such as a metropolitan area may have a comparative advantage with respect both to a rural and peripheral location and to a network of intermediate urban centres. That is especially important in those economic activities, which imply high transaction costs, such as modern business services or high-tech industries.

Thus, actors concentrate when a dispersed location pattern would imply too high transaction costs. That process is very similar to the case when the vertical integration within a large firm of the various production phases becomes the most appropriate organization mode, since the integration through the market mechanism would instead imply too high transaction costs.

An urban centre is not just a territorial concentration of firms and households, but it should be considered as a specific form of organization of the tight relationships among the various local actors or as an appropriate “governance structure”, which allows firms, workers and private and public organizations to minimise the transaction costs in their reciprocal relations.

The decrease of transaction costs leads to an increasing integration among the local actors. In particular, an urban centre, similarly to a "local production system", seems to be characterised by the following types of relationships (Cappellin 1998):

- the relationships of *technological integration,* related with the development of the local production know how, the sharing of knowledge, promoted by learning processes on the job and the continuous education of the workers, the vocational education of the young workers, the joint investments in R&D of local firms and the technological co-operations with external firms,
- the relationships of *integration in the local labour market,* related with the co-operation between the workers and the firms, the high mobility of the workers between the firms belonging to the same sector and also the capability to attract qualified workers from other sectors and from other regions,
- the relationships of *production integration between the firms* or the subcontracting relationships between the firms, which play a crucial role in promoting the diversification of the local productions,
- the relationships of *integration between the service sectors and the manufacturing sectors*, which stimulate the development of modern distribution services, of transport and logistic services and also of qualified services specialised in product quality certification and in technology transfers,
- the relationships of *financial integration between the firms,* which promote pro-active bank-industry relationships, the creation of financial groups made by several local firms, the spin-off from the existing firms of new specialised firms, the attraction of external investments and the development of local firms in other countries and regions,
- the relationships of *territorial integration at the local level,* which require an improvement in the infrastructure endowment and a greater effort in an effective physical planning, aiming to defend the quality of the territory,
- the relationships of *social and cultural integration*, which enhance the development of a local identity and of a sense of belonging and the creation of a consensus on a common development strategy within the local community,
- the *relationships of institutional integration,* which are related with the development of local administrative capabilities and the capability of the local institutions to interact with the regional and the national institutions especially for the implementation of strategic projects.

However, while the decrease in transaction costs may explain spatial agglomeration, other factors may explain the crisis of a too concentrated settlement pattern, such as a very large metropolitan area. In fact, when the number of firms and households increases above a specific threshold, which may vary according to the sector and the period considered, the transaction costs may increase and this may decrease the localization and urbanization economies.

Thus, various factors explain why the most appropriate governance form of the transactions between the firms and in the labour market may not be a large metropolitan area but rather a system of interdependent and smaller urban centres.

Firstly, the cost of the transfer and the elaboration of information between firms, tightly integrated among themselves in a specific production sector, may become very high and unmanageable, due to the congestion existing in a large metropolitan area.

Secondly, a wider disparity between the local actors would lower the belief in common values and the spirit of solidarity among them, with respect to a small or intermediate urban centre. Thus, an informal organization would become ineffective for co-ordinating the disparate and often conflicting aims of the various local actors and a more complex and longer public decision making processes would be required.

Thirdly, the increase of the number of the local firms producing the same or similar products would increase the opportunities for the buyers. The customer-supplier relationships would become more unstable and long term formal and informal agreements would become less convenient. The decrease in the reciprocal loyalty between the buyers and the suppliers would decrease the incentive to make specific or idiosyncratic investments and slow down the process of innovation.

Fourthly, the production know-how may gradually diffuse to other distant areas, and the relationships with distant firms could become less uncertain and complex due the development of learning processes. This may determine a decrease of the transaction costs between two distant firms and reduce the need for a spatial concentration.

Therefore, according to the specific characteristics of the sectors and of the relationships to be considered, the economics of transaction costs explain the comparative efficiency of different forms of spatial organization. Moreover, the economics of transaction costs explain why different spatial patterns may coexist at the same time and why the spatial structure of a country or a region is usually organised by a complex network of larger and smaller urban centres.

3. Knowledge and the Urban Economy

If "knowledge represents the fundamental resource in the contemporary economy and the process of learning represents the most important process" (Lundvall, Johnson 1994), cities can enhance the regional innovation potential and become the core of a "learning region". In fact, cities facilitate the adoption of innovation, as they insure a better access to information on international markets and are characterised by the availability of qualified human resources and of highly diversified service and industrial activities. In particular, the urban agglomeration and the development of interregional relationships among the urban centres may be explained by the factors indicated by many recent contributions in the field of innovation and knowledge economics.

First of all, urban agglomeration promotes the innovation, as it facilitates a process of intense interaction between the local actors and between these latter and the external actors, both through face to face contacts in the case of physical proximity and also through the information and communication technologies (ICT) on long distance. In fact, the creation of new knowledge requires a long and gradual process of individual and collective learning based on the integration of the "tacit knowledge", made by specialised know-how embedded in the local firms, with the "explicit knowledge" transferred from other regional or local production systems (Nonaka, Konno 1998; Cooke, Morgan 1998).

Tacit knowledge concerns technical aspects, which pertain to the working abilities and capabilities, which are often defined as know-how, and it has also a cognitive dimension, which pertains to the ideas, the ideals, the values and the mental models, which are tightly intrinsic in each individual or in a particular local community. Tacit knowledge is highly personal and not formalised, and it requires the sharing of a common work experience and face to face contacts. That makes it difficult to be communicated and shared with others.

On the contrary, the explicit or codified knowledge may be expressed with words and numbers and it is shared in the form of data, scientific formulas, manuals and procedures. This type of knowledge may be easily transmitted among the individuals in a formal and systematic way, even at long distance through the modern ICT and also through more traditional technologies such as mail, telephone and fax.

According to a second perspective, cities contribute to the advancement of knowledge due to their higher internal diversification, being a concentration of public and private activities, of service and manufacturing activities and of a variety of professional profiles. Cities stimulate the dialog among different cultures and the co-operation between different institutions and actors, thus enhancing the design of a common development strategy.

In fact, the advancement of knowledge is promoted by cultural diversity, and the process of innovation is fostered by the combination of different already existing technologies. Thus, an important distinction in the process of innovations is that between "specialised" knowledge and "diversified" knowledge. The first develops within a specific production sector, a given technological trajectory or within a specific world of specialists. The second implies the availability and the integration of the technological and organizational knowledge derived from other sectors and other regions. That requires the capability to understand and to translate languages and models, which may be very different one from the others.

The specialised knowledge, which may be both tacit and explicit, can be easily transferred at long distance, for example through the mobility of the entrepreneurs and experts, as it is indicated by the intense relationships existing at the international scale among the firms, which work in the same production field. On the contrary, the development of the diversified knowledge seems to require the spatial contiguity among various firms and organizations working in different fields or a strong common organizational and institutional framework.

According to a third perspective, the competitiveness of cities is not only determined by "hard" location factors, such as transportation linkages and production costs, but also by "soft" or qualitative factors which decrease the obstacles to innovation, such as the efficiency of the public administration and of the collective governance process, the degree of consensus between the local actors on a common development strategy and the openness with respect to external actors.

In fact, according to recent contributions of the theory of agglomeration ("economie de proximité"), territorial proximity is given by the intersection/overlap of three different dimensions of proximity, which may be classified respectively under the name of "geographical proximity", of "organizational proximity" and of "institutional proximity" (Rallet, Torre 1998).

While the organizational proximity deals with the links in terms of production organization, the geographical proximity deals with the links in terms of distance. The organizational proximity is based upon on the logic of organizational membership and of intrinsic similarity of the actors. Instead, the geographical proximity refers to the natural and physical limits and it includes the effect of the transport infrastructures.

Finally, the institutional proximity means the belief in common representations, models and rules of thought and of action by the agents belonging to a territory. It consists of the development of relationships of intentional nature, like the relationships of co-operation, of trust, of exchange of technological information, of partnership, that determines the strategy of the actors. It implies rules of collective action and the creation of institutions both formal and informal, which perform an often fundamental role in the mechanisms of interaction among the economic actors.

Thus, the geographical proximity allows the development of knowledge interactions, only if this is accompanied by an appropriate organizational and institutional context. In fact, the experience accumulated in the international transfers of technology has demonstrated that the geographical distance is less important as an obstacle to the international co-operation, than the organizational or institutional distance.

In particular, while geographical proximity is mainly given, although it may be improved by new infrastructures and by modern ICT, the organizational and institutional proximity is determined by an interactive learning process, which involves the networks of the local actors. Thus, an urban area combines these three different types of proximity, since the firms and the local actors in an urban area are not only located at a short distance, but they are also tied up among themselves through their similarity and linkages of co-operation.

Moreover, the lower organizational and institutional distance explains why cities are a gateway in the international and interregional relationships and are linked by increasing competitive and co-operative relationships with the cities of distant regions and countries. This characteristic is not only due to the fact the cities are the nodes of the physical communication networks, but also to the fact that cities are characterised by a greater openness to international relationships or by a greater organizational and institutional proximity with distant regions and countries than their respective hinterland region, which is often characterised by a rather parochial attitude or an attitude of "local closure". In particular, the internationalization of the local economy facilitates the access to a diversified knowledge and the learning of new labour skills, of new technologies and of new organizational methods.

4. The Role of Urban Centres in the Regional Economy

A network model of industrial organization emphasises the interdependence between the economy and the territory and the role of urban centres (Cappellin 1997). Thus, cities perform five different functions in a local economy.

They are the administrative centres of their respective regions. That implies the problem of defining a new allocation of the powers between the cities and the national state according to the criteria of subsidiarity, and also of defining the forms of the inter-institutional co-operation with other contiguous urban centres.

Secondly, according to the Christaller model, cities are the centre of economies of agglomeration. In this perspective, urban policies play a crucial role not only in the development of public services, but also in planning the location of the retail trade sector and of business services.

Thirdly, cities are a node in the transport and communication networks at the interregional level and perform the role of nodes or gateways in the relationships of a region with the outside world. In this perspective cities should co-operate with national institutions in the design of the national and European transport networks.

Fourth, cities represent the incubator of innovations and of new productions and are the centres of research and higher education institutions and the preferred locations of high-tech firms. Thus, cities play a crucial role in facilitating the process of re-conversion of the regional economy toward new and more productive sectors.

Finally, cities are the centre of the cultural identity of their region. They may have a strategic role in the education policies, which aim to improve the human capital endowment of a regional production system. Moreover, cities create a cultural "leadership" effect on their hinterland and contribute to the creation of an image, which facilitates the visibility of the region in the international economy.

In particular, these five dimensions of a city may be useful in interpreting the changing role of intermediate cities in the case of the European non-metropolitan regions. During the early phases of development of these regions, in the late 1960s and the 1970s, small and medium size firms have diffused in the rural areas and have mainly concentrated in small country villages. Thus, intermediate cities have only played a rather passive role, as simple supply centres of traditional commercial and public services for the population of their respective hinterland.

The export base of the intermediate regions was in the rural areas rather than in the cities. Thus, the industrial development of these regions seems to have been characterised by a clear anti-urban bias or by a reaction to the "fordist" models of economic and social organization prevailing in the urban areas, where the large industrial firms were concentrated.

On the other side, intermediate cities in the non-metropolitan regions have played a rather subordinate role with respect to the large metropolitan cities of the most developed regions. Moreover, the intermediate cities were characterised by competitive relationships among themselves, since they had a very similar economic structure, which hindered effective complementary relationships.

However, intermediate regions, which during the early phases of their industrial development did not consider the importance of the urban centres, now acknowledge the crucial role that the various intermediate cities, such as their regional capital cities, may have in the process of transformation of their industrial structure.

Thus, the traditional conflict between rural areas and cities is transforming into a more synergetic relationship, where the rural areas maintain their industrial specialization and export orientation, while the intermediate cities assume a crucial role in the supply of modern producer services, fairs centres, research and superior education centres and important commercial transport and communication infrastructures.

Moreover, the increasing complexity of technologies and the process of internationalization of the firms have increased the scope of interregional and international relations, which do not only consist in the exports flows, but are gradually extending to intense exchanges of specialised commercial, financial and technological information.

In particular, the intermediate cities now assume an increasing importance in the interregional and international relationships and are transforming themselves into the gateways of their regions in the relations with the outside world. That is demonstrated by the increase of the international lines operating in the "third level" regional airports, which are not any more only the destination of tourist flows, but have received a new impulse from the increasing international activity of the many small and medium size firms, which have developed in the hinterland of the intermediate cities.

Intermediate cities are also becoming increasingly specialised in particular activities, which give to them a specific identity and are making them more complementary and interdependent. Thus, they may now increasingly compete with the large metropolitan areas in these specific activities. In fact, the recent European experience seems to indicate a decreasing power of the large metropolis and a "renaissance" or a substantial increase in the international standing of smaller urban centres and especially of intermediate cities.

5. Spatial Models of European Integration

European economic integration may occur according to both a functional and a spatial perspective. A functional perspective to the European integration characterises the aim to create a "Single Market" or a new supranational institution, such as the "European Union".

Differently from these functional approaches, the concept of the "Europe of regions" emphasises a spatial approach to the European integration (Peschel 1997) and suggests various models of organization of the European territory

The most common spatial model in the European regional policies is the *dualistic model,* which underlines the relationships between a "core", made by well developed regions, and a "periphery", made by economic lagging regions or "*assisted areas*", which are defined as Objective 1 and Objective 2 regions.

A second spatial model is that of the *"North-South corridors",* such as the "Blue Banana" or the "Adriatic Belt", which indicate the direction of the process of gradual diffusion of economic development. This concept emphasises the positive or negative polarization effects between the most and the less developed regions, rather than the internal homogeneity and the disparity of the individual regions, as the core-periphery model.

While these two models refer to the traditional objective of decreasing regional disparities, the aim of promoting a greater interregional integration and the development of co-operative relationships between the various regions in the European territory suggests different spatial models. In particular, spatial integration may be fostered by policies based on the model of the European *"macro-regions"* (Cappellin 1993). These are broad transnational areas made by various contiguous administrative regions, which co-operate among themselves and compete with the regions belonging to other macro-regions.

However, the process of internationalization is promoting tighter relationships between distant or non contiguous regions and cities; thus the model of the European "macro-regions" may evolve toward the model of the *"interregional networks"* made by various regions or urban centres, which may perform a complementary role at the European scale.

In fact, the concept of "macro regions" and of "networks" have an increasing role as tools for the analysis of the recent trends in the restructuring of the European territory and as spatial framework of the programmes of the European regional policy.

Wide areas of interregional and transnational co-operation have been first indicated in the document "Europe 2000+" (European Commission 1994) and now represent the geographical framework of the Community Initiative "Interreg IIC". On the other hand, the networks of urban centres and of various local and regional authorities are the model adopted in some EU programmes, such as "Recite", "Ecos-Ouverture" and "Urban". Both the concept of "macro-regions" and that of "networks" play a crucial role in the recent "European Spatial Development Perspective" (E.S.D.P.) document (European Commission 1999).

6. The Urban Dimension of European Regional Policies

The role that urban centres have on the performance of regional economies and the increasing interregional and international integration of the urban centres indicates that the field of the urban policy does not only consist in the supply of infrastructures and in the elaboration of physical plans, but it should be extended to the broader field of territorial policies. These latter aim to the objectives of a better organization of territory at the regional level and of a better quality of life in the urban and rural areas.

On the other hand, national and European regional policies, which traditionally have only aimed at attracting investments and creating employment opportunities, should reorient their strategy and scope, as the territorial policy should be included among the sectors of competence of the European Union. In fact, the concept of economic and social cohesion should not only imply a decrease of the development disparities, but it should include also the aim to a well-ordered European territory (Cappellin 1999).

An urban perspective in the organization of the European territory is different from a regional perspective. While this latter accentuates the dualism between the economic lagging areas, or the areas of industrial crisis, and the most developed regions of the European Union, an urban perspective underlines a multipolar perspective and lifts common problems and challenges of a strategic character.

Moreover, the European Union regional policy should not continue to overburden the regional level of administration, since the enhancement of the economic development requires to mobilise a variety of actors and the most appropriate territorial framework for really operational interventions often is the sub-regional level, as in the case of provinces or of rather large inter-municipal basins.

Taking into account the five dimensions indicated above of the role of cities in a regional and national economy, a first field of a European urban policy could be represented by the culture, since the European civilization is born in the cities, and it is still founded on the crucial role of various institutions, which are localised and interact among themselves within the cities.

Moreover, cities represent the main area of incubation of innovations and are a local technology system, where, similar to a science park, different public and private research and higher education institutions tightly interact among themselves. Therefore, the European research and innovation policy should consider the network of urban centres as a strategic policy framework and should enhance a greater synergy between the various institutions existing within a specific urban centre and among the various urban centres.

A third field of a European urban policy is represented by a territorial co-ordination of the policies dealing with the service sectors, since cities represent the supply centre of private and public services for the their hinterland. That relates to the problems of the development of tourism and of modern commercial distribution services. But it also deals with the problems of organising the health, the welfare and the social policies, since the largest part of the European population is concentrated in the cities, where the social problems often are the most acute.

A fourth field of a European urban policy is represented by the transport and communication policy, since the cities represent the nodal centres of the infrastructure networks. It is crucial that the European Union assures a priority to the projects in favour of the small and averages cities and that it avoids that the creation of the large Trans-European networks (TEN) could lead to an increase of the attraction of the metropolitan areas and could penalise the accessibility of the small and medium size cities.

Therefore, it is necessary to design such infrastructure networks according to a non-radial but transversal structure and to link the intermediate and small cities to the new Trans-European networks, through the creation of intermodal exchange centres, the development of international lines in the "third level" airports and the creation of local ICT networks also in the small and medium size cities.

Finally, an urban policy of the European Union should have an institutional dimension, as cities do not only represent a specific geographical area, where the European policies should intervene. They are also specific political institutions, which have been democratically elected and can represent a partner in the process of inter-institutional co-operation with the European Union, according to the principle of subsidiarity.

In particular, an urban policy of the European Union seems to require mechanisms of organization, which are different from those traditionally used in the regional European policy, such as the regional "Community Support Frameworks". Rather than detailed plans for each individual region, it is crucial to have a well defined strategic framework, such as the "European Spatial Development Perspective" (ESDP), for the overall territory of the European Union and for the various European "macro-regions" (European Commission 1999).

Due to its mainly strategic characteristics, the ESDP should be capable to orient the local administrations to the adoption of new initiatives, having the nature of pilot projects, experimental programs and exchange of experiences, and it should facilitate a synergetic relationship between the Community and the local institutions. Thus, a European urban policy should combine the demand of a long term spatial planning with the respect of bottom-up decision-making processes, and it should enhance the capabilities of endogenous initiative.

References

Cappellin R (1988) Transaction Costs and Urban Agglomeration. Revue d'Economie Regionale et Urbaine 2: 261-278

Cappellin R (1993) Interregional Co-operation in Europe: An Introduction. In: Cappellin R, Batey P (eds) Regional Networks, Border Regions and European Integration. Pion Editor. European Research in Regional Science, London, pp 1-20

Cappellin R (1997) The Economy of Small and Medium-size Towns in Non-metropolitan Regions. Document prepared for OECD. Programme of Dialogue and Cooperation with China, SG/CHINA/RUR/UA(97) 3, Paris

Cappellin R (1998) The Transformation of Local Production Systems: Interregional Networking and Territorial Competitiveness. In: Steiner M (ed) From Agglomeration Economies to Innovative Clusters. Pion Editor. European Research in Regional Science, London, pp 57-80

Cappellin R (1999) The Enlargement of the European Union and the Future of the European and National Regional Policies. Regional Contact XIII/14: 29-40

Cooke P, Morgan K (1998) The Associational Economy: Firms, Regions and Innovation. Oxford University Press, Oxford

European Commission (1994) Europe 2000+: Cooperation for European Territorial Development. Office for Official Publications of the European Communities, Luxembourg

European Commission (1999) European Spatial Development Perspective (ESDP): Toward Balanced and Sustainable Development of the Territory of the EU. Final Discussion at the Meeting of Ministers Responsible for Regional/Spatial Planning of the European Union. Potsdam, May 10-11, 1999

Lundvall BA, Johnson B (1994) The Learning Economy. Journal of Industrial Studies 1: 23-42

Nonaka I, Konno N (1998) The Concept of "Ba": Building a Foundation for Knowledge Creation. California Management Review 40: 40-54

Peschel K (1997) Globalization and Northern European Integration. Paper Presented at the 37th European Regional Science Congress, Rome, August 26-29, 1997

Rallet A, Torre A (1998) On Geography and Technology: Proximity Relations in Localised Innovation Networks. In: Steiner M (ed) From Agglomeration Economies to Innovative Clusters. Pion Editor. European Research in Regional Science, London, pp 41-56

Williamson OE (1981) The Modern Corporation: Origin, Evolution, Attributes. Journal of Economic Literature 19: 1537-1568

Knowledge Creation, Knowledge Diffusion and Regional Growth

Dirk Dohse

Institut für Weltwirtschaft, Kiel

Kiel Institute of World Economics

Kiel, Germany

1. Introduction

There seems to be unanimity among economists that new knowledge is one of the most important sources of economic growth. The spatial dimension of knowledge, however, is often neglected. Obviously, the costs of information transfer over large distances have been rapidly decreasing during the last decades. So, at first glance, in the age of internet, fax and e-mail spatial aspects may seem of ever decreasing influence. This is, however, not the whole story: Recent empirical studies have shown that knowledge spillovers are geographically localized (e.g., Glaeser et al. 1992; Jaffe et al. 1993; Audretsch, Feldman 1996; Keller 2000). This may be due to the fact that new knowlege is often unstructured and highly complex (tacit knowledge) and can thus best be transferred face to face (Polanyi 1958). Furthermore, new knowledge is often produced cooperatively in joint ventures or innovation networks. In these cases, the advantage of spatial proximity is not so much the reduction of information costs but the fact that only close personal relationships allow for the evolution of incentive and sanction mechanisms necessary for the keeping of the implicit cooperation contracts (Bröcker 1995).

Compared to the classical factors of production (land, labour and capital), knowledge shows great resemblance to capital as both are accumulative factors of production. Thus, some authors view knowledge just as a special kind of capital and speak of "knowledge capital" (e.g., Carr et al. 1998). This is, however, misleading for a couple of reasons.

- Other inputs perish in the production process or are at least subject to depreciation (e.g., physical capital). In contrast, knowledge originates and/or grows in the production process. As a by-product of the main production it is input and output at the same time.
- This is not to deny that knowledge is also subject to depreciation (we call this "forgetting"), but knowledge becomes obsolete when it is not used, whereas

the depreciation on other inputs is the higher the more often/the more intensively they are used.

- New knowledge can be the result of a planned search process (learning by searching) or emerge by chance. The accidental character of knowledge creation is, however, also present in planned search processes. Thus, knowledge creation is never fully deterministic but always involves a stochastic element.
- Knowledge has characteristics of public goods as well as characteristics of private goods. As Paul Romer has stated, "Discoveries differ from other inputs in the sense that many people can use them at the same time" (Romer 1994: p12). This principal non-rivalry in consumption (which characterizes a public good) goes hand in hand with excludability (which characterizes a private good), i.e., an individual that creates new knowledge has a certain control over it and can claim a price for transfering it to others.
- Knowledge has an explicit spatial and temporal dimension: It spreads over geographic space and changes its very nature in the course of the diffusion process. Parts of the original knowledge are lost, other parts are added or substantially modified. Thus, knowledge creation and knowledge diffusion cannot be separated and should therefore be analyzed simultaneously.

To capture the spatial and temporal dimension in what follows, I define knowledge as a *local public good* (or, to be more precise: a local public factor) *with dynamic spillover effects*. In contrast to a classical (Tieboutian) local public good, knowledge that originates in some region does not stick to that region but spreads over regional and national borders in the course of time. I analyze the flow of knowledge and its impact on regional growth in a simple two country model. The setting of my model is similar to the dynamic incubation model by Davelaar, Nijkamp (1990), however, the mechanisms driving knowledge diffusion and growth are quite different.

2. The Model

There are two countries I and II producing a new, knowledge-intensive commodity X, which can be used as a consumption good or as an investment good. I call country I the domestic country and country II the foreign country. Each country has a simple trichotomic spatial structure, i.e., it can be subdivided into a central region (c), an intermediate region (i) and a periphery (p). Population density is highest in the centre and lowest in the periphery. New technological knowledge originates in the core regions (the centres) of the two countries. The transmission of knowledge to the periphery and to the other country is impeded by geographic distance and national borders, inter alia.

The world demand for the innovative product is given by *Equation (1):*

$$(1) \quad X_t^N = X_{t-1}^N + k \cdot \left[\frac{X_{t-1}^N}{X_{\max}} \cdot \left(1 - \frac{X_{t-1}^N}{X_{\max}} \right) \right] \cdot X_{\max} .$$

Let the maximum demand level (or saturation level) be $X_{\max}$. World demand in period t increases with the demand proportion already reached in the previous period $(X_{t-1}^N / X_{\max})$ and with the remaining demand potential $(1 - X_{t-1}^N / X_{\max})$. The parameter k ($0 \leq k \leq 1$) measures the speed of adoption to the maximum demand level. *Equation (1)* is an s-shaped function of time typical for complex and expensive innovations (see Alderman 1990, Davies 1979 for a more detailed discussion).

Equation (2) states that aggregation of regional production (output in the centre, in the intermediate region and in the periphery) gives national or aggregate output, whereas *Equation (3)* postulates that the sum of aggregate output in country I and country II exactly meets the world demand in each period of time.

$$(2) \quad X_t^A = \sum_r X_{r,t}^A \; r = c, i, p \qquad \text{and} \qquad X_t^{A*} = \sum_{r*} X_{r*,t}^A \; r* = c*, i*, p*.$$

$$(3) \quad X_t^N = X_t^A + X_t^{A*} \qquad t = 1, \ldots, T.$$

Regional production functions have a similar structure for all domestic and foreign regions, see *Equation (4)*. Regional output is a function of capital input (K), labour input (L) and the stock of knowledge (σ) available in that region in each period of time (Uzawa 1965 and Zhang 1991 use a similiar production function). It is assumed that capital is perfectly mobile while labour is a fully immobile factor of production.[1]

$$(4) \quad X_{R,t}^A = \sigma_{R,t}^{\rho} \cdot K_{R,t}^{\beta} \cdot L_R^{\chi} \qquad R = r, r*.$$

Perfect mobility of capital (interregionally and internationally) implies that the marginal product of capital (the return to capital, respectively) must be the same everywhere, i.e.:

$$(5) \quad \frac{\partial X_{c,t}^A}{\partial K_{c,t}} = \frac{\partial X_{i,t}^A}{\partial K_{i,t}} = \frac{\partial X_{p,t}^A}{\partial K_{p,t}} = \frac{\partial X_{c*,t}^A}{\partial K_{c*,t}} = \frac{\partial X_{i*,t}^A}{\partial K_{i*,t}} = \frac{\partial X_{p*,t}^A}{\partial K_{p*,t}} .$$

The equilibrium stock of capital in each region and each period of time ($K_{R,t}$) depends on the world demand in the respective period, on the constant distribution of labour among regions and on the time-dependent distribution of knowledge among regions, see *Equation (6)*:

[1] For mere simplicity it is assumed that labour supply does not change over time.

$$(6)\quad K_{R,t} = \left(\frac{X_t^N}{ZW_{R,t}} \right)^{1/\beta} \qquad R = r,\, r^*\,,$$

$$\text{with } ZW_{R,t} = \sigma_{R,t}^{\rho} \cdot L_R^{\chi} + \sum_{R' \neq R} \sigma_{R',t}^{\rho} \cdot L_{R'}^{\chi} \cdot \left(\frac{\sigma_{R,t}^{\rho} \cdot L_R^{\chi}}{\sigma_{R',t}^{\rho} \cdot L_{R'}^{\chi}} \right)^{(\beta/\beta-1)} \qquad R' = r,\, r^*.$$

Regional investment depends on the entrepreneurs' expectations with respect to the world demand of the next period, the expected regional distribution of knowledge (and labour),[2] the given depreciation rate on capital (δ) and the capital stock of the respective region in period t, see *Equation (7):*

$$(7)\quad I_{R,t} = \left(\frac{X_{t+1}^{N^e}}{ZW_{R,t+1}^{e}} \right)^{1/\beta} - (1-\delta) \cdot K_{R,t}\,.$$

3. The Flow of Knowledge

New technological knowledge originates in the core regions (the centres) of the two countries where population density is highest. The initial stock of knowledge in the central regions ($\overline{\sigma}_{c,0}$ and $\overline{\sigma}_{c^*,0}$, respectively) is given exogenously. It grows in a process of learning-by-doing and learning by imitation as described by *Equation (8)* for the domestic country. The growth of knowledge in the foreign centre is analogously determined:

$$(8)\quad \sigma_{c,t} = \overline{\sigma}_{c,0} + \left(\sum_{t'=0}^{t-1} I_{c,t'} \right)^{\alpha} - h \cdot \sigma_{c,t-1} + \frac{1}{1+f_t} \cdot \left(\sigma_{c^*,t-1} - \sigma_{c,t-1} \right)$$

$$\text{if } \sigma_{c^*,t-1} > \sigma_{c,t-1}\,,$$

$$= \overline{\sigma}_{c,0} + \left(\sum_{t'=0}^{t-1} I_{c,t'} \right)^{\alpha} - h \cdot \sigma_{c,t-1} \quad \text{otherwise.}$$

Following the argumentation in Arrow (1962), cumulative investment (right hand-side of *Equation (8),* second term) is used as an index of *learning-by-doing* since "[e]ach new machine produced and put into use is capable of changing the environment in which production takes place, so that learning is taking place with continually new stimuli" (Arrow 1962: p157). *Learning by imitation* – the last term on

[2] We assume that the regional agents' expectations with respect to X^N_{t+1} and $ZW_{R,\,t+1}$ are correct on average.

the right hand-side of *Equation (8)* – only takes place in the domestic centre if the foreign centre has a technological advantage (i.e., if $\sigma_{c^*,t} > \sigma_{c,t}$). The flow of knowledge between the two countries is impeded by f_t, a "frontier" factor capturing social, cultural and lingual differences between the two countries. It is assumed that these impediments slowly decrease in the period under consideration (see Peschel 1993 on the changing relevance of such barriers to economic interaction in the process of European integration). Furthermore, *Equation (8)* allows for the possibility of knowledge depreciation, with h being the annual depreciation rate on knowledge.

Equations (9) and *(10)* characterize the flow of knowledge within the domestic country:[3]

$$(9) \quad \sigma_{i,t} = (1-h)\cdot\sigma_{i,t-1} + \frac{1}{d_{i,c}}\cdot\left(\sigma_{c,t-1} - \sigma_{i,t-1}\right), \quad t = 2,\ldots,T \text{ and } \sigma_{i,1} = 0,$$

$$(10) \quad \sigma_{p,t} = (1-h)\cdot\sigma_{p,t-1} + \frac{1}{d_{p,c}}\cdot\left(\sigma_{c,t-1} - \sigma_{p,t-1}\right), \quad t = 2,\ldots,T \text{ and } \sigma_{p,1} = 0\,.$$

The stock of knowledge in the intermediate region grows the faster the greater the "knowledge-gap" between the centre and the intermediate region and the less the mean distance ($d_{i,c}$) between them. An analogous assumption is made for the spread of knowledge from the centre to the peripheral region; however, the mean distance from the periphery to the centre is always greater than the mean distance from the intermediate region to the centre ($d_{p,c} > d_{i,c}$).

4. A Reference Scenario

In the reference scenario, we assume that the domestic country has a higher initial stock of knowledge than the foreign country $\left(\overline{\sigma}_{c,0} > \overline{\sigma}_{c^*,0}\right)$. In all other respects, there is perfect symmetry between the two countries: the efficiency of learning-by-doing, the efficiency of learning by imitation, the mean distances between the centre and the intermediate region on the one hand and the periphery on the other hand, the partial production elasticities of labour and capital as well as the depreciation rates are the same for both countries. For mere convenience we assume that, while population density is highest in the centres and lowest in the peripheries, the absolute size of the immobile labour force is the same in all domestic and foreign regions. This assumption is given up later. *Table 1* shows the parameters that were used for the calculation of the reference scenario.

[3] The flow of knowledge within the foreign country is analogously determined.

Table 1: Parameters of the reference scenario

	domestic country	foreign country
initial stock of knowledge in the centre	1	0.1
mean dist. betw. centre and intermed. region	5	5
mean distance between centre and periphery	10	10
efficiency of learning-by -doing (α)	0.5	0.5
depreciation rate on capital (δ)	0.5	0.5
depreciation rate on knowledge (h)	0	0

valid worldwide	
world demand in first period	1
maximum demand level	100
adoptiveness parameter (k)	0.2
frontier factor f_t	$\max[(f_0 - \varepsilon t);5]$
initial frontier factor f_0	25
partial production elastic.	β=0.4; χ=0.4 ρ=0.7

In this reference scenario there is no path dependence at all (*Figure 1*). Although the domestic centre has an initial advantage (an initially higher stock of knowledge), in the long run there is convergence of regional output with each region producing approximately 1/6 of world output. This is not too surprising since knowledge is created with decreasing returns and spreads nearly perfectly in the course of time.

Figure 1: The reference scenario

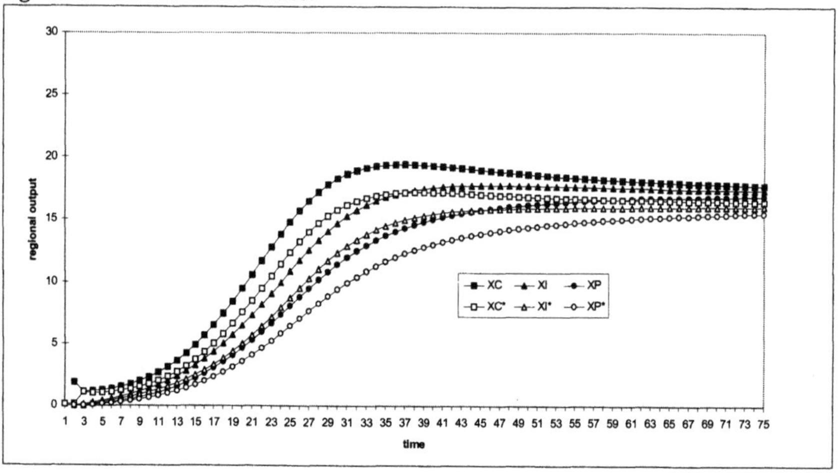

5. Some Comparative Dynamics

We turn now to some sensitivity analysis investigating the dynamics resulting from parameter changes.

An increased capital productivity

An increase in the partial production elasticity of capital (β) implies that a given world demand can be satisfied with less factor input. Since labour supply is fully inelastic, capital and knowledge have to adapt. This adaption process can only be brought about by a reduction in investment as investment determines both the stock of capital and the stock of knowledge. A reduction in investment leads to less knowledge creation and diffusion as production becomes more capital intensive and less knowledge intensive. So, it takes a longer time span to make up for an initial advantage in the stock of knowledge or, to put it a little differently, the speed of convergence decreases if capital productivity increases.

Depreciation of knowledge

Considering the possibility of knowledge, depreciation ($h = h^* > 0$) in the course of time has a twofold effect: convergence between the two countries is accelerated, whereas regional convergence within each country is retarded. The explanation is that depreciation of knowledge accelerates the use up of the domestic centres' initial advantage such that the foreign centre needs less time to close the knowledge gap. Or, to put it differently: newly created knowledge becomes relatively more important than the initial endowment with knowledge. For the same reason, the intermediate and peripheral regions are unable to catch up with the centres if knowledge depreciation is high, because they cannot create new knowledge themselves but have to appropriate the knowledge produced elsewhere (in the centres) in an indirect and time-consuming fashion (*Figure 2*).

Figure 2: Depreciation of knowledge

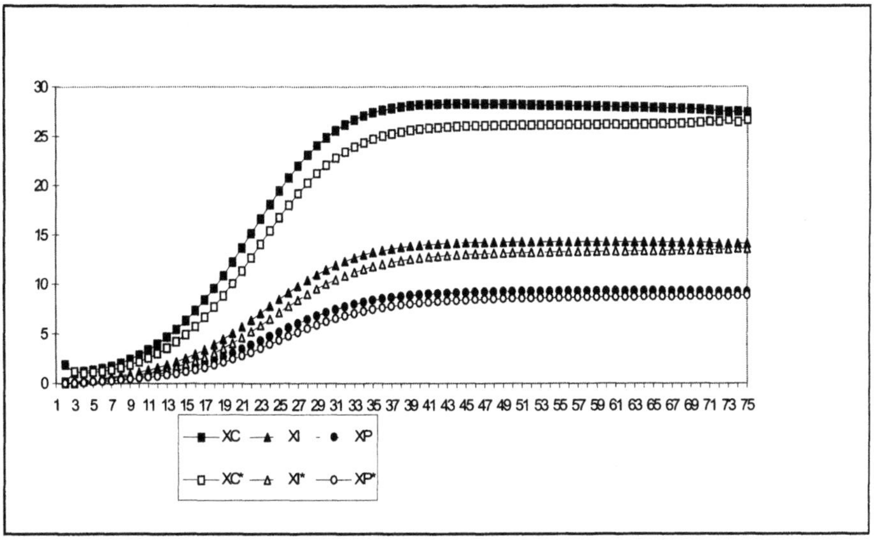

Regional differences in the size of the labour force

Up to now, we have assumed that the size of the labour force is the same in all regions, although population density in the centres is highest and the population density in the periphery is lowest. If we allow for different sizes of the labour force, the results depend on the production elasticities of labour and capital (χ and β). *Figure 3* shows the case in which the size of the labour force in the centres is three times the size of the labour force in the periphery and 1.5 times the size of the labour force in the intermediate regions. With increasing returns to scale in labour and capital input ($\chi + \beta > 1$), the output per head is the higher the higher the size of the regional labour force. The opposite is true if we have decreasing returns to scale (illustrated in *Figure 3b*). Only in the constant returns case ($\chi + \beta = 1$) is long run output per head independent of the regional population size (see *Figure 3a*).

Figure 3a: Uneven size of the labour force—output per head, constant returns case

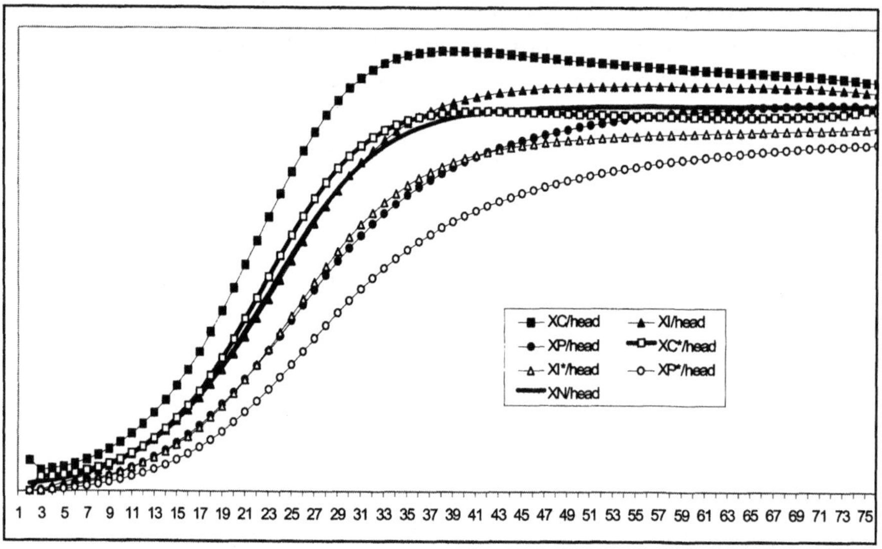

Figure 3b: Uneven size of the labour force—output per head, decreasing returns case

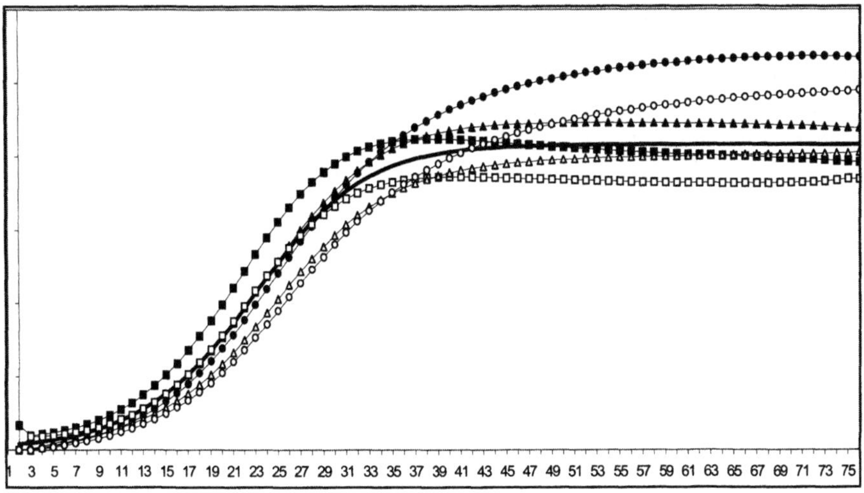

A higher efficiency of learning-by-doing in the foreign country

If $\alpha < \alpha^*$, learning-by-doing in the foreign country is more efficient than learning-by-doing in the domestic country, because the same aggregate investment leads to a higher stock of knowledge. As can be seen from *Figure 4,* a higher efficiency of learning-by-doing in the foreign country leads ceteris paribus to a permanently higher output in the foreign country.

Figure 4: A higher efficiency of learning-by-doing in the foreign country

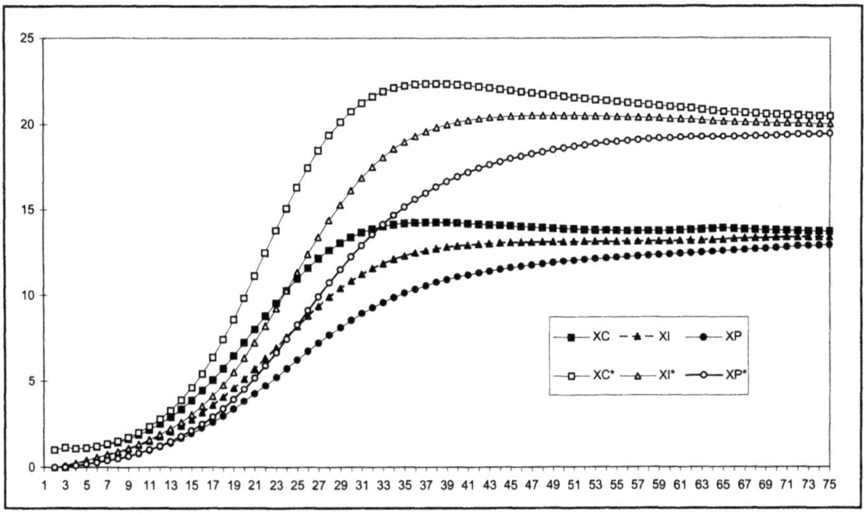

There is, however, a limiting case in which there is a tendency towards convergence in spite of a different efficiency of learning-by-doing in the two countries: if we allow the frontier factor f_t to approach zero, learning by imitation becomes almost perfect. The lagging country is able to catch up even if its capacity of learning-by-doing is permanently below the other countries' capacity. So, a higher efficiency of learning-by-doing is sufficient for a permanent advantage if – and only if – integration between the two countries is less than perfect.

An increased speed of adoption

An increase of the adoptiveness parameter k implies a higher speed of knowledge creation, since higher investments in earlier periods are necessary to meet the rapidly increasing world demand. The country with the higher efficiency of learning- by-doing profits most as production becomes more knowledge intensive.

The possibility of historical lock in

Even if the efficiency of learning-by-doing is the same in both countries, an initially higher stock of knowledge in one country can matter (lead to a permanent advantage) under very special circumstances: if k is high such that the saturation level is reached relatively early, f is high such that learning by imitation plays only a minor role, α (the efficiency of learning-by-doing) is low and capital productivity β is high such that relatively little investment is needed to satisfy the maximum demand level, an initially higher stock of knowledge in the domestic country will lead to a permanently higher output in this country (*Figure 5*).

Figure 5: Historical 'lock in'

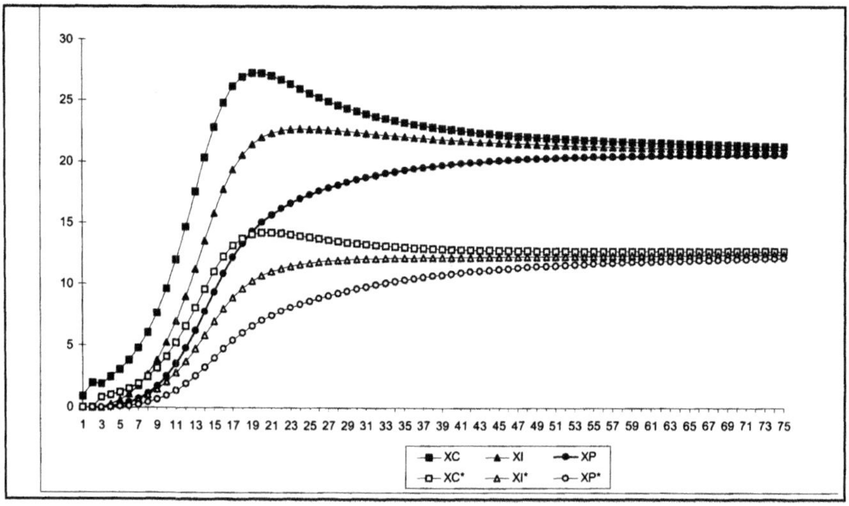

6. Conclusion

A simple two country simulation model with a trichotomic regional structure has been constructed in order to show that small variations in the parameters determining the creation and flow of knowledge may have substantial impact on the spatial distribution of economic activity. Further research – especially an in-depth analysis of the role of the public sector in shaping the economic landscape of knowledge based societies – is warranted.

References

Alderman N (1990) Methodological Issues in the Development of Predictive Models of Innovation Diffusion. In: Ciciotti E, Alderman N, Thwaites A (eds) Technological Change in a Spatial Context. Theory, Empirical Evidence and Policy. Springer, Berlin, Heidelberg, New York, pp 148-166

Arrow KJ (1962) The Economic Implications of Learning by Doing. Review of Economic Studies 29: 155-173

Audretsch DB, Feldman MP (1996) R&D Spillovers and the Geography of Innovation and Production. American Economic Review 86: 630-640

Bröcker J (1995) Koreferat zum Referat Agglomerationen und regionale Spillovereffekte von D. Harhoff. In: Gahlen B, Hesse H, Ramser HJ (eds) Standort und Region. Neue Ansätze zur Regionalökonomik. Wirtschaftswissenschaftliches Seminar Ottobeuren, Band 24. J. C. B. Mohr (Paul Siebeck), Tübingen

Carr DL, Markusen JR, Maskus KE (1998) Estimating the Knowledge-Capital Model. NBER Working Paper 6773. Cambridge (Massachusetts)

Davelaar EJ, Nijkamp P (1990) Technological Innovation and Spatial Transformation. Technological Forecasting and Social Change 37: 181-202

Davies S (1979) The Diffusion of Process Innovation. Cambridge University Press, Cambridge, New York

Glaeser EL, Kallal HD, Scheinkman JA, Shleifer A (1992) Growth in Cities. Journal of Political Economy 100: 1126-1152

Jaffe A, Trajtenberg M, Henderson R (1993) Geographic Localization of Knowledge Spillovers as Evidenced by Patent Citations. Quarterly Journal of Economics 108: 577-598

Keller W (2000) Geographic Localization of International Technology Diffusion. NBER Working Paper 7509. Cambridge (Massachusetts)

Peschel K (1993) Perspectives of Regional Economic Development Around the Baltic. In: Lundqvist L and Persson LO (eds) Visions and Strategies in European Integration – A North European Perspective, pp 19-31

Polanyi M (1958) Personal Knowledge: Towards a Post-Critical Philosophy. University of Chicago Press, Chicago

Romer PM (1994) The Origins of Endogenous Growth. Journal of Economic Perspectives 8: 3-22

Uzawa H (1965) Optimal Technical Change in an Aggregative Model of Economic Growth. International Economic Review 6: 19-31

Zhang WB (1991) Economic Growth, Creativity and Spatial Diffusion of Knowledge, Socio-Spatial Dynamics 2: 19-30

Regional Development in a Restructuring Economy. The Examples of the Urban Areas of Kiel and Nuremberg

Uwe Blien, Alexandros Tassinopoulos[1]

Institut für Arbeitsmarkt- und Berufsforschung (IAB)

an der Bundesanstalt für Arbeit Nürnberg

Nuremberg, Germany

1. Introduction

In the following we focus on the basic features and the development of the labour market of two West German cities: Kiel and Nuremberg (Nürnberg). The preparation of an analysis for Kiel is motivated by the fact that Karin Peschel has been the director of the "Institute for Regional Research" in Kiel since 1975, and she has been the Rector of the University of Kiel 1992–1996. But apart from the personal connection, a view on Kiel and – to have a reference for comparison – on Nuremberg is of interest to highlight some general economic processes which are developed in Section 2. In Section 3, we look at some empirical developments concerning the industry structure and the labour market of the two cities of Kiel and Nuremberg. Section 4 is a conclusion.

2. Employment, Product Cycle and Structural Change

In the empirical part of the paper, it is shown that the economy of the two cities, Kiel and Nuremberg,, is specialized up to a certain degree. Models developed by Krugman (1991) and colleagues (Fujita, Krugman, Venables 1999) and by land use theory (Puu 1997) provide explanations. Firms of the same region which specialize in the same industry use the advantages of a joint regional labour-force pool, the availability of intermediate products, the technological spillover effects and the easy transfer of information by personal contacts. Localization effects of this kind lead to specialization of regions according to individual industries: it is

---

[1] The authors would like to thank Johannes Bröcker, Volker Daumann and Klaus Mehnert for helpful advice. The responsibility for this analysis remains with the authors.

advantageous for a firm to select a location in which other firms with a similar product are already located.

If an economy is specialized up to a certain degree, it is affected by business cycles specific for its most important products. Therefore, the product cycle thesis (influenced by ideas of Schumpeter 1939; Appelbaum, Schettkat 1993; Appelbaum 2000; Schettkat 1997) can be used to explain the destiny of specialized regions. In a very simple model outlined in the following, the dynamics of the regions are explained by an interaction of changes of productivity and of product demand. The effects of innovations with respect to the production process are ambivalent, since they are associated with gains of employment if the product demand is elastic, and with employment losses if the demand is inelastic. Product innovation, however, i.e., the development of new products, has favourable effects on the development of regional employment.

One implication of the product cycle hypothesis is that products usually do not meet indefinitely with profitable demand. As can be shown by the example of the gramophone being replaced by the record player and this again being superseded by the CD player (and in the future – may be – by the DVD player), many products have only a finite "life". Whenever a region has specialized predominantly in a specific product, it experiences a crisis if this product reaches a saturation level or the end of its "life cycle". Therefore, the occurrence of innovations within regions is of crucial importance for the fate of a specialized region. If structural change in the direction of "new" industries is present in a regional economy, employment is increased.

To develop a clearer picture of the problem, a rudimentary model structure is shown in the following which is based on several assumptions: the gains of productivity progress are passed on to prices by the firms; capital and labour are employed in fixed proportions; only Hicks-neutral technical progress is allowed. Then, the development of employment can be expressed by the development of productivity and the demand elasticity. This may be shown by starting from the following equations:

$$(1) \quad \pi_{ir} = \frac{Q_{ir}}{N_{ir}} \quad ,$$

$$(2) \quad P_{ir} = \frac{kW_{ir}}{\pi_{ir}} \quad ,$$

$$(3) \quad Q_{ir} = f(P_i), \quad \text{with} \quad dQ_{ir}/dP_{ir} < 0 \, ,$$

where π is productivity, Q is the amount of a product and N is employment of an industry i in a region r. *Equation 2* is a price setting function, with k as a mark-up which includes capital cost. W is the wage. *Equation 3* is a decreasing demand function. If ε is the demand elasticity, it can be formulated for growth rates:

$$(4)\quad \hat{N}_{ir} = \hat{Q}_{ir} - \hat{\pi}_{ir} ,$$

$$(5)\quad \hat{P}_{ir} = \hat{W}_{ir} - \hat{\pi}_{ir} ,$$

$$(6)\quad \hat{Q}_{ir} = -\varepsilon_{ir} \cdot \hat{P}_{ir} .$$

Then, we obtain the following expression for employment growth:

$$(7)\quad \hat{N}_{ir} = \hat{\pi}_{ir}(\varepsilon_{ir} - 1) - \varepsilon_{ir} \cdot \hat{W}_{ir} .$$

If we assume a situation with constant wages, the employment *Equation 4* implies that productivity gains are connected with increases of employment if the demand elasticity ε is greater than one (demand is elastic). If demand is inelastic (ε is smaller than one), the increases in productivity are accompanied by employment losses. If the demand function is linear (or "nearly" linear), it shows an elasticity shift as a consequence of price decreases. Then, technical progress might be accompanied by employment gains in a first phase of the product cycle and by employment losses in a later phase.

The described effect might be very relevant to describe the process of structural change in a regional economy. There is empirical evidence showing the effectiveness of the shifts of the demand elasticity. With macroecononmic data, Möller (2000) found decreases of the elasticities for a number of industries during the last few decades. Oberheitmann, Wenke (1994) presented empirical analyses of the German product markets, including estimates for the price elasticity of consumer goods. The elasticity fell from a figure of about two to one close to zero between 1976 and 1989. In business economics, it is a standard theorem that the market saturation of single products is increasing during the time span of their "lives" (Ansoff et al. 1999, Porter 1998). Therefore, the product cycle hypothesis and its consequences for structural change and for employment are used as a background for the situation of the two German cities of Kiel and Nuremberg.

3. Structure and Development of Employment

A common property of the two cities of Kiel and Nuremberg is that they are medium sized urban agglomerations, away from other German industrial centres. Kiel as well as Brunswick (Braunschweig) and Regensburg (see *Table 1*) is rated as a core city with conurbational features, according to a common classification of the German Federal Office for Building and Regional Planning (*Bundesamt für Bauwesen und Raumordnung BBR*, see Görmar, Irmen 1991). Nuremberg is even a core city within a major agglomeration, since this municipality is larger than its counterpart and represents the centre of a city cluster. The number of inhabitants and of people gainfully employed can be seen from *Table 1*. Generally, both cities reveal large differences in the structure and in the development of employment as can be seen from the table, which shows two additional cities, in order to have an extended comparison.

Table 1: City sizes

	Inhabitants 1997 (1)	Employment 1998 (2)	Labour market participation = (2)/(1)
Kiel	242,300	101,100	0,42
Nuremberg	491,700	254,600	0,52
Brunswick	250,400	106,100	0,42
Regensburg	125,100	83,700	0,67

Source: Statistical Yearbook 1999, Federal Employment Services

Kiel has two special features: it is the capital of a federal state (Schleswig-Holstein), and it is located by the sea. The name of Kiel is well known in the world for the "Kieler Woche" (Kiel's week), one of the world's biggest sailing events, which has also a considerable commercial impact. It takes place every year and has a long tradition, starting in the year 1882. The sea dominated the history of Kiel and its economy for a long time, especially after it fell to Denmark in 1773. In the medieval age, the city had been a member of the "Hanse" (the Hanseatic League), but it was not one of its major trading places. During the 19th and in the first decades of the 20th century, shipbuilding, harbour, navy and related industries were very important. The Kiel region (*"Raumordnungsregion Schleswig-Holstein Mitte"*) showed a relatively high density of industry in the 19th century (Bröcker 1989). But sea transport lost its importance relative to other forms of transport, and therefore Kiel region's economy has developed not so favourably during the last decades.

Figure 1 reveals a more or less weak position of the city of Kiel in comparison to others. It might be argued that Kiel's losses are compensated by a favourable development in its suburbia. If we regard to a "labour market region" which includes Kiel's adjacent districts, we can see a growth rate that is better than that of the city. But the region's figure is still below the national average, too. And even if Kiel's neighbourhood wins, Kiel itself loses employment. Many cities are affected by suburbanization effects which means that they lose economically to the advantage of the surrounding region.

But the focus of this paper is not the region but the city. In a first approach, the problems of Kiel city can be seen very clearly from *Figure 1*, which compares the employment development of Kiel with selected other cities. The development of the city of Kiel was worse than that of Nuremberg, also worse than that of the average of cities of the same type. In a broad sense, Regensburg and Brunswick are cities that can be compared with Kiel (e.g., with respect to their size, *Table 1*).

Regensburg shows a very positive labour market development, Brunswick recently reached the West German average, after a sharp decline through the mid 1990s.

Figure 1: Regional employment 1987-1997: selected types of cities and regions

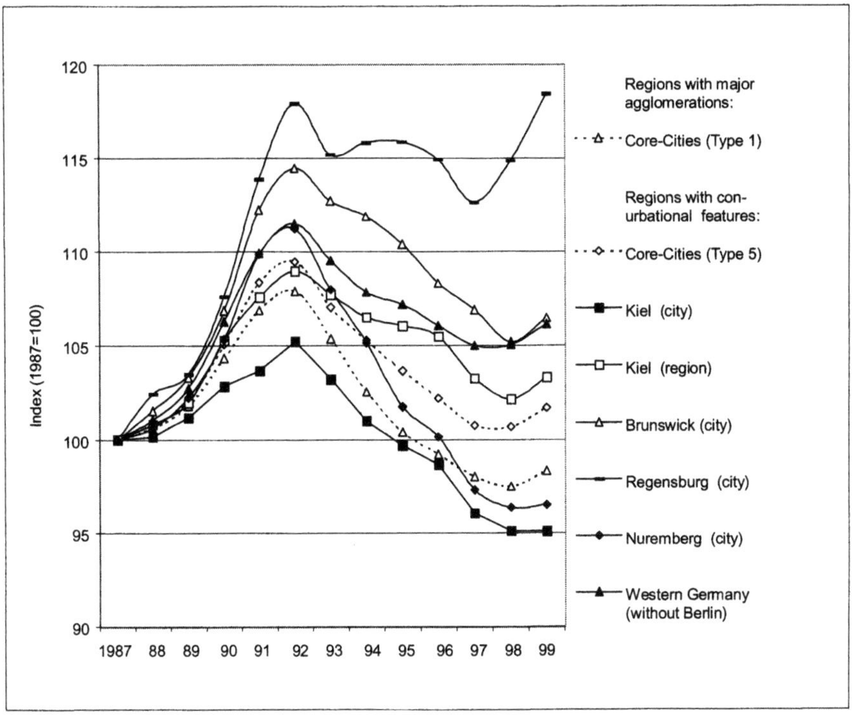

Source: Federal Labour Office, Employment Statistics; authors' calculations

From *Tables 2* and *3*, the structure and changes of employment are visible. *Table 1* shows the low level of labour market participation and *Figure 2* the corresponding high unemployment rates. Today, Kiel still has the largest shipyard in Germany, but compared to former years, the shipbuilding industry is small, since it has been shrinking for a long time, and so have related industries. The decreasing importance of sea transport can be seen from the shrinkage of trades in Kiel.

A remarkable fact is that the service sector in Kiel is growing at lower rates than in Western Germany as a whole, whereas manufacturing of machinery is performing better. The construction sector has developed worse in Kiel than in Western Germany. Car manufacturing is one of Germany's leading industries, but it is not settled in Kiel. Since Kiel is the capital of Schleswig-Holstein, the public sector is large but shrinking, too. The whole area of public administration is underrated in *Table 3*, since 13.2 % of all employment in Kiel are civil servants, which are not included in the employment statistics. In addition, there are large parts of German's naval forces stationed in the city. The labour market participation rate in

Table 1 should be interpreted in the light of these facts. The university of Kiel is important, especially compared to Nuremberg which shares a university with Erlangen.

Table 2: Change of employment 1987–1998

Sector	Change of Employment 1987-1998 (%)		
	Kiel	Nuremberg	West-Germany
Primary sector	36,16	24,18	-12,28
Energy	-10,05	-10,87	-5,46
Mining	..	..	-50,01
Manufacture of chemicals, chemical products	-37,41	-43,51	-22,93
Manufacture of rubber and plastics	-9,68	5,39	14,64
Pharmaceutical industry	-19,00	-0,67	-10,31
Refining	58,33	-14,90	24,43
Manufacture of basic metals and quarrying	23,27	-32,09	-21,89
Heavy industry	-8,61	-15,38	16,31
Engineering	11,98	-37,74	-15,56
Manufacture of motor vehicles	-26,60	43,90	-5,89
Manufacture of ships	-33,48	..	-48,85
Manufacture of airplanes	..	..	4,46
Manufacture of general electrical equipment	14,29	224,59	-27,53
Manufacture of other electrical equipment	210,88	-55,35	-19,08
Manufacture of precision electrical/optical equipment	-67,50	-6,36	-2,10
Manufacture of wood and woodproducts	-11,22	-32,53	-1,87
Manufacture of pulp paper and paper products	25,63	-19,17	-8,71
Manufacture of leather, textiles, clothing	-35,91	-52,10	-50,11
Manufacture of food products and beverages	-41,48	-30,22	-9,73
Construction	-9,29	-33,37	-3,29
Trade, renting	-2,16	-8,23	11,71
Post, telecommunication	-19,07	-25,69	-20,54
Distributive services, transport	8,75	24,05	24,51
Financial services	-2,74	10,93	11,02
Business consultancy, engineering activities	48,39	67,85	86,97
Services for society	-3,07	-7,96	9,87
Health and social work	16,38	117,95	39,04
Science, Education	10,88	17,52	25,64
Service activities for private households	51,83	54,80	39,44
Public administration	-21,84	-21,83	-8,17
Total	-4,89	-3,63	4,89

Source: Employment statistics of the Federal Employment Service, own calculations.

If we exclude the public sector for a moment, most of the stated facts fit into a picture of Kiel as having a rather specialized manufacturing sector, consisting of industries which are "old", interpreted with the background of the product cycle idea of Section 2. Though no direct econometric evidence is presented here and no hard test feasible, at least qualitatively there is a correspondence to the empirical developments. Kiel's industry is strong in the delivery of military equipment, e.g., ships and ship equipment. The demand for these products is very inelastic.

Table 3: Employment structure 1998

Sector	Patterns of Employment 1998 (%)		
	Kiel	Nuremberg	West-Germany
Primary sector	0,24	0,43	0,91
Energy	1,73	1,04	1,07
Mining	0,00	0,02	0,50
Manufacture of chemicals, chemical products	0,09	0,80	2,01
Manufacture of rubber and plastics	0,08	0,37	1,44
Pharmaceutical industry	0,78	0,64	0,55
Refining	0,02	0,22	0,30
Manufacture of basic metals and quarrying	0,30	1,44	2,89
Heavy industry	0,96	0,89	1,73
Engineering	4,55	2,28	4,16
Manufacture of motor vehicles	1,65	2,12	4,31
Manufacture of ships	3,38	0,00	0,09
Manufacture of airplanes	0,00	0,00	0,27
Manufacture of general electrical equipment	0,02	0,08	0,66
Manufacture of other electrical equipment	0,73	4,55	3,34
Manufacture of precision electrical/optical equipm.	2,78	7,89	2,98
Manufacture of wood and woodproducts	0,45	0,31	1,71
Manufacture of pulp paper and paper products	0,64	2,39	1,58
Manufacture of leather, textiles, clothing	0,11	0,36	1,25
Manufacture of food products and beverages	1,16	1,81	2,86
Construction	4,41	4,04	6,24
Trade, renting	14,66	16,85	14,25
Post, telecommunication	1,88	2,94	1,18
Distributive services, transport	2,99	4,88	3,84
Financial services	6,29	5,92	4,25
Business consultancy, engineering activities	9,70	15,51	8,57
Services for society	5,09	4,24	4,69
Health and social work	11,58	6,94	9,32
Science, Education	6,46	1,86	3,66
Service activities for private households	6,23	3,39	3,33
Public administration	11,04	5,80	6,05
Total	100,00	100,00	100,00

Source: Employment statistics of the Federal Employment Service, own calculations.

In some respects, Nuremberg is similar to Kiel. The city in the North of Bavaria is an industrial centre, specialized in the manufacturing of electrical equipment and machines. This industry structure is "old", too, its products are in a late phase of the product cycle. Like Kiel, Nuremberg was industrialized early in the 19th century (Bröcker 1989). The long history is a disadvantage in so far the switch to a modern structure was not completely successful. Nearly all industries of the secondary sector develop unfavourably in Nuremberg with respect to employment. But many firms located in this city are highly productive (Tassinopoulos 2000b). And this is also a feature of many firms in Kiel, e.g., in shipbuilding. A strength of Nuremberg is the manufacturing of medical, precision and optical instruments. Business consultancy, marketing research and related activities are rather important in this city. The proportion of these industries is extraordinarily high and so are their growth rates.

Figure 2: Development of unemployment 1990-1998

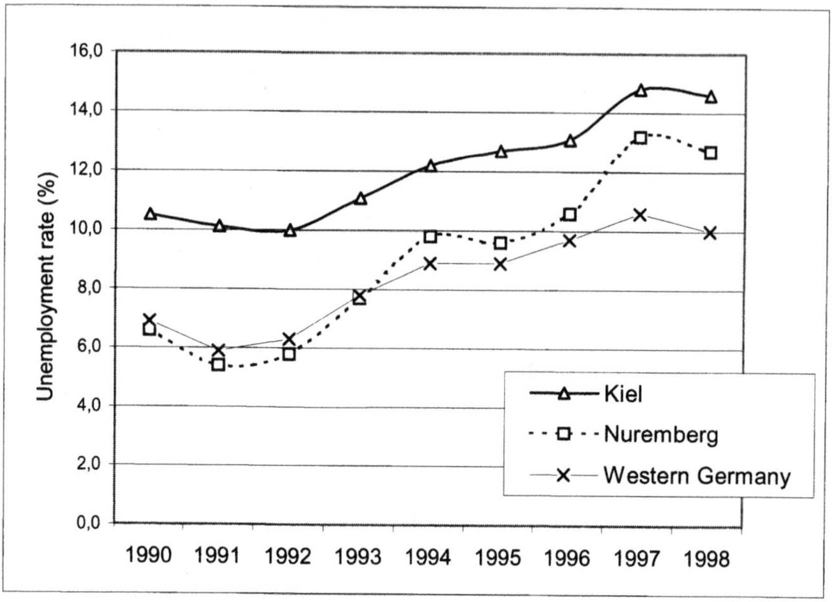

Source: Federal Employment Services

So far, the discussion of empirical development figures has concentrated on employment. *Figure 2* adds a comparison of the unemployment rates of our two cities. Above-average unemployment rates are typical for larger municipalities in Western Germany. Employment growth in these cities has been below average, since all are affected by well-known suburbanization effects. Many innovative industries leave the urban centres and move to the suburbs. Kiel shows the highest rates of unemployment during the last years. A pronounced deterioration of the situation revealed Nuremberg.

Apart from the factors emphasized up to now, other developments are relevant to understand the situation of Kiel and Nuremberg. Changes in the international division of labour are in favour of newly industrialized countries. These are able to attract part of the demand in important industries, e.g. in shipbuilding, that has been traditionally relevant for the industrialized countries in Europe.

The present situation of Kiel's economy is not favourable, but there are prospects for a better future. Though the city is located distant to the main economic centres of Germany, which has been a restriction for the development of the city, at the moment, the quality of the location is changing. The large area of Scandinavia is integrating, partly due to the construction of large bridges, connecting the main islands of Denmark with Jutland in the recent past and with Sweden from July 2000 on. A bridge passing the Fehmarn Belt is planned.

For the West, the opening of the Baltic countries has facilitated new trade flows, which can include Kiel. Bröcker (1998) has shown that Poland in particular will gain from economic integration in the EU. Though an integrated Baltic Sea region is not expected to develop, a Scandinavian-Baltic economic space could arise (Peschel 1998). These effects of economic integration, especially with respect to Scandinavia and the Baltic Sea, has been a focus in Karin Peschel's thinking and the work of the Institute for Regional Research (e.g., Peschel 1995).

The developments mentioned above are favourable for the location of Kiel. The city is no longer outside the network of trade flows but in the centre of an integrating economic system. The unfavourable development of trades might be reversed soon because of the city's facilitated access to new markets (Niebuhr, Peschel, Radtke 1999). Innovative industries might choose Kiel as an appropriate place.

4. Conclusion

In Section 2, it was argued that regional economies might suffer from a shift in demand elasticities in the course of the product cycle of its dominating industries, and that this may cause a loss in employment. Kiel and Nuremberg might represent examples of the effectiveness of these developments. Both cities have been highly specialized in industries which represented great strength for a long time, but then their industry structure became partly outdated.

Though the empirical facts shown so far are in accordance with this basic idea, the evidence they represent is not exclusive. A crucial factor in the model is the demand elasticity, for which – apart from some qualitative indicators – no regionalized information is available. Therefore, other approaches could be more relevant to explain the decline of Kiel and Nuremberg, e.g., a pure demand shift in the process of structural change (Gundlach 1994). Undoubtedly, other developments contribute to the situation of Kiel, among others a shift in the international division of labour.

The basic idea of Section 2, however, implies the advantage of explaining striking features of the production and the labour market in both cities. Some firms located there are highly productive. But this competitive position – e.g., in Kiel's shipbuilding – is not accompanied by employment gains. The contrary is the case. Our conclusion is therefore, that this qualitative information confirms the theoretical model.

If the interpretation suggested here is correct, strategies to overcome the employment problems of Kiel and Nuremberg should not the attempt to preserve the old strengths by any means. If the reason for the employment decline is a decreasing demand elasticity, it will not be sufficient to secure productivity gains. The decrease in employment would not stop, even if the industries of both cities were most competitive. The strategy can only be to develop new strengths, i.e., to facilitate the development of new and innovative industries accompanied by increases in demand. Another – or a complementary – option would be the opening of new markets, a process which is developing with respect to Kiel.

References

Appelbaum E (2000) Are Prices Unimportant? The Changing Structure of the Industrialized Economies. In: Baumol WJ, Schettkat R (eds) Structural Change and Employment (forthcoming), Amsterdam

Appelbaum E, Schettkat R (1993) Employment Developments in Industrialized Economies. Discussion Paper FS I 93-313, Wissenschaftszentrum Berlin

Appelbaum E, Schettkat R (1994) The End of Full Employment? On Economic Development in Industrialized Countries. Intereconomics 29: 122-130

Ansoff HI, Declerck RP, Hayes RL (1999) From Strategic Planning to Strategic Management. In: Hahn D, Taylor B (eds) Strategische Unternehmungsplanung – Strategische Unternehmensführung. Physica, Heidelberg, pp 105-144

Baumol WJ, Schettkat (2000) (eds) Structural Change and Employment (forthcoming), Amsterdam

Blien U (1999) Arbeitslosigkeit und Entlohnung auf regionalen Arbeitsmärkten. Theoretische Analyse, ökonometrische Methode, empirische Evidenz und wirtschaftspolitische Schlußfolgerungen für die Bundesrepublik. Habilitation Thesis, Publication in Preparation

Blien U, Herrmann H, Koller M (1994) (eds) Regionalentwicklung und regionale Arbeitsmarktpolitik. Beiträge aus der Arbeitsmarkt- und Berufsforschung 184. Bundesanstalt für Arbeit, Nuremberg

Bröcker J (1989) Determinanten des regionalen Wachstums im sekundären und tertiären Sektor der Bundesrepublik Deutschland 1970 - 1982. Florentz, Munich

Bröcker J (1998) How would an EU-Membership of the Visegrád-Countries Affect Europe's Economic Geography? Annals of Regional Science 32: 91-109

Carlin W, Soskice D (1990) Macroeconomics and the Wage Bargain. A Modern Approach to Employment, Inflation and the Exchange Rate. Oxford University Press, Oxford

Fujita M, Krugman P, Venables AJ (1999) The Spatial Economy: Cities, Regions and International Trade. MIT Press, Cambridge (Massachusetts)

Görmar W, Irmen E (1991) Nichtadministrative Gebietsgliederungen und -kategorien für die Regionalstatistik. Raumforschung und Raumordnung 49: 387-394

Gundlach E (1994) Demand Bias as an Explanation for Structural Change. KYKLOS 47: 249-267

Herrmann H (1994) Wirtschafts- und Arbeitsmarktentwicklung in Schleswig-Holstein unter dem Eindruck der Grenzöffnung. In: Blien U, Herrmann H, Koller M (1994) (eds) Regionalentwicklung und regionale Arbeitsmarktpolitik. Beiträge aus der Arbeitsmarkt- und Berufsforschung 184. Bundesanstalt für Arbeit, Nuremberg, pp 232-265

Krugman P (1991) Geography and Trade. MIT Press, Cambridge (Massachusetts)

Möller J (2000) Income and Price Elasticities in Different Sectors of the Economy. In: Baumol WJ, Schettkat R (eds) Structural Change and Employment (forthcoming), Amsterdam

Möller J, Tassinopoulos A (2000) Zunehmende Spezialisierung oder Strukturkonvergenz? Eine Analyse der sektoralen Beschäftigungsentwicklung auf regionaler Ebene. Jahrbuch für Regionalwissenschaft 20: 1-38

Niebuhr A, Peschel K, Radtke GP (1999) Zukunftsszenarien Schleswig-Holstein im Jahr 2010. Peschel K (ed) Beiträge aus dem Institut für Regionalforschung der Universität Kiel. No. 28, Kiel

Peschel K (1996) (ed): Regional Growth and Regional Policy Within the Framework of European Integration. Physica, Heidelberg

Peschel K (1998) Perspectives of Regional Development Around the Baltic Sea. Annals of Regional Science 32: 299-320

Porter M (1998) Competitive Strategy. Techniques for Analyzing Industries and Competitors. Free Press, New York

Puu T (1997) Mathematical Location and Land Use Theory. Springer, Berlin, Heidelberg, New York

Schettkat R (1997) Die Interdependenz von Produkt- und Arbeitsmärkten. Mitteilungen aus der Arbeitsmarkt- und Berufsforschung 30: 721-731

Schumpeter JA (1939) Business Cycles. New York

Tassinopoulos A (2000a) Die Prognose der regionalen Beschäftigungsentwicklung. Beiträge aus der Arbeitsmarkt- und Berufsforschung. Publication in Preparation. Bundesanstalt für Arbeit, Nuremberg

Tassinopoulos A (2000b) Regionalanalyse Nuremberg. Discussion Paper of the Institut für Arbeitsmarkt- und Berufsforschung. Publication in Preparation, Nuremberg

Part III

Economic Integration, Trade and Migration

Migration and the Efficiency of European Labour Markets[1]

Sule Akkoyunlu, Roger Vickerman

Department of Economics

The University of Kent at Canterbury

Canterbury, United Kingdom

1. Introduction

The role of borders in adding to the costs of trade and of cultural ties, such as language, in reducing such costs have been a major element in the contributions of Karin Peschel to our understanding of the development of spatial patterns of trade. With the elimination of most direct costs of borders on trade in goods and services within the European Union, attention has been increasingly focused on imperfections in the European labour market. In this paper, we focus on the role of migration in achieving greater efficiency in the labour market. This is important because of the role of labour market flexibility in meeting the conditions for a successful monetary union and because of the concerns raised by the perceived "threat" of potential mass migrations from future enlargement of the EU.

The Heckscher-Ohlin model of trade assumed that factors were immobile between countries, although mobile within them. Equalisation of factor rewards between countries was effected through the differing factor intensities of goods, specialization depending on factor endowments. Migration thus had only a limited role in the determination of trade patterns, largely as an internal mechanism by which factors moved between sectors within countries in response to changes in the factor rewards.

Alternative explanations were needed for the international migration of labour. Major migrations were a response to some major event in the origin country to which the domestic market could not react sufficiently quickly. Natural disasters, wars, political oppression or a sufficiently large asymmetric shock in one country would lead to a substantial push to encourage population to leave. Once mobile, people would seek the location which offers the best rewards. This two-stage mo-

[1] Acknowledgement: The work reported in this paper is supported by the UK Economic and Social Research Council through the One Europe or Several? Research Programme (Grant No L213252042).

del of migration introduced by Sjaastad (1962) has been generalised more recently in Zimmermann's (1996) identification of push and pull factors.

In the so-called "new trade theory" and "new economic geography", there is a wider interpretation of the specialisation of regions and the concentration of industries which depends on the presence of scale economies in imperfectly competitive markets interacting with trade costs. In such a representation, it becomes feasible to view migration of factors such as labour and trade in goods and services as both complements and substitutes of the same process (see Faini et al. 1999 for alternative approaches).

Two pressing issues require a more consistent approach to the migration question in Europe. Firstly, the move to a single currency poses important questions about labour mobility. The optimal currency area (OCA) literature specifies that labour mobility is required to ensure efficient adjustment to asymmetric shocks within a single currency zone in the absence of independent monetary policy or exchange rate adjustment (Mundell 1961). The evidence suggests labour mobility in the EU is substantially less than in the US (Krugman 1993).

Secondly, the potential expansion of the EU to include Central and Eastern European countries (CEEC) raises fears of a sustained increase in migration from these countries and indeed from the excluded countries further to the east across more difficult to control eastern borders. This form of "economic migration", arising where the potential pay-off to the migrant is large, has become regarded, at least by some politicians and pressure groups, as a bad outcome. The impacts on wages and productivity in the recipient countries are assumed to be negative whilst the donor countries lose skilled workers, hence the net outcome on welfare is seen as negative.

Thus, we have policy pressures for increased mobility within the EU, but for restricting mobility into the EU. In this paper, we review the state of the art in migration literature in order to demonstrate firstly that the effect of increased mobility into and out of the EU is in fact generally positive and, secondly, that geographical mobility, although sufficient for achieving an OCA, may not be necessary. Increased flexibility and efficiency of European labour markets is desirable, but simply increasing internal geographic mobility whilst restricting inward mobility from external origins is not the most efficient solution.

The remainder of the paper is in four Sections. In Section 2, we provide a brief overview of the trends in international migration. In Section 3, we review the recent theoretical literature on international migration. In Section 4, we discuss the implications of the new economic geography for understanding labour market flexibility and the concentration of economic activity. In Section 5, we offer some conclusions on likely impacts.

2. Migration in Europe

Large scale migration has been a feature of European populations throughout history. Migrations of pre-historic and early modern times took place in the face of climatic change and the secular rise and fall of military power, both within and on the fringes of Europe. Out-migration towards new continents occurred in the 19th and early 20th centuries. In the last half century major movements were occasioned by both war and its aftermath and the unequal economic growth experienced on the continent.

For much of history, a simple model of migration would suffice, people moved from poor conditions towards better conditions and in so doing they raised the ultimate standard of living in both. This model would also apply to the pattern of migration in the early part of the post-Second World War period. Despite the great movements of displaced persons in the immediate aftermath of war (estimated at around 20 million people) and the political division which Europe faced for the next 40 years, the essential characteristic of the European economy in the 1950s and 1960s was labour shortage in the face of unprecedented rates of economic growth.

The faster growing economies of northern Europe relied on immigration to meet the growing demand for labour. The United Kingdom and France relied on colonies in the Caribbean, Africa and Asia to provide this labour. Industrial northern Europe, especially Germany, received large numbers of immigrants (around 5 million people, 3.6 million workers respectively, according to Zimmermann 1996) from the poor regions of the Mediterranean including Turkey. These early immigrants were less skilled or at least were prepared to accept less-skilled jobs. Essentially, a dual labour market was created, which preserved a separation between immigrant and resident workers. This allowed the wages of immigrant workers to rise relative to their country of origin, whilst not impacting so much on the wages of indigenous groups in the recipient countries.

Problems arose as the rate of growth of the European economy slowed down in the 1970s and 1980s. By this time, the second generation of immigrant families was entering the workforce with the benefit of education (and expectations) equivalent to that of the home population. Rising unemployment amongst both, the more and the less skilled, and blurring of the distinction between the two labour markets led to conflict. Ethnic tension from the concentration of families of immigrant origin in certain areas of major cities and increasing competition for scarcer jobs became more widespread across Europe (see Wrench et al. 1999, for a valuable survey of these problems). In most countries, these groups could no longer be regarded just as immigrants, in that they had been resident for a substantial period of time, increasingly had been born there, and in many cases (Germany being the major exception) they had acquired full citizenship rights. However, the perceived problems arising from the presence of such groups led to increasing problems with new immigrants.

New flows started to arrive in increasing numbers in the late 1980s with the collapse of the communist systems in the countries of Central and Eastern Europe. If we take Germany as an example of the general pattern of flows, partly because of its rather better data on migrant flows than most other European countries and partly because its size and position produces rather more consistent patterns of flow, this trend is clear. Peaks in immigration are followed quickly by increasing outflows, and the long-term rate of net migration is fairly stable, usually due to strict controls. Cyclical trends in the European economy are also reflected with a sharp downturn in net immigration in the 1970s and 1990s.

These flows were added to in the 1990s by the victims of the wars and resulting social upheavals in the former Yugoslavia. However, despite the upsurge in immigration, it is interesting to note how quickly this reversed. In-migration rose from 66,000 in 1990 to over 384,000 in 1992, but then fell to under 54,000 by 1997, by which time annual out-migration to these areas was already more than 153,000. Although the inflow 1990–1998 was over 1.4 million, the total outflow over this period was nearly 950,000.

Turning from flows to stocks, some 8.7 % of the German resident population is of non-German citizenship. The largest group of these (34 %) is of Turkish origin, more than from the whole of the EU which contributes just 25 % of the immigrant population. Clearly, the stocks of migrants from Central and Eastern European countries have not been able to develop to the same extent as those from the much longer established flows, although even here the largest stocks are those from the recent asylum seekers in the former Yugoslavia. Poles, for example, only number the same as Austrians in the total population.

The working population is the same share of the total, but the share of those actually in work is rather smaller at 7.9 %, reflecting an unemployment rate of foreigners of 18.9 % compared with 10.9 % unemployed in the total population. What is difficult to know here is whether those unemployed for long periods are more or less likely to return home and thus whether the unemployment rate is a true reflection of actual unemployment propensity. Considering occupation, 59 % of foreigners were classified as workers (*Arbeiter*) compared with 34 % in the workforce as a whole, but this figure was 75 % for Turkish residents, who also faced an unemployment rate of 23.5 %. Poles, on the other hand, had a profile much more like Italians, with 58 % classed as workers (60 % for Italians) and 16.2 % unemployed (14.9 % for Italians).

Straubhaar, Wolburg (1998) note, however, that there is evidence that immigration is self-selective: the share of persons who are highly qualified in foreign residents exceeds the share of such persons in the home population. Migration from Central and Eastern Europe to Germany caused the average level of human capital in Germany to increase, whereas the opposite occurs in the sending countries. This is a classic case of the so-called "brain drain", which Korcelli (1994) argues will continue for Poland, particularly among those with the highest educational qualifications and skill levels, such as scientists and medical doctors.

Straubhaar, Zimmermann (1993) argue that a selective immigration policy could be used to attract the highly qualified workers needed in innovative industries. However, the employment of foreigners is relatively weak in export-oriented, research-intensive industries (Zimmermann 1996). Foreigners have been more attracted to those industries that face high import competition and employ less qualified workers. The competitive effects of this type of immigration are ambiguous (Zimmermann 1995): cheap, low-quality immigrant labour may lead to a loss of competitiveness, since it induces a slowdown in the adjustment process to higher quality production. However, declining relative wages for less skilled work are an incentive for the home population to engage in human capital formation and earn higher wages in the long-run. Immigration can increase labour market flexibility, provide incentives to slow down wage growth and thus increase employment.

Empirical analyses also suggest that the size of the inflow will not be as dramatic as some have argued. The *Eurobarometer* survey in 1992 suggested, for example, that less than 5 % of the population in Poland, Czech Republic, Slovakia and Hungary had any strong desire to emigrate, although nearly 5 % of Poles surveyed had already acquired some experience of working in Western Europe. The aspiration for emigration was much higher in countries like Albania, where 60 % said they would definitely or probably emigrate (Papapanagos, Sanfey 1998).

This fairly low potential is consistent with other more recent survey evidence. Orlowski, Zienkowski (1998) estimate potential emigration from Poland to the EU during the period of 10–12 years after accession is at most 1.5 million if the current GDP relatives were to be maintained. However, assuming EU membership will allow Poland to continue its fast rate of GDP growth, this will reduce the demand for emigration. Fertig (2000) also predicts only a moderate increase in immigration to Germany, especially for the first round accession candidates. He predicts the stock of migrants from Czech Republic, Estonia, Hungary and Poland in Germany to rise from 371,665 in 1995 to 1.06 million in 2015, an average immigration flow of 33,000 people *per annum*.

Thus, the evidence is that it is not so much free access into the German labour market which leads to immigration, but rather the demand by German industry for workers to undertake less skilled jobs. The inflow from the candidate countries for EU membership is following a pattern more like that of existing EU partners, rather than the forced and temporary migrations of refugees and asylum seekers. In the following Section we turn to theoretical explanations of migration behaviour to examine, what light these shed on the processes observed above.

3. Migration Theories

3.1 Neo-Classical Models

The traditional model of migration is the neo-classical/labour-flow approach, in which migration is viewed as a response to regional labour market disequilibrium. Regions with a shortage of labour relative to capital have a high equilibrium wage, whereas regions with a large supply of labour relative to the endowment of capital are faced with low equilibrium wages. This wage differential induces a migration flow from low wage to high wage regions, in response to which wages in the high wage region will fall, while the wages in the low wage region will rise. In equilibrium, factors of production will receive the same real return in any region, thus producing a narrowing of real wage differentials (Smith 1776, Ravenstein 1889, Hicks 1932).

Empirical studies verify that net migration does typically occur from low wage to high wage regions, but without reducing regional wage differentials. Market imperfections are a first explanation. Regional differences in skill or education may be self-perpetuating because higher skilled and better educated individuals are the most likely to migrate out of the depressed regions (Daly, Ghatak 1999). Union or government restrictions on hiring, restrictive land tenure laws, discrimination and high wage policies of governments, private employers or unions may also be a cause of such failure. Later models used *expected* rather than *actual* earning differentials (earnings weighted by the probability of finding employment in the destination region) as the determinant of migration, and introduced further factors such as the costs of moving, differences in the cost of living, occupational structure (Harris, Todaro 1970; Aghion, Blanchard 1994; Hatton 1995).

The main disadvantage of the labour-flow models, however, is that it is difficult for these models to explain differences in migration behaviour for what otherwise appears to be comparable individuals. These models also do not incorporate time into the decision calculus. The costs and benefits of a move occur at different times.

3.2 Human Capital Models

Human capital models treat migration as an investment decision in which individuals calculate their present discounted value of expected returns in every location (Becker 1962, Schultz 1961, Sjaastad, 1962). The expected gains from a move derive from the higher real wage less the cost of migration. The cost includes the monetary expenses of the move, the earnings foregone during the migrating, searching and settling periods, plus any loss of job seniority, pension plans and other job-related benefits.

Empirical modelling of flows relates the expected present value of a move to individual characteristics. The key variables are age, education, occupation, employment status, sex, race, marital status and family size, of which two are particularly important. Younger persons are expected to be more mobile than older persons because they can expect more years of enjoying the benefits received from migration. Education determines general human capital which is easily transferable to different locations and reduces the risks of migration.

In general, it is expected that an increase in immigration would cause a decline in wages in the receiving country. With wage rigidity this could lead to increased unemployment in the destination country, but Schmidt, Stilz, Zimmermann (1994) and Zimmermann (1996) show that this is not necessarily the case. Declining wages and increasing unemployment in the receiving country could make it beneficial for individuals to move to another region or to return back home. On the other hand, wage and employment opportunities in sending countries rise due to the emigration of labour, which may also improve the incentives for return migration. Only in the case of free labour mobility with perfectly competitive labour markets, will wages in the sending and receiving regions perfectly adjust and result in no unemployment.

However, there are difficulties with the human capital model. A move is normally viewed as an irrevocable lifetime decision and, in concentrating on income, the model ignores many non-pecuniary aspects of a move, differences in the consumption activities of the potential migrant and financing the move.

3.3 Household Migration Models

Mincer (1978) showed that increased female labour force participation rates lead to increased interdependence with the partner's migration decision, which results in less migration. Furthermore, migration is a decreasing function of family size, since household size and the number of working family members increases the sources of costs and benefits from migration. Those family members who do not move of their own initiative often have to expect reduced earnings and fewer employment opportunities in the labour market of the destination country. Therefore, a family will only migrate if the gains of one family member internalise the losses of other family members (Sandell 1977).

However, migration can also be considered as risk-sharing behaviour within families, even in the absence of wage differentials (Stark 1991). The family wants to maximise income, but also to minimise risks to the family income, which can be achieved by some family members working in labour markets where wages and employment conditions are negatively or weakly correlated with those in the home region. This hedging strategy enables a family to secure their economic well-being in the case of an economic deterioration in local labour market through remittances from family members working abroad (Poirine 1997). Furthermore, migration of some members may improve the relative income of the household in the home region. Thus, not only income differentials between regions, but also the income distribution in the original location affects the migration decision (Stark, Taylor 1989).

3.4 Asymmetric Information

The failure of markets to adjust fully may be due to asymmetric information about workers skills. Migrants have full information about their skills, but potential employers cannot observe their true skill levels and thus offer all immigrants a wage reflecting the productivity of the average immigrant. This can produce a positive wage differential for migrants with low skills (Stark 1991) and a resulting reduction in the quantity and quality of migration. In the long-run, as employers learn the true skill level of the immigrants, wages will adjust to reflect actual productivity. The prospect of higher wages in the future results in a rising migration of highly skilled individuals and therefore in a rising short-term wage for low-skilled persons. The most skilled migrants have the highest probability of investing in signalling devices like certificates. This will result in a U-shaped migration pattern with respect to skill level, meaning that only the lowest and the highest skilled individuals will migrate.

3.5 Networks

There is evidence of strong flows between certain pairs of countries and not others, and that immigrants from one country often cluster in specific cities in the host country. This suggests the importance of networks which link new migrants with previous migrants by ties of ethnicity, kinship and friendship (Bauer, Zimmermann 1997a). Migration becomes a self-perpetuating process because the costs and risks of migration for subsequent migrants are lowered by social and informational networks. This leads to a higher net return from mobility and therefore to an increasing migration probability. Rising wages in the home country and falling wages in the receiving country weakens the self-sustaining process and lowers the possible benefits of moving (Hugo 1981, Massey 1990a and 1990b, Massey, Espana 1987).

3.6 Regional Amenities, Life Cycle and Household Production

As well as network ties, there may be other external influences such as differences in the range of regional amenities. These include public or merit goods such as educational opportunities, health care systems and general living conditions or externalities in consumption through the variety and kinds of market goods which are available. As a society becomes more prosperous, regional amenities replace pecuniary motives in the migration process; such as the familiar decentralising moves from large cities. This movement can lead to clustering of households with similar preferences for public services (Tiebout 1956). As consumers move to a region to purchase amenities, land rents may rise until households are in equilibrium. Hence, migration is seen as equilibrating both the labour market and the land market.

The choice of location may vary systematically with the life cycle even if tastes remain unchanged, depending on income, household formation, children, job changes, education, entertainment needs, health care etc. (Mincer 1978). The decision to migrate may further depend on the impact of a move on the productive household activities of the household members. A move can change both the composition of the household's costs of production and its income. Location affects the household's budget not only because it influences wage rates or the prices of goods, but also because it affects shadow prices through differences in the availability of regional amenities which affect the household's ability to produce various commodities.

Strategic behaviour may result in individuals not taking the once for all decision to change location implied by the human capital approach, but to migrate for shorter periods as part of the process of human capital acquisition. It is quite consistent with this view that a worker can take an occupation below his or her skill level, if this helps the gaining of experience of different working practices and allows the accumulation of financial capital, which can be used to start a business in the home region in the future. Migrants in such a model may respond in an apparently perverse way to signals in the home market, moving as unemployment falls, since the potential pay-off to migration will rise with the opportunities on return (Papapanagos, Vickerman 2000).

4. Migration in the New Economic Geography

The migration theories considered above have taken an increasingly sophisticated view of individual and household behaviour in labour markets which are far from perfectly competitive, not least in terms of the lack of perfect information. Recently, there has also been the development of theories which look at the implications for relative regional development in the presence of imperfect competition in the goods markets. These introduce a specific spatial element, which has been missing from much economic theory for some time and have been termed new economic geography (see Fujita, Krugman, Venables 1999 for a summary).

These models look at the relative performance of regions in the presence of scale economies and costs to trade and transport, and hence imperfect competition, in at least one sector. Labour in these models is considered free to move in response to changes in real returns, but the existence of the imperfect competition may prevent this have an equilibrating effect. Any labour moving into a region constitutes additional "home" demand for a region's industries, which then sustains the continuing development of this region's incomes through the strength of the backward and forward linkages. Labour mobility is not actually necessary for this process to occur, as it is the vertical linkages between sectors (of which labour is one) which are the main determinants (Venables 1996).

The interesting feature of the model is that it is highly parameter dependent and can produce different outcomes depending on the initial values and the degree of change in critical parameters. We can find again U-shaped relationships, in which a given change in one parameter, say the border costs of movement, can in certain circumstances be centralising (increasing regional disparities) and in others decentralising (reducing regional disparities). This is particularly important in our understanding of the impacts of migration on relative regional development, since it implies a very important result that we cannot simply transfer the experience of migration on receiving and donor regions through either space or time.

There remains an important further step to effect an integration between these models of spatial markets and the more detailed understanding of the non-pecuniary influences on labour mobility discussed in the previous section.

5. Conclusions

What can the theoretical insights on the process of migration and its impacts on relative regional development tell us about the two main questions which were posed at the start of this paper? The initial view is that any restriction on mobility must be inefficient from the point of view of the European economy as a whole, but increasing overall efficiency may imply winners and losers amongst groups of the population and regions. However, the more detailed the consideration given both to the factors influencing movement and to the markets' responses, the less clear cut can our answer be. The distribution of winners and losers is not simply a case of labour losing through falling wages in regions facing in-migration, given the skill mix and demand potential of the in-migrants. Out-migration regions may lose some skilled workers, but also gain through accumulations of human capital and financial capital.

Two reviews by Borjas (1994) for the USA and Zimmerman (1996) for Europe show that there is no consistent evidence that immigration necessarily causes declining wages and increasing unemployment in the host region. Bauer, Zimmermann (1997b) show that, if workers in host countries are predominantly unskilled, then the immigration of further unskilled or manual workers may cause unemployment and create losses. However, the immigration of skilled or non-manual workers may help considerably, if these two types of labour are complements, since this would moderate the unemployment problem independent of the wage flexibility of trade unions. On the other hand, emigration countries are likely to lose at first sight, since capital loses significantly even if native workers may benefit. However, this ignores the role of migrants. If labour outflow is temporary, remittances may cause net gains: remittances are important for labour-exporting countries, so it is more likely that the emigration country also benefits.

De New, Zimmermann (1994a, 1994b) identified some negative effects for Germany, but they conclude that these remain in an acceptable range. While Winkelmann, Zimmermann (1993) suggested that a larger share of foreign labour had increased the frequency of unemployment of Germans in the 1970s, Mühleisen, Zimmermann (1994) have found no effects for the 1980s, perhaps because wages adjust more flexibly.

De New, Zimmermann (1999) suggest that trade has had a more significant effect than migration on the German labour market, with male wages negatively affected by the trade deficit ratio. This affects skilled workers at least as much as unskilled workers. In contrast, immigration has no effect on low-skilled workers, but a positive effect on the wages of the high-skilled. Winter-Ebmer, Zweimüller (2000) show for Austria that there is only a modest impact of immigration on the unemployment risk of home employees and, in an earlier paper, that the wage effects of immigration are negligible or even positive (Winter-Ebmer, Zweimüller 1996).

In a general equilibrium model, Hille (2000) suggests that the greatest winners of free labour mobility are the migrants themselves. Although emigration has a negative overall welfare consequence for the CEEC, it leads to an increase of real wages of skilled and unskilled workers in the CEEC. With respect to the EU, welfare effects of immigration are positive but almost negligible. The arrival of further economic agents providing work and consuming goods expands overall economic activity, which eventually increases aggregate wealth. Real wages for skilled workers increase but for unskilled workers decrease.

Faini, Venturini (1993) argue that trade policy is most likely to affect both supply and demand factors in migration flows. EU policies such as the Common Agricultural Policy and the continuation of restrictive trade practices in the textile and clothing sector may have contributed to increased migration pressures. Their findings suggest that the completion of the internal market in Europe, in particularly the abolition of remaining barriers to labour mobility, should not lead to a substantial increase in intra-European migrations. Thus, trade is likely to remain a more efficient market stabiliser than migration. Labour market flexibility is needed within each regional labour market (what we could term vertical flexibility) rather than between regional labour markets (horizontal or geographical flexibility).

References

Aghion P, Blanchard OJ (1994) On the Speed of Transition in Central Europe. Discussion Papers in Economics, No. 87. Nuffield College, Oxford

Bauer T, Zimmermann KF (1997a) Network Migration of Ethnic Germans. International Migration Review 31: 143-149

Bauer T, Zimmermann KF (1997b) Looking South and East: Labour Market Implications of Migration in Europe and Developing Countries. In: Memedovic O, Kuyvenhoven A, Molle WTM (eds) Globalisation of Labour Markets: Challenges, Adjustment and Policy Response in the EU and the Less Developed Countries. Kluwer, Dordrecht

Becker GS (1962) Investments in Human Capital: A Theoretical Analysis. Journal of Political Economy, Supplement 70: 9-49

Borjas GJ (1994) The Economics of Immigration. Journal of Economic Literature 32: 1667 -1717

Daly V, Ghatak S (1999) East-West European Migration: Questions and Some Answers. Paper Presented at the Conference on "Migration and Mobility: The European Context" at Kingston University, United Kingdom

De New J, Zimmermann KF (1994a) Blue Collar Labour Vulnerability: Wage Impacts of Migration. In: Steinmann G, Ulricj R (eds) Economic Consequences of Immigration to Germany. Physica, Heidelberg

De New J, Zimmermann KF (1994b) Native Wage Impacts of Foreign Labour: A Random Effects Panel Analysis. Journal of Population Economics 7: 177-192

De New J, Zimmermann KF (1999) Wage and Mobility Effects of Trade and Migration. In: Dewatripont M, Sapir A, Sekkat, K (eds) Trade and Jobs in Europe. OUP, Oxford

Faini R, Venturini A (1993) Trade, Aid and Migrations: The Evidence of Southern Europe. European Economic Review 37: 435-442

Faini R, de Melo J, Zimmermann KF (1999) Migration: The Controversies and the Evidence. Cambridge University Press for CEPR, London

Fertig M (2000) The Economic Impact of EU-Enlargement: Assessing the Migration Potential. Paper Presented at the Workshop on Borders, Migration and Labour Market Dynamics in a Changing Europe. University of Kent at Canterbury, February 11-12, 2000

Fujita M, Krugman PR, Venables AJ (1999) The Spatial Economy: Cities, Regions and International Trade. MIT Press,.Cambridge (Massachusetts)

Harris JR, Todaro MP (1970) Migration, Unemployment and Development: A Two Sector Analysis. American Economic Review 60: 126-142

Hatton TJ (1995) A Model of UK Emigration, 1870-1913. Review of Economics and Statistics 77: 407-415

Hicks J (1932) The Theory of Wage. Macmillan, London

Hille H (2000) Assessment of the Amount of Potential CEEC-EU Migration and Analysis of its Effects Using a Computable General Equilibrium Model. Paper Presented at the Workshop on "Borders, Migration and Labour Market Dynamics in a Changing Europe". University of Kent at Canterbury, February 11-12, 2000

Hugo GJ (1981) Village-Community Ties, Village Norms, and Ethnic and Social Networks: A Review of Evidence from the Third World. In: De Jong GD, Gardner RW (eds) Migration Decision Making: Multidisciplinary Approaches to Microlevel Studies in Developed and Developing Countries. Pergamon Press, New York

Korcelli P (1994) Emigration from Poland After 1945. In: Fassmann H, Munz R (eds) European Migration in the Late Twentieth Century. Edward Elgar, Aldershor

Krugman PR (1993) Lessons of Massachusetts for EMU. In: Torres F, Giavazzi F (eds) Adjustment and Growth in the European Monetary Union. CUP, Cambridge

Massey DS (1990a) The Social and Economic Origins of Immigration. Annals of the American Academy of Political and Social Sciences 510: 60-72

Massey DS (1990b) Social Structure, Household Strategies, and the Cumulative Causation of Migration. Population Index 56: 1-26

Massey DS, Espana FG (1987) The Social Process of International Migration. Science 237: 733-738

Mincer J (1978) Family Migration Decisions, Journal of Political Economy 86: 749-773

Mühleisen M, Zimmermann KF (1994) A Panel Analysis of Job Changes and Unemployment. European Economic Review 38: 793-801

Mundell RA (1961) The theory of Optimal Currency Areas. American Economic Review 51: 657-665

Orlowski WM, Zienkowski L (1998) Potential Size of the Emigration from Poland After Joining the European Union: An Attempt of a Forecast. In: Research Centre For Economic and Statistical Studies of the Central Statistical Office and the Polish Academy of Sciences (ed) Research Bulletin 7: 23-31

Papapanagos H, Vickerman RW (2000) Borders, Migration and Labour Market Dynamics in a Changing Europe. In: van der Velde M, van Houten H (eds) Borders, Regions and People. European Research in Regional Science, Vol. 10. Pion, London

Poirine B (1997) A Theory of Remittances as an Implicit Family Loan Arrangement. World Economy 25: 589-611

Ravenstein E (1889) The Laws of Migration. Journal of the Statistical Society 52: 214-301

Sandell SH (1977) Women and the Economics of Family Migration. Review of Economics and Statistics 53: 157-163

Schmidt CM, Stilz A, Zimmermann KF (1994) Mass Migration, Unions and Government Interventions. Journal of Public Economics 55: 18-201

Schultz TW (1961) Investment in Human Capital. American Economic Review 51: 1-17

Sjaastad LA (1962) The Costs and Returns of Human Migration. Journal of Political Economy 70: 80-93

Smith A (1776) Inquiry into the Nature and Causes of the Wealth of Nations. Strahan/Cadell, London

Stark O (1991) The Migration of Labour. Basil Blackwell, Oxford

Stark O, Taylor JE (1989) Relative Deprivation and International Migration. Demography 26: 1-14

Straubhaar T, Wolburg M (1998) Brain Drain and Brain Gain in Europe: An Evaluation of the East-European Migration to Germany. Paper Presented at Winter 1998 Workshop on Managing Migration in the 21st Century: CIIP and Institute on Global Conflict and Co-operation at Centre for US-Mexican Studies. University of California, San Diego

Straubhaar T, Zimmermann KF (1993) Towards a European Migration Policy. Population Research and Policy Review 12: 225-241

Tiebout CM (1956) A Pure Theory of Local Expenditures. Journal of Political Economy 64: 416-424

Venables AJ (1996) Equilibrium Locations of Vertically Integrated Industries. International Economic Review 37: 341-359

Winkelmann R, Zimmermann KF (1993) Ageing, Migration and Labour Mobility. In: Johnson P, Zimmermann KF (eds) Labour Markets in an Ageing Europe. CUP, Cambridge

Winter-Ebmer R, Zweimüller J (1996) Immigration and the Earnings of Young Native Workers. Oxford Economic Papers 48: 473-491

Winter-Ebmer R, Zweimüller J (2000) Do Immigrants Displace Young Native Workers: The Austrian Experience. University of Linz, mimeo, Austria

Wrench J, Rea A, Ouali N (1999) Migrants, Ethnic Minorities and the Labour Market. Macmillan, London

Zimmermann KF (1995) Tackling the European Migration Problem. Journal of Economic Perspectives 9: 45-62

Zimmermann KF (1996) European Migration: Push and Pull. International Regional Science Review 19: 95-128

Regional Market Areas at the EU Border

Klaus Schöler

Universität Potsdam

Wirtschafts- und Sozialwissenschaftliche Fakultät

Lehrstuhl für Volkswirtschaftslehre, insbesondere Wirtschaftstheorie

Potsdam, Germany

1. Introduction

With the enlargement of the European Union (EU) and the negotiations with potential member countries and further candidates, the question arises how to form the relationship to non-EU countries. The enlargement leads to new borders in new areas and to enlarged external frontiers with cross-frontier trade and markets. Therefore, at the new EU border many new regional markets will emerge, in which – on the basis of lower production costs in many industries in non-EU countries – an import pressure arises. This import pressure calls for a political answer. In the past, the EU gave many different regional answers which produced preferential trade for more than 25 % of the whole EU trade with non-EU countries. In 1996, there was a hierarchy of EC trade regimes: in Eastern and South-Eastern Europe, a free-trade area (Europe Agreements) covered Bulgaria, the Czech Republic, Estonia, Hungary, Latvia, Lithuania, Poland, Romania, the Slovak Republic and Slovenia. In the Mediterranean area, there was a custom union with Turkey; free trade areas included Israel, Cyprus and Malta. Non-reciprocal contractual preferences were agreed with Algeria, Egypt, Jordan, Morocco, Lebanon, Syria and Tunisia (Sapier 1998). This trade policy followed the lines of general foreign policy, and the traditional policy of some EU states was based on interests in certain regional areas. Furthermore, the trade policy of the EU may not be understood without an investigation of the design and evolution of EU institutions (Bilal 1998).

This paper tries to give a theoretical and model based economic answer to the question, which trade policy is appropriate to raise the welfare of EU regions near borders. For this purpose, we concentrate our investigations on two extremes, on the one hand on free trade, and on the other hand on trade policy with import tariffs and export subsidies of non-EU countries. There is no doubt about the results of the applied model: trade policy raises the welfare effects of the EU area and lowers these effects of the non-EU countries, which are in a position to make compensation payments to the EU to avoid a system of import tariffs and contrary export subsidies. Free trade also produces the highest world welfare.

This essay combines elements of international trade theory with a model of spatial oligopoly, i.e., with at least one supplier's market area stretching across the border. In an early paper, Benson, Hartigan (1983) demonstrate that import tariffs may reduce the (profit-maximizing) mill price, even that of the domestic firm. In further papers, these authors also tackle the effects of import quotas (1984) and the distributional incidence of tariffs (1987). An early discussion of welfare effects in the mentioned analytical framework can be found for certain special cases in Porter (1984) as well as, with endogenous revenue and protective tariffs, in Schöler (1990). Heffley, Hatzipanayotou (1991, 1993) investigate the impact of tariffs on population distribution and land rents as well as on consumers' mobility. Furthermore, alternative conjectural variations and heterogenous goods are treated by Heffley, Hatzipanayotou, Mourdoukoutas (1993) in a spatial market model with tariffs. Hass (1996, 1997/98) extends the analysis to alternative models of spatial competition on the one hand, and to endogenous welfare maximizing tariff rates on the other hand. This kind of endogenous welfare maximizing tariff, though calculated in a different fashion, is also applied by Schöler (1997). Hass, Schöler (1999) reach a differentiated welfare-theoretical assessment of export subsidies. Finally, there are two papers published by Schöler (1999a, 1999b), in which different trade policies are compared. In this paper, we want to investigate the trade policy of setting welfare maximizing tariffs for imported goods by the EU and the reactions of non-EU countries, which pay welfare maximizing export subsidies to their domestic industries.

The paper is organised as follows: In Section 2, the assumptions and the spatial market model with trade policy are developed. In Section 3, we discuss the welfare effects of free trade and of trade policy (tariffs and export subsidies) by using a numerical example. In Section 4, we summarize the results of our spatial model of trade policy.

2. Model with Trade Policy

For simplification, we want to introduce the following notations: in the sense of our model, the EU area is the domestic state or country and all non-EU areas are foreign states or countries. Therefore, the world is the sum of the EU and non-EU countries. The regional markets at the EU border are represented by a one-dimensional space, which is divided by the EU border. It is appropriate to formulate some further assumptions (A) common to the spatial pricing literature in order to keep the model manageable:

A1 Domestic and foreign consumers continuously occupy a homogenous line $\overline{0R}$ at uniform density equal to 1. The locations of the firms are exogenously given at the left and right ends of this line, i.e., at 0 for the domestic firm and at R for the foreign competitor. The foreign firm exports part of its production to the domestic market, so that it serves the foreign market between its location R and the EU border R_G as well as the domestic market between the EU border R_G and the market area boundary R_C. The domestic firm delivers to the remaining part of the domestic market, covering $\overline{0R_C}$.

0---------------------R_C---------------------R_G---------------------R

A2 To keep the algebra less cumbersome, we assume domestic and foreign individual consumer demand to be identical with respect to utility and expenditure functions, and represented by a linear function of the respective delivered price $p(r)$:

(1) $q_i = 1 - p_i$ and $p_i = m_i + r, \quad i = I, A, D, \quad r \in [0, R]$.

The delivered prices of the domestic firm $p_I(r)$, of the foreign firm in the domestic market area $p_A(r)$ and in the foreign market area $p_D(r)$ are the sum of the mill prices m_I, m_A, or m_D, respectively, and the transportation costs between the production and consumption locations r, with r signifying the distance between the two locations. The freight rate per quantity and distance unit for domestic and foreign transportation is assumed to equal 1.

A3 Production technology and cost functions are identical in both countries. Hence, the cost functions read

(2) $K_I = vK_A + (1 - v) K_D = K_f$,

with variable costs set to zero. The parts of the fixed costs of the foreign firm which are attributable to the exports are vK_f with $v \in [0, 1]$.

A4 The firms aim at maximizing their profits under Löschian competition. The consumers aim at maximizing their consumers' surplus and purchase the good from the firm which offers the lowest delivered price.

A5 The trade policy of the domestic government (EU) comprises welfare maximizing import tariffs t^*, and the answer of the foreign government (non-EU) is the grant of welfare maximizing export subsidies s^* .

A6 The model is confined to the short run analysis, i.e., relocations are neither undertaken nor expected by the competitors.

The existence of a spatial market implies the following conditions:

(a) $m_I < m_A + R$ and $m_A < m_I + R$, respectively: a firm cannot be entirely pushed out of the market via price undercutting by the competitor at the former firm's own location.

(b) $1 - m_I + R_C > 0$ and $1 - m_A + R - R_C > 0$, respectively: at the competition boundary R_C, the delivered price is not allowed to be higher than or equal to the prohibitive price, which is: $R \leq m_I - m_A + 2R_C$.

Due to the fact that at the competition boundary the delivered prices of both firms are identical, we get the admissible distance R between the firms' locations, with R_C being less or equal to the monopoly market size. If at least one of these two conditions is not fulfilled, the market will be divided into one or two spatial monopolies.

Under the assumptions A1 to A6, spatial competition under free trade can be modeled with $t = 0$ and $s = 0$. In the case of trade policy the model is the following. The domestic firm's profit is given by

$$(3)\quad \Pi_I = m_I \int_0^{R_c} (1 - m_I - r)dr - K_f .$$

The profit-maximizing domestic mill price, as a function of the market area size, reads

$$(4)\quad m^*_I = 0.5 - 0.25R_C .$$

Given assumption A1, the foreign firm serves the foreign market between R_G and R as well as a part of the domestic market $\overline{R_C R_G}$. The profit is given by

$$(5)\quad \Pi_{A/D} = m_D \int_0^{D} (1 - m_D - r)dr + (m_A + s)\int_0^{R_G - R_C} (1 - m_A - D - t - r)dr - K_f ,$$

where t is the domestic tariff on the quantity of imports, s the foreign export subsidies on the quantity of exports and $D = R - R_G$. In the presence of tariffs, the foreign firm may determine a common mill price for its foreign market (m_A) and domestic market (m_D) and separate prices in the sense of spatial price discrimination. The profit-maximizing foreign mill price for the domestic market, as a function of the domestic market size, tariff, and subsidies, reads

$$(6)\quad m^*_A = 0.25[R_C - 2D - R_G + 2(1 - s - t)] ,$$

and the profit-maximizing foreign mill price for the foreign market

$$(7)\quad m^*_D = 0.5 - 0.25D .$$

Due to the fact that, according to A4, the delivered prices of both firms are identical at the competition boundary R_C:

$$(8)\quad m^*_A + D + R_G - R_C = m^*_I + R_C ,$$

this boundary with profit-maximizing foreign and domestic mill prices m^*_A, m^*_I can endogenously be derived as

$$(9)\quad R^*_C = (1/6)[2D + 3R_G - 2(s - t)] .$$

Inserting this result (9) into the price equations (4) and (6), the mill prices will read

(10) $m^*_{\mathrm{I}} = (-1/24)[2D + 3R_G - 2(s - t + 6)]$

and

(11) $m^*_{\mathrm{A}} = (-1/24)[(10D + 3R_G + 2(7s + 5t - 6)]$,

with $\partial m^*_I/\partial t = -1/12$, $\partial m^*_I/\partial s = 1/12$, $\partial m^*_A/\partial t = -5/12$, and $\partial m^*_A/\partial s = -7/12$.

The domestic tariff revenue equals

$$(12)\quad T = t \cdot \int_0^{R_G - R_C^*} (1 - m_A^* - D - t - r)dr\,,$$

and the foreign expenditures for export subsidies is

$$(13)\quad S = s \cdot \int_0^{R_G - R_C^*} (1 - m_A^* - D - t - r)dr\,.$$

Under exogenous tariff and subsidy rates, the domestic revenue and foreign expenditures depend solely on the transport costs between the locations of the firms and the border between the EU and non-EU countries.

To calculate the welfare maximizing tariff and subsidy rates, we have to choose an appropriate definition of welfare. One plausible definition of the domestic welfare would be the sum of the profit of the domestic firm, the domestic consumers' surplus and the tariff revenue. Following this definition, welfare reads $\Omega_I = \Pi_I + \Lambda_I + \Lambda_A + T$, where Π_I is the profit of the firm, Λ_I is the consumers' surplus in the market area of the domestic firm, and Λ_A symbolizes consumers' surplus in the domestic market area of the foreign firm. Therefore, the foreign welfare reads $\Omega_{A/D} = \Pi_A + \Pi_D + \Lambda_D - S$, where Π_A is the profit of the foreign firm in the domestic market area and Π_D in the foreign market area, and Λ_D symbolizes the consumers' surplus in the foreign market area of the foreign firm. The consumers' surpluses are

$$(14)\quad \Lambda_I = \int_0^{R_C^*} 0{,}5(1 - m_I^* - r)^2\,dr\,,$$

$$(15)\quad \Lambda_A = \int_0^{R_G - R_C^*} 0{,}5(1 - m_A^* - D - t - r)^2\,dr\,,$$

$$(16)\quad \Lambda_D = \int_0^{D} 0{,}5(1 - m_D^* - r)^2\,dr\,.$$

Under consideration of R^*_C and the equations (3), (5) and (12) to (16), the welfare effects are functions of the distance between the locations of the firms and the border as well as t and s. If we maximize the domestic welfare function Ω_I with respect to t and the foreign welfare function $\Omega_{A/D}$ with respect to s, we get a system of two equations with two unknown variables:

$$(17)\quad t = (-1/98)[[1600D^2 - 32D\,(67R_G + 100s + 47) + 1465\,R^2_G + 8R_G\,(268s + 173) + 16(100s^2 + 94s - 47)]^{0.5} + 2(29D - 16R_G - 29s - 20)]\,,$$

$$(18)\quad s = (1/70)[2[400D^2 + 20D(2(20t - 17) - 9R_G) + 351R^2_G - 36R_G\,(5t + 8) + 4(100t^2 - 170t + 109)]^{0.5} + 30D - 33R_G + 2(15t - 4)]\,.$$

If we solve the equations (17) and (18) simultaneously and put the results for t^* and s^* into the welfare equations, these terms only depend on R_G and D :

$$(19)\quad \begin{matrix} \Omega_1 = \Omega_1(R_G, D) \\ \\ \Omega_{A/D} = \Omega_{A/D}(R_G, D) \end{matrix} \qquad \text{with} \qquad \begin{cases} s = s^*, t = t^*, \\ m_I = m_I^*, m_A = m_A^*, \\ m_D = m_D^*, R_C = R_C^* \end{cases} .$$

To evaluate the welfare results, it is appropriate to assume numerical values for the exogenous variables R_G and D, because the solutions of the equation system (17, 18), and hence the equations in (19), are very extensive.

3. Some Numerical Results

First of all, it is convenient to reduce the three-dimensional problem (R_G, D, Ω) into a two-dimensional space. For this purpose, we assume $R_G/3 = D$, which means that the ratio of the distances between the location of the domestic firm and the border and the location of the foreign firm and the border is always 1/3. The range of distance between the domestic firm and the border is $R_G \in [0, 1]$, because in a linear spatial market under the applied assumptions the maximal distance between both competitive firms is $R \leq 4/3$. *Figure 1* shows the downward-sloping curves of tariffs and subsidies for the range of $R_G \in [0, 1]$. For the spaceless market $R_G = 0$, the optimal tariff rate and the optimal subsidy rate are $t^* = s^* = 0.5$. With maximal distance between the locations $R_G = 1$, we get $t^* = 0.205$ and $s^* = 0$.

To understand *Figure 2*, it is necessary to remember the fact that we apply a constant relation between R_G and D. Therefore, it is not appropriate to compare the domestic and foreign welfare, but it is worth to make a comparison for the free trade and trade policy cases. Import tariffs raise the welfare of the country which collects the customs duty and lower the welfare of the exporting country, if the foreign country answers with export subsidies and if, in addition, both countries are welfare orientated in their trade policies.

Figure 1: Welfare maximizing tariff and subsidy rates

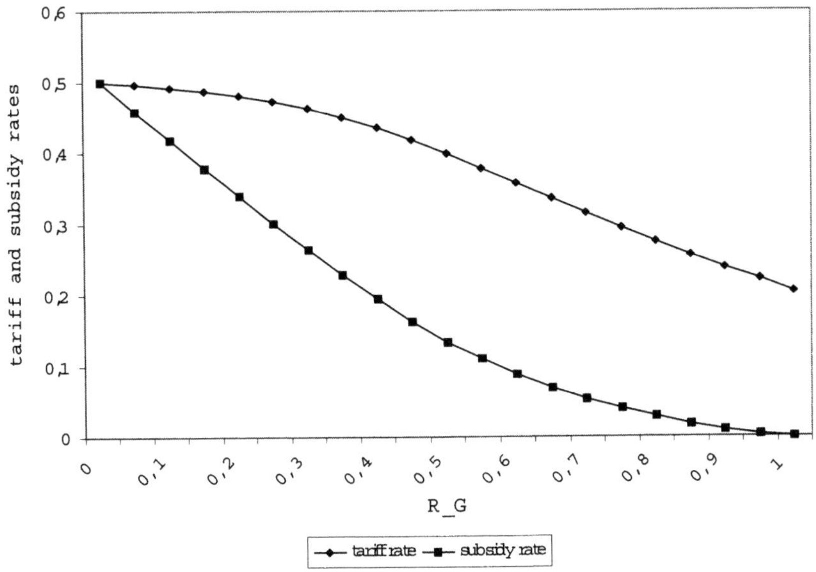

Figure 2: Welfare effects of free trade and trade policy

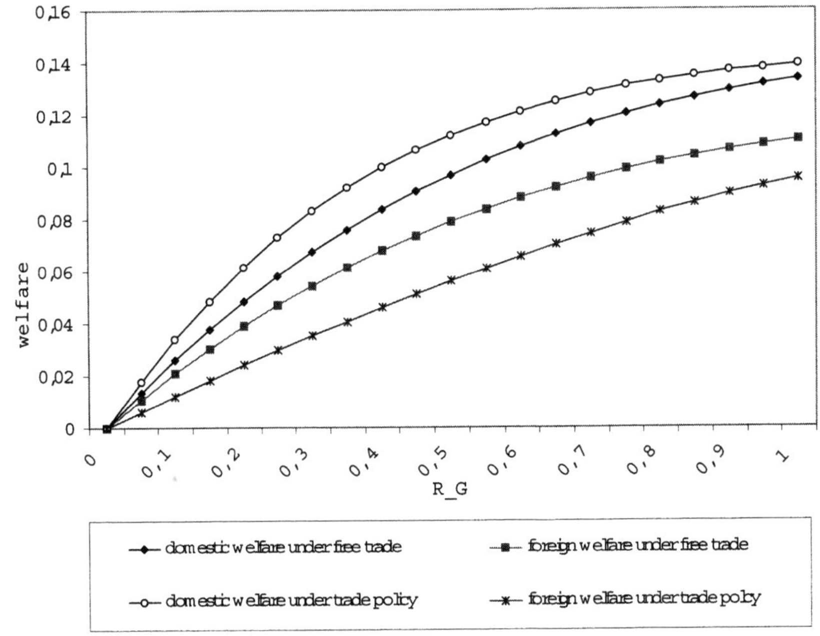

Figure 3: Comparison of trade regimes

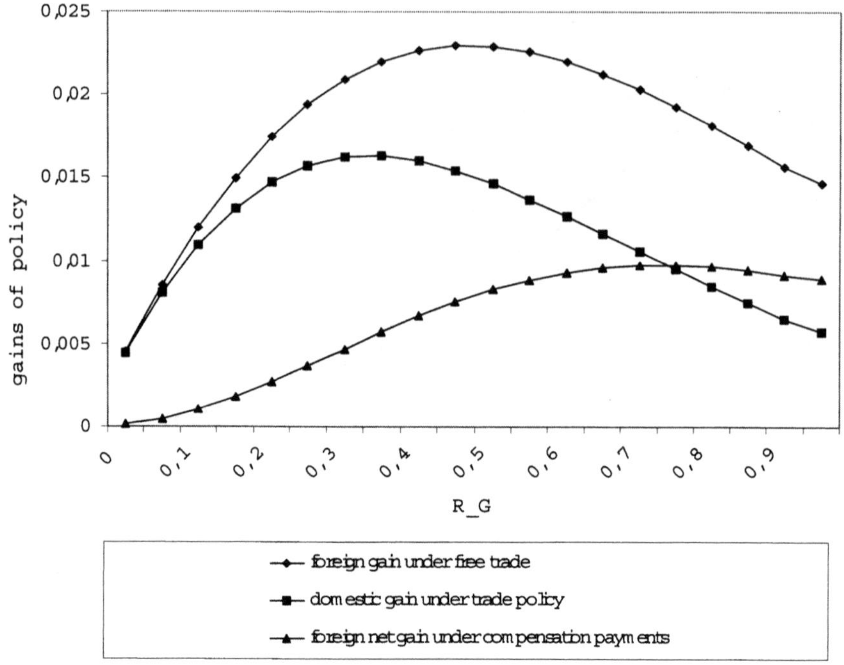

Figure 4: Tariff revenue and subsidy expenditure

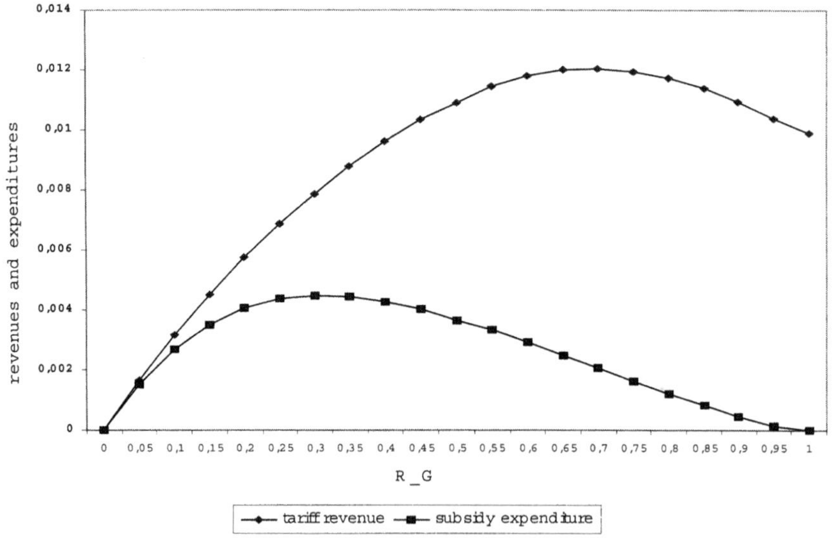

In *Figure 3*, we define the foreign gain under free trade (*FG*) as the difference between welfare under free trade and welfare under trade policy. The definition of domestic gain under trade policy (*DG*) is similar and is defined as welfare under trade policy minus welfare under free trade. The world welfare is always higher under free trade policy, because for all $R_G \in [0, 1]$ we obtain $FG > DG$. The foreign country (non-EU country) is in the position to take compensation payments of *DG* to the EU country to avoid the trade policy of import tariffs and export subsidies and remains the foreign net gain $FG - DG$.

Figure 4 shows us the tariff revenue *T* of the domestic administration and the subsidy expenditure *S* of the foreign government. Both curves have maximums at certain geographic dimensions: $T_{max} = 0.012037$ at $R_G = 0.7$ and $S_{max} = 0.004487$ at $R_G = 0.3$. For simplification, we assume in this model that the production costs are the same in both countries with variable costs equal to zero and $K_I = vK_A + (1 - v) K_D = K_f$. All results will be influenced by different production costs and a tariff policy without subsidies (Schöler 1997) or export subsidies without tariffs (Hass, Schöler 1999).

4. Conclusions

The market results of a spatial bordercrossing dyopoly as shown above depend on the distance parameters R_G, *D* and hence on *R*, the distance between the producers' locations. The national welfare effects and the design of an optimal trade policy also depend on the distance between the location of the producer and the EU border. Furthermore, the solutions of the model depend on the choice of the policy instruments (tariff and subsidy), the conjectural behaviour of the market members (Löschian competition), their pricing strategy (price discrimination and fob-pricing), and the number of acting firms and administrations.

Which results and conclusions can be drawn for the foreign policy of the EU, if we assume that all involved administrations adjust the policy instruments to the goal of welfare maximization? First of all, the answer to the import pressure of non-EU countries in border-adjacent EU areas is to establish import tariffs, also in the case of reactions by those countries with export subsidies. But in this situation, the welfare losses of the non-EU countries amount to such a considerable volume that they agreed on paying compensations to achieve international free trade. These compensations may be granted in different ways, not only by financial transactions, but also by demonstrating a certain political behaviour in various political fields. Under rational behaviour of governments, the announcement of free trade in the tariff case (or the announcement of tariffs in the situation of free trade) may be sufficient to lead to monetary or political payments. It may be possible indeed that such circumstances explain the actual findings of many different regional arrangements and free trade areas.

References

Benson BL, Hartigan JC (1983) Tariffs Which Lower Price in the Restricting Country: an Analysis of Spatial Markets. Journal of International Economics 15: 117-133

Benson BL, Hartigan JC (1984) Tariffs and Quotas in a Spatial Duopoly. Southern Economic Journal 50: 965-978

Benson BL, Hartigan JC (1987) Tariffs and Location Specific Income Redistribution. Regional Science and Urban Economics 17: 223-243

Bilal S (1998) Political Economy Considerations on the Supply of Trade Protection in Regional Integration Agreements. Journal of Common Market Studies 36: 1-31

Hass D (1996) Internationaler Handel in einem räumlichen Oligopolmarkt. Florentz, München

Hass D (1997/98) Optimale Zölle in einem internationalen Dyopol. Jahrbuch für Regionalwissenschaft 18: 21-35

Hass D, Schöler K (1999) Exportsubventionen im internationalen räumlichen Oligopol. Jahrbücher für Nationalökonomie und Statistik 218: 45-62

Heffley D, Hatzipanayotou P (1991) Tariff Protection in an Open Spatial Economy. Journal of Regional Science 31: 1-15

Heffley D, Hatzipanayotou P (1993) Tariff Effects in a Spatial Oligopoly with Land Markets and Mobile Consumers. Regional Science and Urban Economics 23: 629-643

Heffley D, Hatzipanayotou P, Mourdoukoutas P (1993) Tariffs, Price Conjectures and Welfare in an Open Spatial Economy. Papers in Regional Science 72: 87-100

Porter RH (1984) Tariff Policies in a Small Open Spatial Economy. Canadian Journal of Economics 17: 270-282

Sapir A (1998) The Political Economy of EC Regionalism. European Economic Review 42: 717-732

Schöler K (1990) Zollwirkungen in einem räumlichen Oligopol. Zeitschrift für Wirtschafts- und Sozialwissenschaften 110: 393-411

Schöler K (1997) Tariffs, Factor Prices, and Welfare in a Spatial Oligopoly. Annals of Regional Science 31: 353-367

Schöler K (1999a) Internationaler Handel und räumliche Märkte – Handelspolitik aus Sicht der räumlichen Preistheorie. Volkswirtschaftlicher Diskussionsbeitrag Nr. 28 der Wirtschafts- und Sozialwissenschaftlichen Fakultät der Universität Potsdam, Potsdam

Schöler K (1999b) Wohlfahrt und internationaler Handel in einem Modell der räumlichen Preistheorie. Volkswirtschaftlicher Diskussionsbeitrag Nr. 31 der Wirtschafts- und Sozialwissenschaftlichen Fakultät der Universität Potsdam, Potsdam

Specialization and Concentration in the European Union, 1965–1985

Jan A. van der Linden

Policy Research Institute

Antwerp, Belgium

Jan Oosterhaven[1]

Department of Economics, University of Groningen

Groningen, The Netherlands

1. Introduction

We are obliged to the contributions of Karin Peschel to the spatial analysis of international trade and the consequences of economic integration (e.g., Peschel 1985, 1999). In this paper, we like to honour those contributions by analysing the relation between economic integration and the sectoral specialization and spatial concentration of production.

Assuming full competition, traditional trade theory predicts inter-industry trade to increase when there are inter-country differences in resource endowments or technology at the beginning of the integration process (e.g., Balassa 1961). Consequently, sectoral specialization and spatial concentration of output will occur. Modern trade theory adds product heterogeneity, economies of scale and monopolistic competition, and predicts an increase in intra-industry trade (e.g., Dixit, Norman 1980). Thus, opposed to traditional trade theory, modern trade theory implies a decrease in sectoral specialization and spatial concentration. Finally, both traditional location theory (e.g., Isard 1956) and modern location theory (Krugman 1991, Bröcker 1995) explain spatial concentration within sectors and between sectors as the outcome of a trade-off between the cost of overcoming space and economies of scale. In spite of its theoretical importance, the extent of, and the changes in sectoral specialization and spatial concentration have hardly been analysed

---

[1] Respectively, senior researcher at the Policy Research Institute, Antwerp, and professor of regional economics at the University of Groningen. This paper is an extension and revision of Chapter 6 from Van der Linden (1998).

empirically. While series of authors have paid attention to the increase of intra-industry trade, only few authors investigated whether inter-industry trade and, consequently, production specialization increases or not (for an overview of these empirical studies see Van der Linden 1998).

This paper will attempt to fill this gap in the economic integration literature with regard to the EU. Firstly, it will pay attention to the *extent* of specialization; to see which EU-countries are more and which EU-countries are less specialised. Secondly, it will pay attention to the *pattern* of specialization, to see which commodities each member state is specialised in and which commodities are relatively absent. Finally, it will pay attention to the *changes* in specialization, to see whether the expected increases have indeed taken place. Methodologically, this approach builds forth on an earlier study by Oosterhaven (1995). Besides adopting a more detailed sector classification and more recent data, two other elements stand out.

Firstly, along with the sectoral specialization by country, the spatial concentration by sector will be analysed. The analysis of spatial concentration, in fact, complements the analysis of sectoral specialization because of its emphasis on small sectors and large countries, whereas the analysis of specialization emphasises large sectors and small countries.

Secondly, besides export and output specialization, domestic demand specialization is analysed. The reason for this is that attributing increasing specialization to economic integration will be misleading when the output specialization is induced by an increase in domestic demand specialization. Moreover, theoretically, domestic demand-induced output specialization is not expected to have a direct positive impact on the welfare of the countries involved, whereas export-induced output specialization is expected to increase welfare unequivocally.

In modern trade theory, however, a domestic demand-induced specialization of output may lead to economies of scale. And, more importantly, demand-induced specialization may stimulate producers to acquire an innovative edge, as described in the "demand conditions" corner of Porter's (1990) diamond. In this way, demand-induced specialization may even lead to export specialization. For these reasons, the analysis of output specialization in the EU is complemented by the analysis of the specialization of both export and domestic demand.

Note that an analysis of import specialization will not be made. This is on purpose, as the empirical analysis will be based on a set of 5-yearly inter-country input-output tables for the EU for 1965-1985. The use of such tables makes an analysis of import specialization redundant, since these tables satisfy the accounting identity between total commodity supply and demand, i.e., domestic production + imports = domestic demand + exports. This identity, normally, would not be satisfied when sectorally detailed National Accounts and Foreign Trade Statistics are combined.

Further reasons to use input-output data are their overall internal consistency and completeness; i.e., their use of the same commodity classification, the same sector classification, and the same valuation standard for all transactions, as well as in their inclusion of trade in services, next to the trade in goods. Moreover, these tables have a high level of intercountry as well as intertemporal comparability (see Van der Linden, Oosterhaven 1995 for details).

A final reason to use input-output data is found in their ability to distinguish between different sources of demand. Here, only the distinction between productive and consumptive demand is made. *Productive demand* is defined as the demand for intermediate and investment goods by the business sector. *Consumptive demand* is defined as the demand for consumption and investment goods by the household sector and the government sector. The reason for distinguishing between productive and consumptive demand specialization lies in the difference in the causes for their specialization. As regards export demand, a distinction is made between *internal EU-exports* and *external EU-exports*, as the differences in resource endowments among EU member states will both be smaller, and of an other nature, when compared to non-EU countries.[2]

This paper is further built up as follows. Section 2 defines the specialization ratio used, and presents the results of the empirical analysis of specialization, thereby elaborating the relationships between output, domestic demand and export specialization. Section 3 defines the concentration ratio used and discusses outcomes of the spatial concentration of output, domestic demand and export. Section 4 summarizes and concludes the analysis.

2. Analysis of Sectoral Specialization per EU-Country

2.1 Hypotheses and Methodology

Traditional trade and economic integration theory emphasises the importance of similarity *versus* dissimilarity of factor endowments. Interdependence would grow anyhow, specialization only in as far as the endowments are dissimilar. As the countries of the EU do not differ much in their endowments, it may be expected that the European integration has only had a minor effect on specialization. Section 2 analyses whether this is the case or not. To measure the specialization of EU-country r, compared to the total of the EU e, we use the following *specialization ratio*:

$$(1) \quad SX_r = 0.5 \cdot \sum_i \left| \frac{x_i^r}{x_\cdot^r} - \frac{x_i^e}{x^e} \right| \cdot 100 \qquad r = 1, \ldots R,$$

[2] The disaggregation can be further refined to analyse the specialization pattern of entire rows of the inter-country input-output table. This implies that the package of goods delivered to one sector will be interpreted as one "commodity", while the package of goods delivered to an other sector will be seen as a different "commodity".

where i refers to a certain sector, a dot to a summation over the appropriate index, x to either production, exports or domestic demand, and the e only to seven EU-countries: the old EU-countries Germany, France, Italy, the Netherlands and Belgium for the whole of the period 1965–1985, augmented by the United Kingdom and Denmark for the period 1975–1985.[3]

The ratio itself is used to analyse the *extent* of specialisation and *changes* therein. The elements of the ratio are used to analyse the commodity *pattern* of output, export and domestic specialisation. The range of the ratio is [0,100), which may be interpreted in terms of percentage points. The closer to 100, the more a country is *specialised*, and the closer to 0, the more its production, export or domestic demand structure looks alike the EU-average. When it is equal to the EU-average, it may be labelled as being completely *diversified.*

Note that the empirical outcomes of are dependent on the level of aggregation. The more detailed the level of aggregation, *ceteris paribus*, the higher the ratio will be. This has two relevant implications. Firstly, the outcomes have no absolute meaning, but only a comparative one. Secondly, for a proper comparison of different types of specialisation ratios, a uniform sector classification is needed and is, in fact, used (see Appendix for details).

2.2 Extent, Development and Pattern of Output Specialization

Between 1965 and 1985, but especially up to 1975, there has been a moderate increase in specialization within the EU (see *Figure 1*). Between 1975 and 1980, specialization decreased in most countries except Italy and Belgium. Between 1980 and 1985, specialization rose again. Denmark and the Netherlands have the most specialised economies, whereas the French economy is most diversified, having a specialization ratio that is about three times as small as the Danish one.

These outcomes suggest that specialization does not systematically decrease because of integration or of other reasons, while the extent of specialization appears to be determined by the size of the country at hand. Smaller countries like the Netherlands and Denmark seem to be more dependent on specialization and international exchange than the larger member states. Nevertheless, the specialization of both countries has decreased since 1975, whereas the third small country (Belgium) only had a moderate extent of specialization in all years. So, there is more to specialization than size and economic integration.

Though the extent of output specialization generally increased since 1965, the *pattern* of specialization has remained quite stable. Therefore, only the 1985 values

[3] For comparability reasons, two intercountry input-output tables are used for 1975: the first inclusive of Value Added Tax and exclusive of the United Kingdom and Denmark, the second exclusive of VAT and inclusive of the United Kingdom and Denmark (see Van der Linden, 1998 for details).

are shown (see *Table 1*). For each of the seven member states, this table shows the sectors that have an output share with a large deviation from the EU-average. In Germany, for example, the output shares of motor vehicles and other market services are between 1.5 and 2.0 percentage points higher, whereas those for oil and gas are between 1.5 and 2.0 percentage points lower than their respective EU-averages. *Table 1* thus characterises Germany as being *specialised* in metals and in metal processing activities. France, though strongly diversified, has some specialization in agriculture and services. Italy has a strong position in textiles and retail trade. The Netherlands is oriented towards agriculture, other food products, chemicals and petrochemicals. Belgium, like Germany, has a metal oriented economy, but one that is confined to basic metals and does not extend into processed metals. The United Kingdom, though relatively diversified, has become specialised in petrochemicals because of the rise of the offshore oil production. Denmark, finally, is characterised by agriculture, transportation and (public) services.

Figure 1: Development of specialization ratios for sectoral output, 1965-1985

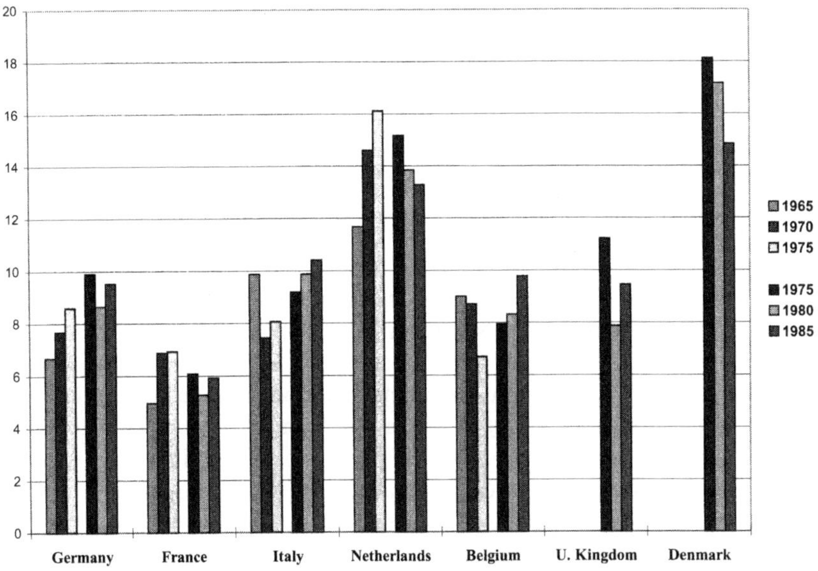

What is *relatively absent* in a country, is also of interest. In Germany, for example, agricultural and petrochemicals are relatively absent. This suggests a strong connection to the Netherlands, which is close-by and specialised in both. In the Netherlands, this holds for all metal producing and processing sectors, which suggest a strong connection to Germany in return (see Van der Linden 1998 for confirmation). In France, machinery is the only sector that falls significantly behind the EU-average. In Italy, motor vehicles and several services are relatively absent. In the United Kingdom, basic metals, chemicals, agriculture and some services sectors are relatively absent. In Denmark, finally, this holds for many manufacturing industries, so this small country is indeed dependent on international exchange.

Table 1: Sectoral pattern of output specialization 1985

%-point deviation from EU-average	Pattern of specialization				Pattern of relative absence			
	> +2.0	+2.0/ +1.5	+1.5/ +1.0	+1.0/ +0.75	-0.75/ -1.0	-1.0/ -1.5	-1.5/ -2.0	< -2.0
Germany		Moto, Mser	Meta, Aima	Chem		Agri, Buil, Retr	Petr	
France	Mser	Agri				Aima		
Italy	Text, Retr			Lodg, Leat	Util, Moto		Mser	Pser
The Netherlands	Petr, Ofoo	Agri	Chem	Pser	Metp, Lodg	Meta, Aima, Mser	Moto, Text	
Belgium	Meta		Chem	Ofoo, Moto Trsp	Aima	Metp, Elgo		Pser
United Kingdom	Petr	Pser	Beve		Agri, Meta Chem			Mser
Denmark	Agri, Trsp, Pser	Meat	Buil, Retr	Milk	Text, Lodg	Elgo	Petr, Chem	Meta, Moto

For sector abbreviations see Appendix.

What is *relatively absent* in a country, is also of interest. In Germany, for example, agricultural and petrochemicals are relatively absent. This suggests a strong connection to the Netherlands, which is close-by and specialised in both. In the Netherlands, this holds for all metal producing and processing sectors, which suggest a strong connection to Germany in return (see Van der Linden 1998 for confirmation). In France, machinery is the only sector that falls significantly behind the EU-average. In Italy, motor vehicles and several services are relatively absent. In the United Kingdom, basic metals, chemicals, agriculture and some services sectors are relatively absent. In Denmark, finally, this holds for many manufacturing industries, so this small country is indeed dependent on international exchange.

Since the pattern of specialization has been quite stable since 1965, the increased overall specialization suggests that the EU-members included in the analysis have successfully exploited their initial output specialization. Nevertheless, there have been some remarkable changes too.

In Germany, the specialization in basic metals, motor vehicles, chemicals and other market services has increased strongly. In France, other market services have come up, though with strong fluctuations. In Italy, the specialization in agricultural and food products has made room for specialization in textile and leather. Furthermore, it lost its position in oil products, but gained a position in trade and lodging. Especially during the 1960s, Italy went through a strong phase of industrialization, giving it a bigger similarity to the other member states and a more diversified output structure. The Netherlands lost some specialization in electrical goods and transport, but gained a position in oil and gas and chemical products, and strengthened its position as an agricultural economy. Belgium remained strongly metal oriented, but after 1975 it also became specialised in chemical products and transport services. In the United Kingdom (after 1975), the specialization in oil and gas increased strongly, while the specialization in transport and public services decreased. In Denmark (after 1975), a specialization in transport has come up.[4]

2.3 Relations with Domestic Demand and Export Specialization

The above analysis indicates that, despite the similarity in endowments between the EU-countries, there is a distinct pattern of output specialization that is intensifying. However, this pattern may not only be related to the specialization of exports due to economic integration, but may also be related to traditional differences in the structure of domestic demand. To investigate this, *Table 2* shows the correlations between the levels and the changes in the levels of sectoral specialization ratios by EU-countries.

Table 2: Pearson correlations between different types of specialization, levels (lower left) and changes (upper left) 1965-1985

Correlation coefficients	Changes in SX	Changes in IN	Changes in EX	Changes in CD	Changes in PD
SX = production specialization		.121	-.092	.338	.529*
IN = internal EU-exports spec.	.873**		.475*	.263	-.186
EX = external EU-exports spec.	.804**	.756**		-.019	-.095
CD = consumptive demand spec.	.771**	.817**	.563**		-.231
PD = productive demand spec.	.667**	.448*	.638**	.482**	

The lower left shows the correlations between the *levels* of specialization (n=30=6 years x 5 countries, where 1975 is measured both inclusive and exclusive VAT). The upper right shows the correlations between the *changes* in specialization (n=20=4 periods x 5 countries). Two stars (**) indicate a two-tailed significance of 1 %, and one star (*) indicates a two-tailed significance of 5 %.

---

[4] These and other detailed results are not shown in any of the paper's tables but are available upon request, or they can be calculated from the tables themselves which are available through the Steinmetz Archive in Amsterdam.

Almost all correlations between the *levels* of specialisation, in the lower left part of *Table 2*, are significant at the 1 %-level. This means that both internal and external EU export specialisation, and both productive and consumptive demand specialization, are high/low for countries and periods for which the extent of output specialisation is high/low too. The first column further shows that the correlation between the extent of output specialization and that of internal EU-exports is slightly larger (0.873) than the correlation with consumptive demand specialization (0.771). The mutual correlations between these potential explanatory variables, however, are too large to draw any definite conclusions as regard their relative importance. The only further corroborative hint about the relative importance follows from the fact that for most years and for most countries the extent of export specialization is larger than that of output specialization, which on its turn is mostly larger than that domestic demand.

More important, however, is the question whether *changes* in the extent of the different types of demand specialization are correlated with changes in the extent of output specialization. The top row of *Table 2* answers this question. Only changes in productive demand specialization show a significant correlation with the changes in total output specialization. The direction of causality, however, is two ways. Due to input-output relations between sectors, output specialization directly and indirectly determines the sectoral specialization in intermediate and investment goods. On the other hand, however, a specialization in intermediate and capital goods forms an important part of the specialization in total output.

Furthermore, the upper right part of *Table 2* shows that both types of export specialization move in the same direction despite the fact that rather different markets and factor endowments are involved. Finally, contrary to the evidence on the correlation between levels of specialization, note that the changes in consumptive demand specialization are at least weakly correlated with changes in output specialization (0.338), whereas changes in export specialization are not (0.121 and minus 0.092). Hence, the relative importance of export specialization and consumptive demand specialization for output specialization will not differ too much.

The correlation between the aggregate ratios, however, does not necessarily imply that the *pattern* of specialization is similar, too. *Table 3* exemplifies this for output and domestic demand. The middle columns, "output & demand", sum all sectors that have demand and output shares that deviate in the same direction from the EU-average with at least 0.75 percentage points. These well filled middle columns show that not only the levels but also the *patterns* of output and domestic demand specialization are correlated.

The left columns of either side show sectors for which output specialization is clearly stronger than domestic demand specialization, thus indicating the commodities for which there is a strong scope for inter-industry *export* specialization. The right columns on either side show sectors with clearly larger demand specialization than output specialization, thus indicating the commodities for which there is a clear scope for inter-industry *import* specialization.

Table 3: The relation between output and demand specialization patterns 1985

	Specialization in:			Relative absence of:		
	Only output	Output & demand	Only demand	Only demand	Output & demand	Only output
Germany	Chem, Aima, Moto	Meta, Mser			Agri, Buil, Petr, Retr	
France		Agri, Mser				Aima
Italy	Leat	Text, Lodg, Retr			Mser, Pser	Util, Moto
The Netherlands	Chem	Agri, Ofoo, Petr, Pser	Util	Trsp	Meta, Moto, Text, Lodg	Metp, Aima, Mser
Belgium	Chem, Trsp	Meta, Ofoo, Moto	Agri, Petr, Retr	Trsp	Metp, Elgo, Pser	Aima
United Kingdom	Petr	Beve, Pser	Trsp		Agri, Chem, Meta, Mser	
Denmark	Meat, Milk, Retr	Agri, Trsp, Buil, Pser	Aima, Mser		Petr, Elgo, Meta, Text, Chem, Lodg	Moto

The left columns characterise Germany as a potential exporter of high technology goods, Italy as a exporter of shoes, the Benelux countries as exporters of transport services, the United Kingdom as a potential oil exporting country and Denmark as an agricultural country. Note the extreme case of Belgium, with an over-represented production and a highly absent domestic demand for transport services. The central location of the spatially small Benelux countries at the crossroads of the EU obviously represents a geographical kind of endowment. The relatively empty character of right columns in the case of the larger countries reflects their relative self-sufficiency, as opposed to the import dependence of the smaller countries. That import dependence especially concerns machinery, cars and some services.

2.4 Export Specialization in More Detail

Next, in view of its prominence in trade and integration theory, we will pay somewhat more attention to the development of export specialization (*Figures 2* and *3*). Since 1965, the extent of *internal* EU export specialization has increased moderately (see *Figure 2*). Before 1975, it decreased in Germany and Belgium, and after 1975 it only decreased in Denmark. Just as for output, Denmark and the Netherlands are the most specialised EU-countries, followed by the others, with France being the most diversified. Note that *Figure 2* does not yet suggest a maturing of the export specialization growth, since the pace is not significantly slower after 1975 than before 1975. These outcomes are generally confirmed when the analysis is made with inter-country input-output tables in constant prices (Hoen 1999).

Figure 2: The development of specialization ratios for *internal* EU-exports 1965-1985

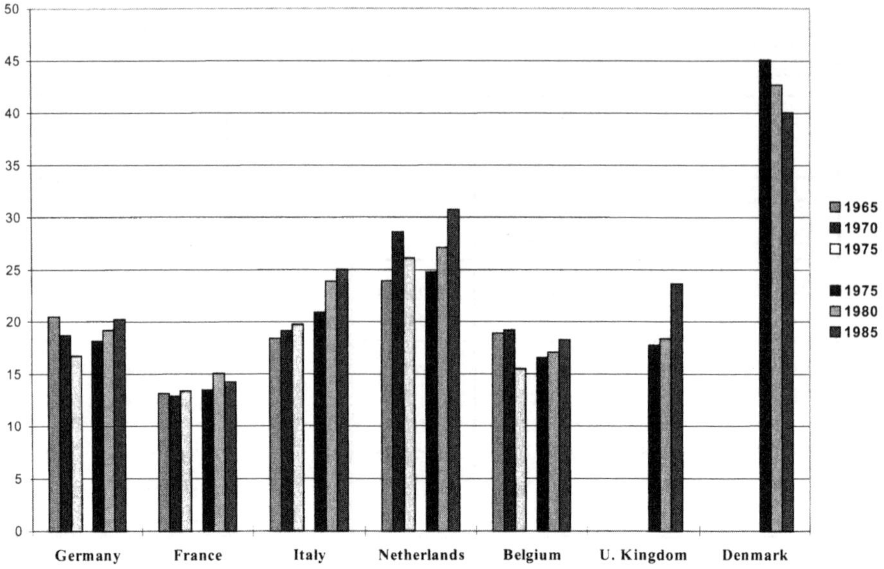

The outcomes for *external* EU export specialization in *Figure 3* are more or less equal to those of *Figure 2*, as was already shown in the correlation analysis. Nevertheless, there are some differences. For Italy, the United Kingdom and Denmark, the internal EU-exports are more specialised. For the Benelux countries, the external EU-exports are more specialised. The development over time is more remarkable and is better shown in *Table 4*, which expresses the external specialization ratio as a percentage of the internal one.

Before 1975, the internal EU specialization increased somewhat more than the external EU specialization. This holds for all five EU-countries included. It may reflect the effects of the early customs union, generating a stronger internal than external increase in trade and specialization because of the removal of (internal) trade barriers. After 1975, the trend reversed and external export specialization increased more than internal export specialization. This may reflect an increasing openness of the EU with respect to the rest of the world, generally as part of the GATT agreements.

Figure 3: The development of specialization ratios for *external* EU-exports 1965-1985

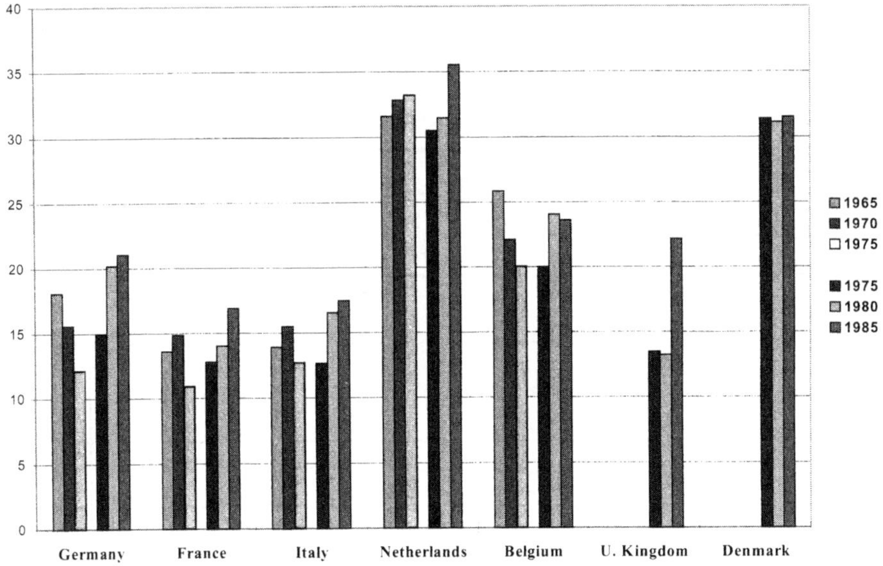

Table 4: External EU export specialization as a percentage of internal EU export specialization 1965-1985

	Ratio gross of VAT			Ratio net of VAT		
	1965	1970	1975	1975	1980	1985
Germany	88	83	72	82	105	104
France	103	115	81	94	93	119
Italy	76	81	64	60	69	69
The Netherlands	132	115	127	123	116	116
Belgium	137	115	130	120	141	128
United Kingdom				76	72	93
Denmark				69	73	79
Unweighted average	102	99	87	84	89	97

As internal and external export specialization – surpringly in view of the endowment differences involved – both have about the same levels and also move globally in the same (upward) direction, we will only show the sectoral *pattern* of specialization for *total* exports (see *Table 5*). For all EU-countries, the specialization of total exports is stronger than the specialization of output, as can be read from the *Figures 1, 2* and *3* and from the ranges given in the comparable *Tables 1* and *5*. Moreover, *Table 5* confirms and differentiates the potential export specialization indicated in *Table 3*.

Table 5: Sectoral pattern of total export specialization 1985

Percentage-points: deviation of EU-average	Pattern of specialization				Pattern of relative absence			
	> +4.0	+4.0/ +3.0	+3.0/ +2.0	+2.0/ +1.5	-1.5/ -2.0	-2.0/ -3.0	-3.0/ -4.0	< -4.0
Germany	Aima, Moto		Elgo		Agri, Retr	Mser		Petr
France		Agri, Mser	Otra	Meta		Aima, Trsp, Retr		Petr
Italy	Text, Leat	Aima			Meta		Petr, Moto	Chem
The Netherlands	Chem, Petr	Ofoo	Agri, Meat, Retr	Milk, Trsp	Otra	Meta, Opma, Text, Mser		Aima, Moto
Belgium	Meta		Text	Chem		Opma, Otra	Elgo	Aima
United Kingdom	Petr		Retr, Mser		Ofoo, Text	Meta, Aima		Moto
Denmark	Meat, Trsp	Ofoo, Retr	Agri, Milk, Wood				Petr, Elgo	Chem, Meta, Moto, Mser

See Appendix for the sector abbreviations.

In most EU-countries, the export specialization pattern has remained relatively stable since 1965. In Italy and the United Kingdom, however, the pattern completely changed. In Italy, the moderate 1965-specialization in agricultural products, oil and gas, transport and other market services ceased, whereas the moderate specialization in textile, leather and machinery strongly increased. The United Kingdom became strongly specialised in the export of its North Sea oil. Furthermore, its 1975-specialization in transport and other market services ceased, whereas a specialization in some other services arose. The Netherlands, finally, though having a quite stable pattern of export specialization, strongly increased its specialization in oil and gas. Furthermore, its 1965-specialization in electrical goods ceased after 1970, and its specialization in chemical products only arose after 1970.

The export specialization pattern is roughly the same for both internal and external EU-exports. There are, however, some differences (not shown in the Tables). These are especially found for the Dutch and British oil and gas products, which are strongly oriented towards the internal market. The same holds for Italian textile and leather and for Danish agricultural and meat products, although to a smaller extent. On the other hand, some specialization is especially oriented towards the external EU market. This is the case for French other transport equipment, Dutch milk, chemicals and transport services and Danish transport services. The Belgian car industry is an interesting case with a strong internal EU export specialization and an almost absence of external EU exports. This reflects its character of an assembly industry, serving the EU-market only. The opposite holds for the Dutch electrical goods industry, which has a relative absence in internal EU-exports and a strong external EU export specialization.

The interesting next question is whether the pattern of export specialization in *Table 5* corresponds to the pattern of output specialization in *Table 1*. This is indicated by the well-filled middle columns on either side of *Table 6*, which has the same structure as *Table 3*.

Table 6: The relation between output and export specialization patterns 1985

	Specialization in:			Relative absence of:		
	Only output	Output & exports	Only exports	Only exports	Output & exports	Only output
Germany	Chem, Meta, Mser	Aima, Moto	Elgo	Mser	Agri, Petr, Retr	Buil
France		Agri, Mser	Meta, Otra	Petr, Retr, Trsp	Aima	
Italy	Lodg	Text, Leat	Aima	Petr, Meta, Chem	Moto	Util, Mser, Pser
The Netherlands	Pser	Agri, Ofoo, Petr, Chem	Meat, Milk, Retr, Trsp	Opma, Otra	Aima, Meta, Moto, Text, Mser	Metp, Lodg
Belgium	Moto, Ofoo, Trsp	Meta, Chem	Text	Opma, Otra	Aima, Elgo	Metp, Pser
United Kingdom	Beve, Pser	Petr	Retr, Mser	Aima, Moto, Ofoo, Text	Meta	Agri, Chem, Mser
Denmark	Buil, Pser	Agri, Milk, Meat, Trsp, Retr	Ofoo, Wood	Mser	Petr, Elgo, Meta, Chem, Moto	Lodg, Text

There are, however, a large number of exceptions, indicating that the correspondence is far from perfect. The left columns on either side show the commodities in which output is specialised and exports are not. In about one third of the cases, this concerns services, indicating that output specialization will also be explained by specialization of consumptive demand, as discussed in Sub-Section 3.2. The right columns on either side show export specializations that have not led to a comparable output specialization. The non-emptiness of these two columns, especially, seems to weaken the case for a relationship between output and export specialization. In more than half of these cases, however, it concerns commodities in which there is still a weak output specialization, just falling below the 0.75 percentage point criterion to enter *Table 1* and thus *Table 5*.

Up to now, the concern has been with specialization. As argued in Section 2, however, the analysis of specialization is biased towards large sectors. Therefore, the analysis of concentration is needed to get a more complete view.

3. Analysis of Spatial Concentration per EU-Sector

3.1 Hypotheses and Methodology

There is a clear analogy and complementarity between the analyses of sectoral specialization and spatial concentration. Specialization adopts the perspective of countries, whereas concentration adopts the perspective of sectors. The spatial *concentration ratio* sums the differences between the EU-country shares in the production of commodity *i* and EU-country shares in the production of all commodities taken together:

$$(2)\qquad CX_i = 0.5 \cdot \sum_r \left| \frac{x_i^r}{x_i^e} - \frac{x^r}{x^e} \right| \cdot 100 \qquad i = 1, \ldots I.$$

Evidently, CX_i has the same features as SX_r. The range of values is also [0,100). The closer to 100, the more a sector is (spatially) *concentrated*. The closer to 0, the more (spatially) *dispersed* a sector is. Again, the individual elements identify the spatial pattern, and the total identifies the extent of spatial concentration.

The reason for analysing concentration lies in the complementarity to the analysis of specialization. The analysis of specialization tends to emphasise not only large sectors, but also small countries, since smaller countries are usually more specialized because of the lack of resources to produce a broad range of commodities on an efficient scale. Besides, diversification of large countries is also a statistical consequence of these countries' larger weight in the EU-average.

The analysis of spatial concentration does the opposite. It tends to emphasise smaller sectors and larger countries. For, when a country is large, a relatively small deviation for a given sector may easily amount to a difference of a few percentage-points and thus have a large weight in the concentration ratio. And, a small sector is more likely to be spatially concentrated, if only because it does not weight so heavily in the EU-average.

3.2 Analysis of the Empirical Results on Spatial Concentration

The empirical results on spatial concentration are given in the Appendix. The middle column gives the *extent* of the spatial concentration of output in 1985. The production of coal is spatially most concentrated, followed by leather, beverages, tobacco, etc., until the services sectors, whose production is quite evenly spread over the member states.[5] Coal, beverages and tobacco are small sectors, each producing about half a percent of the 1985 EU-output. Hence, their deviations from the EU-average output share cannot to be large in absolute terms. So, these sectors do not appear in the pattern of specialization in *Table 1*. At the other end, public services, trade and transport are large sectors, producing 16 %, 10 % and 4 % of the total 1985 EU-output, respectively. Relatively small deviations for these sectors may thus weigh strongly in the extent and pattern of specialization.

The four left columns of the Appendix show the 1965-1985 *development* in the spatial concentration ratio (*Equation 2*) per sector.[6] Since 1965, the production of most commodities has become more spatially concentrated, though not continuously. Only the concentration of coal, leather and textile has increased in all four periods. The concentration of the other sectors has decreased in at least one of the periods. Before 1975, concentration has grown relatively strongly, followed by declines in many sectors between 1975 and 1980. After 1980, the increase of extent of spatial concentration caught-up again.

The *pattern* of output, demand and export concentration is given in the last three columns of the Appendix. It shows which of the elements of the concentration ratio (*Equation 2*) are relatively large. When the deviation is more than 10 percentage points, the country is given in uppercase. When it is between 5 and 10 percentage points, the country is given in lower case. As an example, the production of coal is strongly concentrated in both Germany and the United Kingdom, whereas the demand for and export of coal is strongly concentrated in Germany only. Besides the production of coal, the production of basic metals, motor vehicles and machines is concentrated in Germany, too. Textiles, leather and wood are concentrated in Italy. Oil, beverages, tobacco and other manufacturing are concentrated in the United Kingdom.

---

[5] The high outcomes for beverages and tobacco may also be related to inter-country differences in indirect taxation rather than to spatial concentration proper.

[6] The first two columns (1965 and 1970) are normalised with respect to the 1975 inter-country input-output table measured *gross* of VAT and exclusive of the UK and Denmark. The second two columns (1980 and 1985) are normalised with respect to the table *net* of VAT and inclusive of the UK and Denmark.

The pattern of output concentration has remained roughly the same since 1965. In only eight sectors there have been substantial changes. Of these, textile and leather have become concentrated in Italy since 1970. The concentration of beverages and tobacco changed from Germany and Italy to the United Kingdom. The concentration of oil and gas changed from Italy to the Netherlands and, more recently, to the United Kingdom. The concentration of wood changed from Germany to Italy. The concentration of lodging changed from France to Italy. The concentration of metal products ceased. Until 1975, it was concentrated in Germany.

As argued before, the analysis of concentration emphasises large countries, just as the analysis of specialization emphasises large sectors. In virtually all cases, production is concentrated in the four large countries, the only exception being the concentration of oil and gas in the Netherlands. Note, that the few entries for France again underline the diversified character of its economy. Just like with specialization, domestic demand is less, and exports are more concentrated than production, as appears from the number of entries in the last three columns of the Appendix (23, 17 and 44).

The *domestic demand* for coal and basic metals is concentrated in Germany. The demand for textile and leather is concentrated in Italy. The demand for beverages, tobacco, other transport equipment and transport services is concentrated in the UK. This German and Italian concentration seems to be due to the input demand for the production in which both countries are specialised. The United Kingdom demand concentration of transport services and transport equipment reflects the country's geographic location. Its concentration of beverages and tobacco may be caused by deviations in the tax system, but may also result from some lack of comparability of the British input-output tables to the others.

The "concentration" of *exports*, given in the last column, resembles the pattern of export specialization surprisingly well. As expected, it also resembles the output concentration pattern. Substantial differences are only found for basic metals and lodging. As regards the former, the strong export position of Belgium is confirmed. As regards the latter, the exports are concentrated in the United Kingdom, whereas the production is concentrated in Italy. Just as for specialization, the base material shows that the pattern of internal EU export concentration does not deviate much from the pattern of external export concentration. The British office machines are orientated towards the internal market. The French transport equipment, the British tobacco and the Danish milk are oriented towards the external market.

4. Conclusion

This paper has given a summary analysis of sectoral specialization and spatial concentration in the EU between 1965 and 1985. It thus covers an element in the analysis of European integration that has hardly been studied before. Both for specialization and for concentration its extent, its pattern and its development over time are analysed.

As regards specialization, the *extent* is generally stronger in the smaller member states. Belgium seems to be an exception, because it is relatively diversified. Of the large member states, France is the most diversified. The *pattern* of specialization reveals the commodities in which the countries are specialised. It shows that there is an evident division of labour among the member states. The *development* of specialization shows that there has been a moderate increase since the establishment of the EU. This confirms the traditional trade theory's proposition that European economic integration would lead to specialization and concentration; though a *causal relationship* could not be established. Instead, there appears to be a strong mutual correlation between the levels of specialization of output, domestic consumptive and productive demand, and internal as well as external EU-exports.

The specialization ratio is strongly focused on large sectors and small countries. The complementary analysis of spatial concentration does the opposite. It shows that small sectors, such as coal mining, leather, beverages and tobacco, are strongly concentrated in a few mostly large countries. Just as for specialization, the extent of concentration has also grown since 1965, and just as for specialization spatial concentration is stronger for exports than for production, which on its turn is stronger than that of domestic demand.

All findings taken together, especially, do not substantiate modern trade theory with its emphasis on the growing importance of intra-industry trade. Furthermore, the findings emphasise that, besides EU and non-EU exports, differences in consumptive demand preferences also have a role in explaining differences in specialization and concentration of total output. Possibly, they even play a role in explaining differences in export specialization and concentration.

References

Balassa B (1961) The Theory of Economic Integration. George Allen & Unwin, London

Bröcker J (1995) Chamberlinian Spatial Computable General Equilibrium Modelling: A Theoretical Framework. Economic Systems Research 7: 137-149

Dixit AK, Norman VD (1980) Theory of International Trade. Cambridge University Press, Cambridge (Massachusetts)

Hoen AR (1999) An Input-Output Analysis of European Integration. Labyrint Publication, Cappelle a/d IJssel

Isard W (1956) Location and Space-Economy. MIT Press, Cambridge (Massachusetts)

Isard W (1960) Methods of Regional Analysis. John Wiley and Sons & MIT Press, New York & Cambridge (Massachusetts)

Krugman PR (1991) Geography and Trade. Leuven University Press, Leuven

Oosterhaven J (1995) Changing Specialization and Interdependency of EC-Economies 1959-1975. Australazian Journal of Regional Studies 1: 51-64

Peschel K (1985) Spatial Structures in International Trade: An Analysis of Long Term Developments. Papers of the Regional Science Association 58: 97-111

Peschel K (1999) The Development of Integration Areas in Europe. Paper presented at the 39th European Congress of the RSAI, University College, Dublin

Porter ME (1990) The Competitive Advantage of Nations. Free Press, New York

Van der Linden JA (1998) Interdependence and Specialization in the European Union. Labyrint Publication, Cappelle a/d IJssel

Van der Linden JA, Oosterhaven J (1995) European Community Intercountry Input-Output Relations: Construction Method and Main Results for 1965-1985. Economic Systems Research 7: 249-269

Appendix: Analysis of spatial concentration

Sector	Extent of spatial concentration (1975=100)				Concen-tration ratio	Pattern of spatial concentration in 1985		
	1965	1970	1980	1985	1985	Production	Domestic demand	Total exports
Coal	74	87	115	123	35.67	DE, UK	DE, uk	DE
Leat	20	55	126	156	35.66	IT	IT	IT
Beve	91	131	103	177	23.55	UK	UK	FR, UK
Toba	152	177	150	190	21.08	UK	UK	UK, NL
Moto	121	92	138	181	19.37	DE		DE
Oman	26	11	98	135	19.11	UK	UK	UK, IT
Otra	49	88	79	92	18.97	fr, uk	UK	FR, uk
Petr	79	93	82	135	18.39	UK, nl		UK, NL
Text	39	58	158	181	18.31	IT	IT	IT
Agri	127	114	109	116	17.18	fr		FR, NL
Meta	68	107	78	92	16.22	DE	DE	BE
Aima	91	118	107	125	13.74	DE		DE, it
Opma	87	79	103	85	13.08	DE	de	de
Wood	81	125	124	100	11.62	IT	it	IT, dk
Lodg	60	65	86	90	11.26	it	It	UK
Meat	33	92	66	66	10.68		fr	NL, DK
Util	90	85	78	181	9.79			FR, UK
Milk	72	80	75	58	9.13			NL, DK, fr
Comm	78	41	87	112	8.80	uk	uk	UK
Chem	109	106	125	147	8.69	de		
Metp	127	72	76	82	8.67			de
Mine	84	81	110	106	8.14	it	it	IT
Elgo	97	97	87	78	7.95	de		de
Rubb	87	93	75	86	7.95	de		de
Mser	155	129	84	77	6.89			FR, UK
Ofoo	125	116	77	92	6.34			NL
Pape	99	129	148	133	6.14			de
Retr	34	32	86	98	5.29		it	uk
Trsp	111	122	72	58	5.25		uk	
Buil	55	29	52	102	4.76			DE, BE, nl
Pser	46	112	60	49	4.30			UK

Appendix: Sector abbreviation

Abbrev.	Sector	Abbrev.	Sector
Coal	Coal & lignite	Util	Public utilities
Leat	Leather	Milk	Milk & dairy prod.
Beve	Beverages	Comm	Communication
Toba	Tobacco	Chem	Chemical products
Moto	Motor vehicles	Metp	Metal products
Oman	Other manufacturing	Mine	Non-metallic miner.
Otra	Other transport eq.	Elgo	Electrical goods
Petr	Oil & gas exploit.	Rubb	Rubber & plastics
Text	Textiles & clothing	Mser	Other market serv.
Agri	Agriculture	Ofoo	Other food process.
Meta	Ores & metals	Pape	Paper & printing
Aima	Agric. & ind. mach.	Retr	Trade & repair
Opma	Office & precis. m.	Trsp	Transport services
Wood	Wood & furniture	Buil	Building & constr.
Lodg	Lodging & catering	Pser	Public services
Meat	Meat processing		

Vertical Specialization and Interregional Trade: Turbulence Analogy and Feedback Loops Analysis of the Midwest Economy

Michael Sonis

Regional Economics Applications Laboratory

University of Illinois, USA, and Bar Ilan University, Israel

Geoffrey J. D. Hewings

Regional Economics Applications Laboratory

University of Illinois, USA

Yasuhide Okuyama

Department of Planning

State University of New York at Buffalo, USA

1. Introduction

The renewed interest in international trade has drawn attention to the phenomenon of vertical specialization, the use of imported inputs for producing goods that are exported (Bruelhart, Hine 1999). The term vertical specialization was introduced by Balassa (1967); in a recent paper, Hummels et al. (1998) introduced and discussed the following definition of vertical specialization: "(1) a good must be produced in multiple sequential stages, (2) two or more countries must specialize in producing some, but not all, stages, and (3) at least one stage must cross an international border more then once. Thus, countries link sequentially to produce a final good."

This definition speaks to the role of sequential production and bears an important relationship with the notion of an hierarchy of feedback loops of inter-industry flows elaborated in a series of papers by Sonis et al. (1993, 1995a,b). The further elaboration and visualization of this approach, which is a purpose of this paper, may be shown to be connected with an analogy between the behavior of flows of goods and hydrodynamic turbulence (Richardson, 1922). A flow of energy from large to small scales is one of the main characteristics of fully developed homogeneous isotropic turbulence in three-dimensional space. Energy is pumping into the system at large scales, transferred to smaller scales through a hierarchy of eddies of decreasing sizes, and dissipates at the smallest scale (This cascade of kinetic energy generates the scaling behaviour of eddies). The turbulence analogy is provided through the way in which large, aggregate interregional feedback loops of intermediate input flows are decomposed into feedback loops between economic activities (such as resources, manufacturing and services) and then further decomposed into the loops of flows on the scale of individual industries. Moreover, the scaling of eddies, analogous to the hierarchy of economic subsystems, is presented with the help of so called "Matrioshka" principle (Sonis, Hewings 1990). Thus, the ideas of hierarchical feedback loop analysis can be used for structural economic analysis.

The method of feedback loop analysis used in this paper excluded more complex numerical manipulations with flows and allows the consideration of the non-homogeneous flows of different streams (goods) and the use of turbulence analogy. The need of the feedback loops analysis is justified by the economic phenomenon of vertical specialization of international trade.

Table 1: Vertical trade – two interpretations

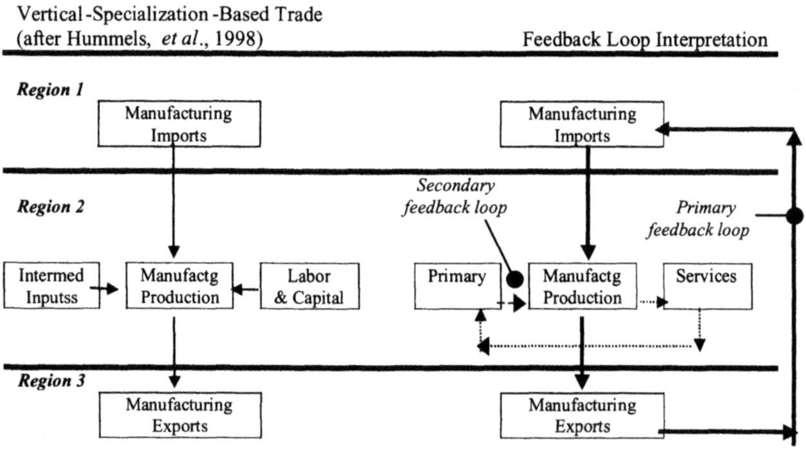

In what way is this approach different from that adopted by Hummels et al. (1998)? *Table 1* provides a comparative perspective for the two approaches; essentially, the non-feedback loop approach may be considered to be an open loop in the sense that flows enter the system as exports from one region to a second, circulate and then exit as exports to a third region. However, there is no connection between the first and third region. Feedback loop analysis, on the other hand, explores the degree to which the pattern of flows just described is completed with the addition of a final flow from the third region back to the first. It is not clear whether the vertical specialization analyses make a distinction between intermediate and final goods; some of the chains of interaction will clearly involve only intermediate flows, but at the final stage, the flows will, in all probability, be to final demand (even in another region/country). In feedback loop analysis, the analysis is confined to intermediate flows only. At some point, it would be appropriate to extend the analysis to total flows between regions.

2. Interregional Trade: Expectations and Structure

The new trade theory associated with Krugman (1991,1993) and others has turned attention to factors other than endowments as a source of explanation for trade. To be sure, initial factor endowments will still allow for specialization to occur with cost advantages leading to a cumulative process of product differentiation. However, at the interregional level, this process could occur simultaneously in two or more regions, leading to the exploitation of increasing returns and thus to increasing trade between regions. However, this trade will be more heavily concentrated in intraindustry trade for many of the reasons provided by Krugman. It so happens these are reasons that find their fullest expression in the state economies of the Midwest of the US. For example, if the economies in question are large, of similar size and with few differences in factor endowments, then something other than comparative advantage has to be proposed to explain trade. Per capita income is high – thus providing opportunities for product differentiation to serve the demand for higher quality products and a greater variety of products. Scale economies exist and capital/labor ratios are high and similar (no comparative advantage here); however, it is the lower transportation costs, the region-wide agglomeration effects, the effectiveness and ease of information flows that all combine to facilitate intraindustry specialization. At the level of trade between regions that is focused on intermediate goods and services, it is unlikely that much of the apparent cross-hauling can be explained by product differentiation. The development of niche products and markets probably accounts for the vast majority of this intra-industry trade.

Complementary evidence for this process may be found in Hewings et al. (1998). In the this analysis, it was observed that establishments at the regional level produced a smaller array of secondary products than similar establishments drawn from throughout the nation. Further, it was noted that the average purchases of locally-sourced inputs declined over the period 1970–1990 in the Chicago region while production did not decline. Taken together, one might infer that the average establishment is focusing production on a narrow range of products and purchasing more of the inputs needed for this production from outside the region. The greater variety of products sought by consumers is being realized in production processes that are extended over many establishments that may be located in different regions; intermediate inputs formerly sourced locally are now imported and a smaller variety of products is being produced at any given establishment. Taken together, the demand for trade has increased.

The next issue addresses methods for analyzing the structure of this trade. Feedback loop analysis is employed since it lends itself readily to the identification of the spatial geographic structure of these flows. Furthermore, a spatial hierarchy of trade flows can be extracted from the flow data, providing additional insights into the nature and strengths of interregional connectivities. In addition, feedback loop analysis operates at a level that is more detailed than traditional macro analysis yet does not provide the potential myriad paths of interaction that can be extracted from structural path analysis (Defourny, Thorbecke 1984). It does, however, share the property that each path in a structural path is part of a global feedback loop that includes the transactions between all sectors.

In the next Section, a brief introduction to feedback loop analysis is provided; further details may be found in Sonis et al. (1993, 1995a,b).

3. The Multiregional Feedback Loop Approach

3.1 Closed Feedback Loops and Block-Permutation Matrices

It is assumed that there are *n* regions in which there exist *m* divisions of the economy, organized into activities and there is a subdivision of activities in the different sub-categories. The central point of the feedback loops decomposition analysis is the use of spatial/functional feedback loops represented by block-permutation matrices. By definition, a block-permutation matrix includes in each block-row and block-column only one non-zero block.

In the two-region case:

$$(1)\quad F = \begin{pmatrix} F_{11} & F_{12} \\ F_{21} & F_{22} \end{pmatrix}.$$

There are only two block-permutation sub-matrices:

$$(2)\quad F_1 = \begin{pmatrix} F_{11} & 0 \\ 0 & F_{22} \end{pmatrix},\quad F_2 = \begin{pmatrix} 0 & F_{12} \\ F_{21} & 0 \end{pmatrix},$$

and

$$(3)\quad F = F_1 + F_2 \,.$$

The matrix $\begin{pmatrix} F_{11} & 0 \\ 0 & F_{22} \end{pmatrix}$ represents the circulation of intermediate goods in the same geographical region, and the matrix $\begin{pmatrix} 0 & F_{12} \\ F_{21} & 0 \end{pmatrix}$ represents the bilateral connections between the two regions.

In the case of n regions, there exist $n!$ different block-permutation matrices, and it is possible to prove that the number of possible additive decompositions of the *Equation (3)* is equal to $(n\text{-}1)!(n\text{-}2)!...2!$. Thus, the problem focuses on the appropriate choices from this very large set of possible decompositions, namely, the decompositions with sound economic meaning. This problem can be solved through the adoption of a hierarchical stepwise approach; the procedure operates at successive levels in the system, but the approach at each stage is similar.

This top-down decomposition may be considered analogously to an exfoliation process in the removal of the layers of an onion, or, using the turbulence analogy to the construction of an hierarchy of feedback loops (whirlpools) ordered with the help of aggregated cumulative flows within the blocks belonging to the loop. The feedback loops on the inner hierarchical level of economic activities should be placed into the loops of the higher levels in the same manner as a set of Matrioshka dolls, in which successively smaller dolls of exactly the same shape and style are nested within the larger dolls. Hence, the Matrioshka approach examines the intra- and inter-regional transactions in terms of the hierarchical structure of feedback effects drawing upon the superposition principle conceptual framework (Sonis 1982). The superposition principle considers the economic system as a decentralized system that is comprised of a set of subsystems acting according to different and often conflicting and non-commensurable objectives. These objectives may be presented in the form of extreme tendencies or trends; the hierarchical viewpoint enables the analyst to extract the tendencies from the most to the least important. In this fashion, the procedure is not unlike that used in principal component analysis. A summary of the methodology for extracting the system of closed feedback loops can be found in Sonis et al. (1993, 1995a,b).

One natural method for dealing with such a large amount of complete feedback loops is of course the derivation of some hierarchical structure. Essentially, the hierarchical feedback loop approach attempts to extract complete feedback loops that successively account for the most "explanation" in each stage of the selection process. The procedure continues until all transaction flows have been included.

The hierarchy of all complete feedback loops is defined as the sequence of quasi-permutation sub-matrices chosen according to the rank-size of their flow intensities. This means that on the top of the hierarchy, one finds the complete feedback loop with the maximal flow intensity. The problem of the determination of the quasi-permutation sub-matrix with the maximal flow intensity is mathematically equivalent to the solution of the optimal personnel assignment of n persons (here rows) between n jobs (columns) in such a way that one person will have one job while profit is maximized (Dantzig 1963). Here, profit is defined by the size of the flows in matrix T. The procedure is summarized in Sonis et al. (1993, 1995a,b).

3.2 Matrioshka Principle for the Description of the Nested Hierarchy of Feedback Loops

It is necessary and possible to combine the interregional and interactivity interdependencies. To this aim, the aggregated table needs to be replaced by the detailed table, describing the interplay between the interactivity and international interdependencies. Further, it is important to stress that the flexible form of the spatio-economic feedback loop analysis employed in this analysis allows an easy extension to the spatio-sectoral level. In such an extension, the analysis will relate to activities per region. Thus, the hierarchy of the feedback loops will reflect the interactivity interdependencies intertwined spatially, enabling one to distinguish the spatial extent of multi-regional industrial complexes.

4. The Midwest Interregional Flows 1992

The methodology used to estimate the interstate trade flows is described more formally in Hewings et al. (1997). Essentially, several sets of data were used; first, for each of the five Midwest states, an input-output table was constructed primarily from the establishment-level data base at the US Bureau of the Census. From this calculation process, estimates were made of vectors of regional imports and exports at the 53-sector level of aggregation (approximately all two-digit SIC). An input-output table was also constructed for the Rest of the US by subtraction of the aggregated Midwest transactions from the US national table. International exports and imports were subtracted using state and MISER estimates. What remained were vectors of interstate inflows and outflows but without any specificity as to their geography. The Commodity Flow Statistics (CFS) were used for the resource and manufacturing sectors. Information was provided for flows for sector specific origins in one state to destination state (but without sector specificity); assumptions underlying the allocation to sector within destination state relied on the column coefficient model (Polenske 1970a,b), namely that the use of imports from another state was proportional to the inflow from that state in comparison to all inflows.

For the remaining sectors, a gravity model was employed with the distances adjusted, so that the resulting flows were consistent with the import/export vector for each state. Some further adjustments were made to handle inconsistencies and to ensure that the system of flows was balanced. Note that the flows that are the focus of this paper represent interindustry transactions and exclude flows to final demand sectors.

5. Hierarchical Feedback Loop Analysis of Midwest Interregional Trade Flows 1992

The analysis was conducted at three levels – at an aggregated level in which all sectors were collapsed into one; at the level of three sectors – primary, secondary and tertiary, and finally, at a six-sector level into which the previous three sectors were each divided into two.

5.1 Interregional Level of Feedback Loop Analysis

Table 2 shows the geographical division of the trade between the Midwest states in 1992. From this table, it is easy to calculate that the global intensity of trade in the Midwest in 1992 reached 3.9 trillion US Dollar, while the interregional trade was 894.9 million US Dollar, which is 22.2 % of all US trade. 85.5 % of Midwest interregional trade includes export and import with the Rest of US; the remaining 15 % that flows among the Midwest states amounts to 135 billion US Dollar. Without a detailed analysis of this table, it would be difficult to identify and interpret the dominant interregional and inter-activities linkages. This is accomplished in the following tables. On the most aggregated regional level of analysis, there is the decomposition of the Midwest trade flows into five feedback loops hierarchically ordered according to the intensity (sum of flows) of trade through this loop. The larger of the five includes 25.9 % of all interregional trade and has the structure:

Rest of US, Michigan, Ohio, Indiana, Wisconsin, Illinois.

This loop includes the largest export flow, from Illinois to the Rest of US, and the largest import flow, from the Rest of US to Michigan.

The second of these two feedback loops accounts for 23.3 % of all interregional trade and has this structure:

Rest of US, Illinois, Wisconsin, Indiana, Ohio, Michigan.

This feedback loop includes the largest inner Midwest trade flow, from Ohio to Michigan. It is important to note that the spatial structure of two largest loops is topologically identical; they differ only in the direction of flows. This means that the Midwest economy is well developed and bilaterally balanced: to each flow, there corresponds the equivalent counter-flow. These two feedback loops together account for 49.2 % of all Midwest interregional trade.

Further analysis reveals three more feedback loops with the bilateral spatial structure (see *Table 2*). Thus, five feedback loops taken together describe the turbulent picture of the interregional Midwest trade. It is important to note that the hierarchy of feedback loops can be defined by the intensity of bilateral connection with the Rest of US and, after that, by the intensity of bilateral connections between individual Midwest states. Note that, on interindustry account, each state has a positive trade balance with the Rest of the US, with Illinois' positive balance being the largest in absolute terms.

Table 2: Interregional feedback loops for Midwest trade flows (1992 million US-Dollar)

	Illinois	Indiana	Michigan	Ohio	Wisconsin	Rest of US
Illinois	154,926	5,042	7,262	3,550	8,828	111,398
Indiana	5,798	61,858	9,220	5,271	2,240	44,317
Michigan	6,190	5,910	104,122	11,158	4,520	90,265
Ohio	3,746	4,647	20,334	139,912	2,172	77,815
Wisconsin	13,688	2,768	9,492	3,819	30,951	90,257
Rest of US	76,202	34,994	83,228	60,998	69,836	2,581,622

First Interregional Loop: (Rest US,Michigan,Ohio,Indiana,Wisconsin,Illlinois) - 25.9 %
Second Interregional Loop: (Rest US, Illnois,Wisconsin, Indiana, Ohio, Michigan) - 23.3 %
Third Feedback Loop: (Rest of US, Wisconsin) (Ohio, Illinois) (Michigan, Indiana) - 20.9 %
Fourth Feedback Loop: (Rest of US,Ohio) (Michigan, Wisconsin) (Indiana, Illinois) - 18.7 %
Fifth Feedback Loop: (Rest of US, Indiana) (Michigan, Illinois) (Wisconsin, Ohio) - 11.3 %

Table 3: Three largest interregional interactivity feedback loops within first interregional loop

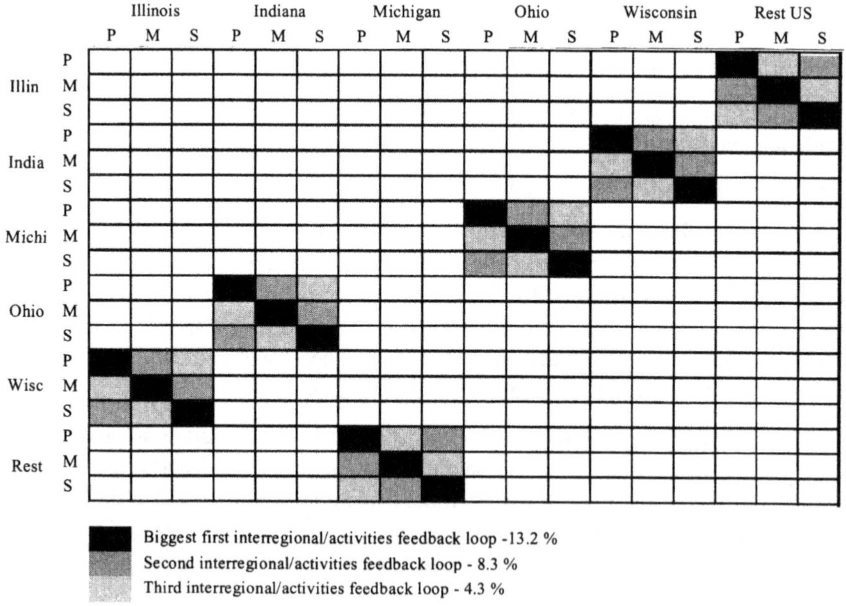

5.2 Inter-Activity Feedback Loop Analysis

The analysis of interregional inter-activity feedback loops can be done on the basis of more detailed trade flows data including three activities: primary (agriculture, forestry and fishing), manufacturing and services. Adopting the "Matrioshka" principle, the following structural decomposition of the first interregional loop into the inner interregional inter-activity loops can be revealed (see *Table 3*). *Table 4* presents the details of this decomposition.

Table 4: Activity tree structure for interregional/interactivity loops

Largest first interregional/activities feedback loop - 13.2 %

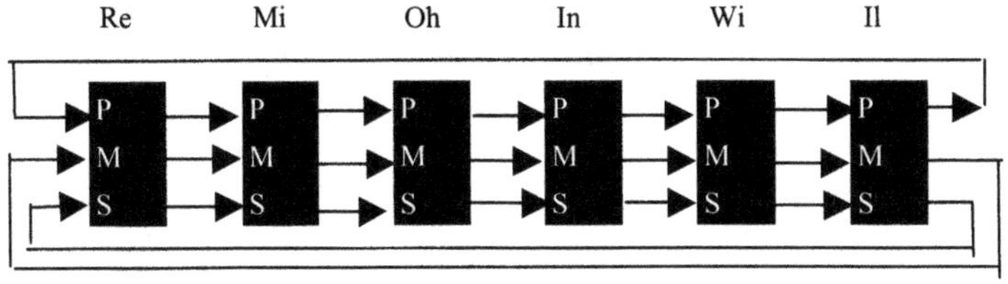

Second interregional/activities feedback loop - 8.3 %

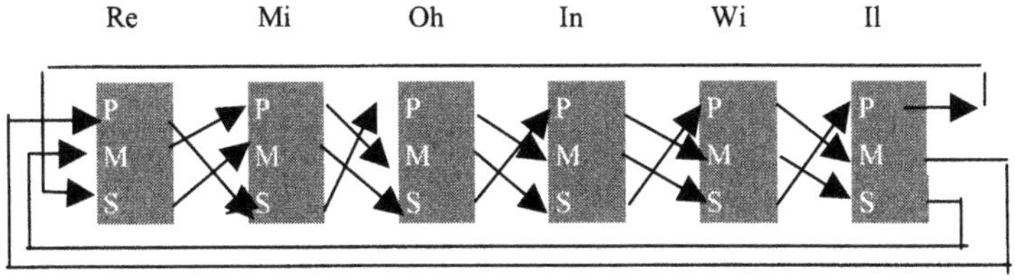

Third interregional/activities feedback loop - 4.3 %

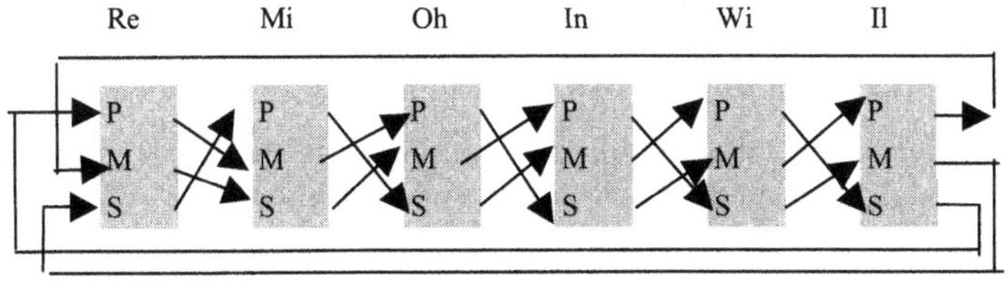

It is important to stress that each inter-regional loop can be decomposed into three inter-activity loops in which the most intensive loop has a block-diagonal form presenting the main tendency of the inter-regional trade to concentrate within the same activity (i.e., intra-industry trade dominates over interindustry trade). This tendency also underlines the "hollowing out" process occurring within the Midwest economy (Hewings et al. 1998) and further reinforces the propositions of the new trade theory that suggests that intraindustry trade will be a feature of economies that share similar characteristics. Clearly, greater levels of disaggregation would need to be adopted to examine the structure of flows and further disaggregation should be explored.

6. Discussion and Conclusions

The feedback loop analysis focuses on self-influence – the journey through the system of economies may be complex or very simple; it may involve all or part of the system and the intensity of interaction may vary significantly. The Midwest case study reveals a set of economies that are interacting very intensively; there are only relatively small differences between the magnitude of the flows accounted for by each of the first three feedback loops. With the possibility of a regular US interregional commodity flow survey, the evolution of this trading regime can be monitored to see whether the expectations of increased interregional at the expense of intraregional flows continues. Early evidence from the European Union (Sonis et al, 1993) found such a pattern to be evolving at the level of nation-states. Feedback loop analysis offers insights into this evolving complexity and geographical transformation, thus complementing and enhancing understanding of trade and spatial economic development.

References

Balassa B (1967) Trade Liberalization Among Industrial Countries. McGraw Hill, New York

Bruelhart M, Hine RC (eds) (1999) Intra-Industry Trade and Adjustment. St. Martins Press, New York

Dantzig GB (1963) Linear Programming and Extensions. Princeton University Press

Defourny J, Thorbecke E (1984) Structural Path Analysis and Multiplier Decomposition Within a Social Accounting Matrix Framework. Economic Journal 94: 111-136

Hewings GJD, Israilevich PR, Okuyama Y, Anderson DK, Schindler GR, Foulkes M, Sonis M (1997) Returns to Scope, Returns to Trade and the Structure of Spatial Interaction in the US Midwest. Discussion Paper 97-P-3. Regional Economics Applications Laboratory. University of Illinois, Urbana

Hewings GJD, Sonis M, Guo J, Israilevich PR, Schindler GR (1998) The Hollowing-Out Process in the Chicago Economy 1975-2011. Geographical Analysis 30: 217-223

Hummels D, Rappoport D, Yi KM (1998) Vertical Specialization and the Changing Nature of Word Trade. Economic Policy Review. Federal Reserve Bank of New York, June

Krugman P (1991) Is Bilateralism Bad? In: Helpman E, Razin A (eds) International Trade and Trade Policy. MIT Press, Cambridge (Massachusetts), pp 9-23

Krugman P (1993) Regionalism Versus Multilateralism: Analytical Notes. In: Melo JDE, Panagaria A (eds) New Directions in Regional Integration. Cambridge University Press, Cambridge (Massachusetts) pp 58-79

Polenske KR (1970a) An Empirical Test of Interregional Input-Output Models: Estimation of 1963 Japanese Production. American Economic Review 60: 76-82

Polenske KR (1970b) A Multiregional Input-Output Model for the United States. EDA Report No. 21, Harvard Economic Research Project, Cambridge (Massachusetts)

Richardson LF (1922) Weather Prediction by Numerical Process. Cambridge University Press, Cambridge (Massachusetts)

Sonis M (1982) The Decomposition Principle Versus Optimization in Regional Analysis: The Inverted Problem of Multiobjective Programming. In: Chiotis GP et al. (eds) The Regions and Erlargement of European Economic Community. Eptalofos, Athens

Sonis M, Hewings GJD (1990) The "Matrioshka Principle" in the Hierarchical Decomposition of Multiregional Social Accounting Systems. In: Anselin L, Madden M (eds) New Directions in Regional Analysis: Integrated and Multiregional Approaches. Pinter, London

Sonis M, Oosterhaven J and Hewings GJD (1993) Spatial Economic Structure and Structural Changes in the European Common Market: Feedback Loop Input-Output Analysis. Economic Systems Research 5: 173-184

Sonis M, Hewings GJD, Gazel R (1995a) The Structure of Multi-Regional Trade Flows: Hierarchy, Feedbacks and Spatial Linkages. The Annals of Regional Science 29: 409-430

Sonis M, Guilhoto JJM, Hewings GJD (1995b) The Asian Economy: Trade Structure Interpreted by Feedback Loop Analysis. Journal of Applied Input-Output Analysis 2: 24-40

Part IV

Transport Infrastructure and the Regions

The Quality of the Transport Infrastructure in European Regions and the Influence of the Trans-European Net

Hans-Friedrich Eckey, Klaus Horn

Universität Gesamthochschule Kassel

Fachbereich Wirtschaftswissenschaften

Kassel, Germany

1. Trans-European Network

1.1 Motives and Aims of a Trans-European Network

The coming together of European economies in a common domestic market is leading to the increasing mobility of people, goods and news, which at the moment are often constricted by an inadequate infrastructure.[1] The various transport infrastructures have been, up until now, mainly designed according to national requirements. "This strategy has led to a number of grave problems, in the view of the Community. These include the lack of suitable connections between the networks of individual countries, gaps and bottlenecks in, as well as obstacles to, the compatibility of these networks; all of which have an enormous influence on performance" (Erdmenger 1996, p 6). As well as the realisation of a unified domestic market for transport services, it must also be the task of the EU to arrange for an efficient international transport network. The Maastricht Treaty appropriately strengthens and lends a new impulse to the correct and consequential development of a Common Transport Policy. This also includes the appointment and promotion of a transport infrastructure, which is seen as essential for the continued growing together of Europe; this shall be known as the Trans-European network. [2]

---

[1] For more information vis á vis the development of international transport and the concomitant infrastructure constrictions, see European Conference of Ministers of Transport (ECMT 1995). International Freight Traffic alone increased by 84.4 % between 1984 and 1989; more than 5,000 km of roads are permanently congested.

[2] The legal Basis is Article 129b-d of the EU Treaty (Commission of the European Communities 1997).

With regard to the Trans-European network, the individual modes of transport will follow three aims: namely, improvement of the operational ability of the domestic market, increased competitiveness of industry (promotion of growth and employment), as well as improved connections between the peripheral and central regions of the EU (Article 129b-d of the EU Treaty). Whilst the first two aims are primarily growth orientated, the third serves to promote regional balance (Wink 1996).

The actions necessary for achieving these results are laid out in Article 129c of the EC Treaty. These are:

- the development of guidelines, in which the objectives, priorities and broad lines of measures should be taken into consideration and projects of common interest should be stated,
- steps of the Community to ensure the interoperability of the networks, in particular the harmonisation of technical norms,
- the possibility of financial support available for the realisation of intended projects.

1.2 The Trans-European Network and Priorities: An Overview

The European Commission has quickly utilised the extra authority that came with the Maastricht Treaty and has, in co-operation with the member states, drawn up guidelines for a Trans-European transport network, which have been accepted by the council of ministers. These include all modes of transport and routes with a European significance[3], including those passing through Switzerland. Furthermore, they also include statements regarding aims for their further development.

A general principle for the guidelines for all modes of transport is that the organisation and further development of the European transport network should be suitable for requirements and also be socially and environmentally acceptable. Moreover, the EU transport network should dovetail with those of neighbouring countries, allowing for the expansion to a transport network for the whole of Europe. In total, 58,000 km of roads, 70,000 km of railways and 12,000 km of navigable waterways need to be taken into consideration when thinking about international long-distance transport routes and the necessary interconnections.[4]

In their "White Paper on Growth, Competitiveness, Employment" (Commission of the European Communities 1993), the EU Commission provides an estimate of the costs involved in the building and expansion of the transport networks. For the Trans-European transport network this estimate is in the region of 400 billion Eu-

---

[3] The routes stipulated have no immediate binding effects on the individual states and the states are not obliged to put them into practice.

[4] A cartographic representation of this Trans-European network can be found, for example, in Erdmenger (1996).

ro. Due to financial shortages and the division of authority, the EU is not in a position to build or expand these routes itself, but simply try, with the help of "golden reins" and some appeals, to influence the actions of the individual countries. For the period between 1995 and 1999, there were relatively modest financial resources available. They amounted to 1.8 billion Euro for the Trans-European network, mainly to support the financial efforts of member states. Chief expenditures included: feasibility studies, loan guarantees and interest allowances. The Cohesion Fund and the Structural Funds provide further sources of finance together amounting to some 30 billion Euro annually, only a part of which, however, may be spent on the transport infrastructure.

Table 1: 14 top-ranking transport projects

Projects	Estimated Total Investment Costs (Billion Euro)
1. High-Speed Train / Combined Transport North–South (Berlin–Leipzig–Erfurt–Nuremberg–Munich–Verona)	15.1
2. High-Speed Train PBCAL (Paris–Brussels–Cologne–Amsterdam –London)	17.2
3. High-Speed Train South (Madrid–Barcelona–Perpignan–Montpellier; Madrid–Valladolid–Vitoria)	14.1
4. High-Speed Train Eastern France–Southern Germany (Paris–Metz–Strasbourg–Karlsruhe, with connections to Metz–Saarbrücken–Mannheim and Metz–Luxembourg)	4.8
5. Conventional Rail / Combined Transport Betuwe Line (Rotterdam–Rhine/Ruhr)	4.1
6. High-Speed Train / Combined Transport France–Italy (Lyon–Turin–Milan–Venice–Triest)	18.3
7. Greek Motorway PATHE and Via Egnatia (North-South-Axis PATHE Patras–Greek/Bulgarian Border; East-West-Axis Via Egnatia Igoumenitsa–Thessaloniki–Kipi–Greek/Turkish Border)	9.2
8. Multimodal Link Portugal–Spain–Central Europe (Lisbon–Formoso–Salamanco–Valladolid)	6.2
9. Conventional Rail Link (Cork–Dublin–Belfast–Larne–Stranraer)	0.4
10. Malpensa Airport (Northern Italy)	1.0
11. Fixed Rail/Road Link between Denmark and Sweden (Øresund Fixed Link)	4.2
12. Nordic Triangle (four sections for rail and road Oslo–Copenhagen, Oslo–Stockholm, Copenhagen–Stockholm, Turku–Helsinki–Russian Border)	10.0
13. Road Link Ireland–United Kingdom–Benelux	3.6
14. West Coast Main Line United Kingdom (High Speed Train / Combined Transport Nort)	3.0

Source: Commission of the European Communities (2000).

For reasons of practicability, the EU has drawn up a list of priorities with the intention of concentrating on the most important projects (see *Table 1*). With this in mind, the European Council appointed a committee under the chairmanship of the then Vice President of the European Commission, Christophersen. The task of the committee was to draw up a list of the most important European transport routes to be prioritised for building or expansion. The list was comprised of 35 transport infrastructure projects, five transport management projects and seven projects to improve connections with non-EU countries. These projects were divided into three groups, expressing the degree of urgency accorded to the implementation of each project. Namely, priority projects, other important projects and projects requiring further appraisal. In a meeting in Essen in 1994, the European Council approved the top ranking projects. The research presented in this paper is concerned with the rail projects 1, 2, 3, 4, 6, 9 and 14, shown in *Table 1*.

The estimated costs for the realisation of these projects amounts to more than 110 billion Euro, of which 80 % is for railway connections, 10 % for the building of new roads and 9 % for road-rail connections. The Council is urging the member states, the European Commission and the European Investment Bank to expedite the 14 top-ranking projects; implementation of which should have begun by the end of 1996 at the latest.

1.3 Economic Evaluation

With regard to the question as to whether the implementation of these projects will be successful, it is still too early to say. We can, however, consider whether the expansion of authority, resolved in the Maastricht Treaty, and the suggestion of the 14 projects based on this are fundamentally reasonable (Laaser 1997). Accordingly, problems should be devolved to those hierarchical levels where the regional effects will be most noticeable, corresponting to the principle of fiscal equivalence, and those most capable of completing the projects. A centralisation of the projects is only sensible if:

- considerable external effects are to be expected at the lower level and the (too) high transaction costs make a solution directly negotiated between those concerned too difficult or even impossible;
- the lower-level personnel are either financially or organisationally unable to complete the necessary project;
- through the implementation of many small projects the advantages of economies of scale associated with mass production arise and so more than compensate for the disadvantages of centralisation.

With regard to Trans-European networks, we are certainly not concerned with the second or third reason. All member states are capable of planning, building and maintaining transport routes on their own. Should financial bottlenecks arise, it is more sensible to provide specified transfers to the lower level than to centralize the project. Similarly, there are no noticeable advantages in mass production. The first argument is, however, valid. Transport routes that are built and maintained by nation-states but have the status of European main routes carrying considerable external effects (at least as long as tolls are not charged to cover the costs). Furthermore, individual routes can never be seen alone but only as part of an extensive network. For the management of cross-border traffic routes this means that the national networks have to be agreed with each other. In cases where a route involves a number of countries, centralisation of the planning and implementation authorities suggests itself, otherwise the transaction costs for those involved would be too high. An expansion of the EU's authority in the field of transport is, therefore, welcome. It should, however, be limited to those cases where the effects clearly go beyond national borders. This is also the view of the EU and the one adopted for the criteria in choosing the priority projects; the common interest of numerous countries and their extraordinary size (Bulletin 1994, Schulze 1996). This basically correct and valid reason needs, however, to be supplemented with the following claims:

- The levying of tolls on transport to cover costs reduces the occurrence of external effects and, therefore, the necessity for the centralisation of authority.
- For every project within the framework of the Trans-European network, there must be evidence that several countries will be (noticeably) affected by it.[5]
- The norms and standards of the EU have to be binding for the member countries; a project has to be implemented if evidence of usefulness on the European level has been provided – unless, that is, either the environment or the people in a member state would be unreasonably aggrieved. The EU must contribute towards the costs of the scheme proportionate to the share in benefits for which other member states do not pay.

2. The Quality of the Transport Infrastructure in the European Region

2.1 Evaluation Concept

Our empirical results presented below serve to answer the following questions:

- How big are the differences in quality of the transport infrastructure in the various European regions?

[5] This criterion does not appear to have been met by all priority projects of the Trans-European network. For example, roads are to be sponsored in Greece, the effects of which will be broadly limited to this member state. In this instance, the EU has clearly allowed itself to be led by the wish and political necessity of taking all member states into consideration.

- How are the regional accessibility and the differences between regions affected by the implementation of the projects?
- How do we ascertain whether several countries will be affected by a transport project, in order to justify a decision in favour of centralisation?

These (and other) questions can be answered with the help of a complex simulation model "VERENA".[6] With this programme, it is possible to analyse the total freight and passenger traffic (road, rail, air and water borne) and to make prognoses. The main constituents are digitalised transport networks[7] with traffic regions and algorithms adapted to the networks. This allows for a variety of indicators regarding regional planning policy, transport policy and environmental policy to be calculated. A comparison of the characteristics of these indicators before and after the adoption of transport policy, in this case the building or expansion of railway lines, shows the effects these actions are likely to have.

Due to reasons of space, multiple limitations are effected.

- Only the priority railway projects will be considered.
- From those, the Berlin–Verona route as well the sum of all projects will be more closely considered.
- From the whole of Europe, only the results for West-Central Europe, the core of the EU and those countries immediately bordering the EU, will be presented.

2.1 Quality of the Transport Infrastructure Today and Changes Likely as a Result of the Priority Projects

Figure 1a shows the present high-speed train network in Europe. Whereas routes with a speed over 150 km/h and those between 100 and 150 km/h are differentiated, the rest of the network is not depicted. Whilst there are considerable differences between countries (France is clearly leading, whilst the Czech Republic has no high-speed routes), of particular interest is that the high-speed routes, with a few exceptions between France and Belgium, all end at the national borders; an international integration of the high-speed networks has not yet occurred.

This unsatisfactory situation will decidedly change, when the priority measures have become reality (*Figure 1b*). Connections, especially between France–Spain, France–Italy, France–Germany and Germany–Austria–Italy, will be greatly improved.

---

[6] VERENA GhK (1999) was developed in the subject area "Empirical Economic Research" in the University Gesamthochschule Kassel GhK and continuously modified to conform to specific questions. A detailed description is available for interested readers.

[7] All railways in Europe currently used for passenger traffic are taken into account. Journey times are taken from the timetables of the railway companies.

Let us then look at the quality of the connections between the NUTS-III regions.[8] This is measured with the help of speed as the crow flies (distance as the crow flies divided by travel time). Underpinning these indicators is the idea that a connection between two places can be said to be good if it is possible to travel from A to B at high speed without any large detours. The particularly poor connections can be seen in *Figure 2a*; here the speed as the crow flies is less than 20 km/h. There are considerable deficiencies to be seen in specific countries (Portugal, Czech Republic, also Germany), but especially due to the separation effect of the national borders. The lack of efficient international connections between the Czech Republic and Germany on the one side and Poland on the other are particularly pronounced. Here, the topography (low mountain range in the border regions) probably also plays a role. There is a similar deficiency between Portugal and Northern Spain and between the Netherlands and Northern Germany.

Figure 2b provides an answer to the question as to which core city connections[9] will be the most enhanced through the priority projects. These are concentrated in the Mediterranean area and the Southern Germany–Austria–Northern Italy strip. At present, the fastest route is between Paris and Lyon with a maximum speed of 164 km/h as the crow flies, followed by Seville–Cordoba (163.3 km/h) and Madrid–Cordoba (161.7 km/h). The greatest improvements to journey speed through the priority projects will be between Halle and Erfurt (+186.9 %), followed by Nuremberg–Erfurt (+162.7 %), Lyon–Torino (+149.6 %), Montpellier–Zaragossa (+132.1 %) and Montpellier–Barcelona (+127.6 %).

If one calculates the speed as the crow flies from one region to all others, one arrives at a weighted arithmetic average[10]. In this way, we can work out a complex indicator for the quality of the various regional transport infrastructures[11] that comprehensively expresses the level of development and connection of an economic area.[12] Proceeding accordingly, Indre-et-Loire assumes the top position. From here, it is possible to travel to the other regions of West-Central Europe at an average speed as the crow flies of 77.4 km/h. With Gironde, Vienne, Sarthe and Cha-

[8] In Switzerland, the analogue unit of observation is called "Kanton", in Poland "Województw" and "Kraj" in the Czech Republic. The purpose of this paper is not to investigate whether the NUTS-III regions in the EU are sensibly delineated, i.e., corresponding to functional regions (regional job markets, "core" integration areas). This is surely not the case.

[9] Since there are no specified core traffic centres in West and Central Europe, places with a population of over 200,000 are regarded here.

[10] The weight corresponds to a gravity approach. The larger the destination regions or the closer they are to the starting point, the more heavily they are weighted.

[11] In the opinion of the author, this indicator is superior to the most common indices, such as length of railway line, surface, presence of an IC-station, connection with a high-speed network, etc., insofar as it is concerned with the developmental quality and not with the mere physical existence of the infrastructure. Furthermore, the inhabitants of other economic areas also benefit insofar as they use these routes as throughways.

[12] For more information regarding the development of rail transport in European regions see Lutter et al. (1992) and Vickermann et al. (1999).

rente, other French regions follow. The Czech economic area is in last place with an average value of around 40 km/h. *Figure 3* shows these regional differences in cartographic form. Most noticeable are the especially well connected economic areas of Western France, Northern Great Britain, large parts of Spain and the lower parts of Northern Germany.

Figure 1a: Current high-speed rail network in West-Central Europe

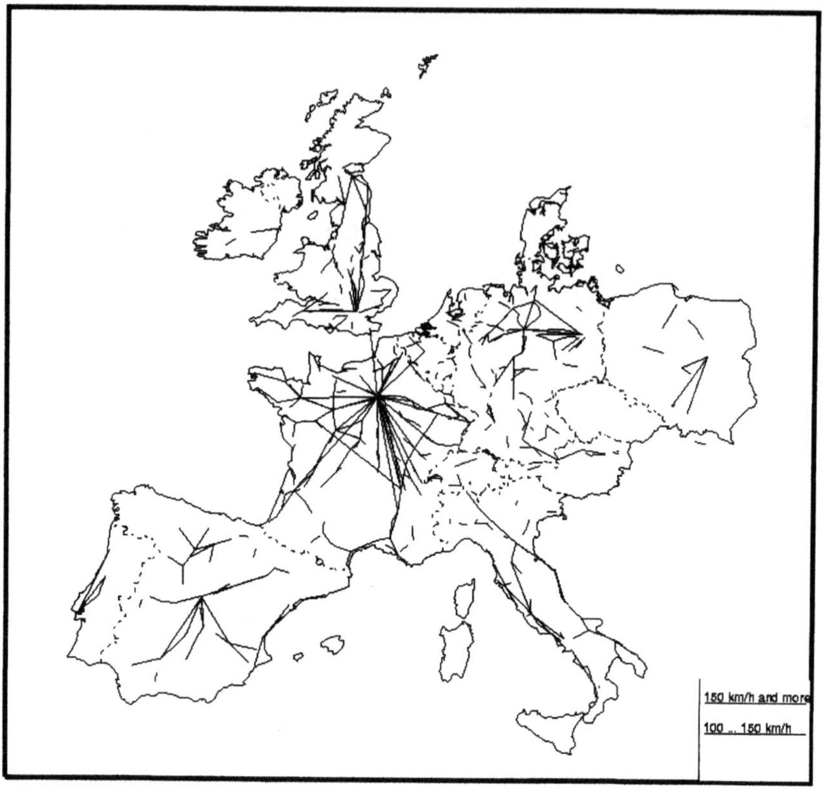

Source: VERENA GhK (1999)

Figure 1b: High-speed rail network in West-Central Europe following the building and expansion of the priority projects

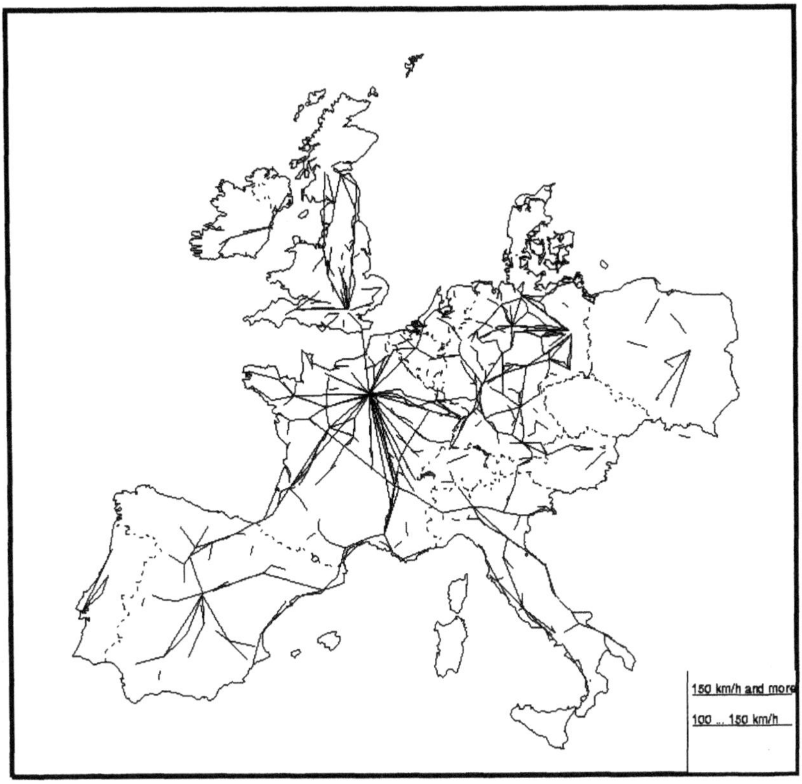

Source: VERENA GhK (1999)

Figure 2a: Connections of particularly poor quality between the NUTS-III regions (1999)

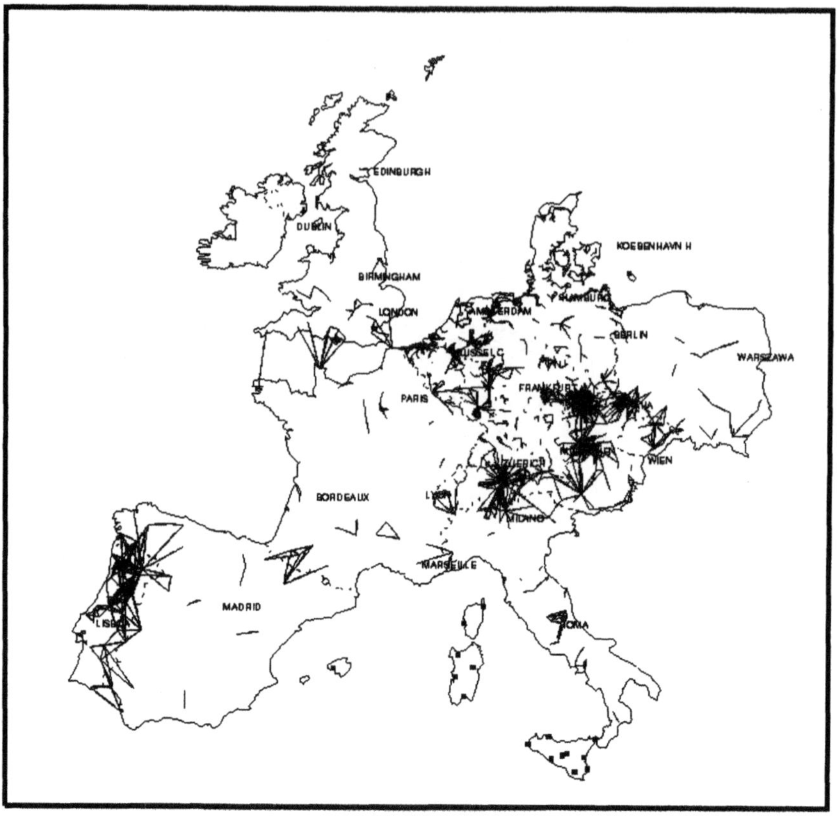

Key: —— Connections <20 km/h as the crow flies

■ NUTS-III regions on islands (not included in the research).

Source: VERENA GhK (1999)

Figure 2b: The connections between core centres most improved by the priority projects

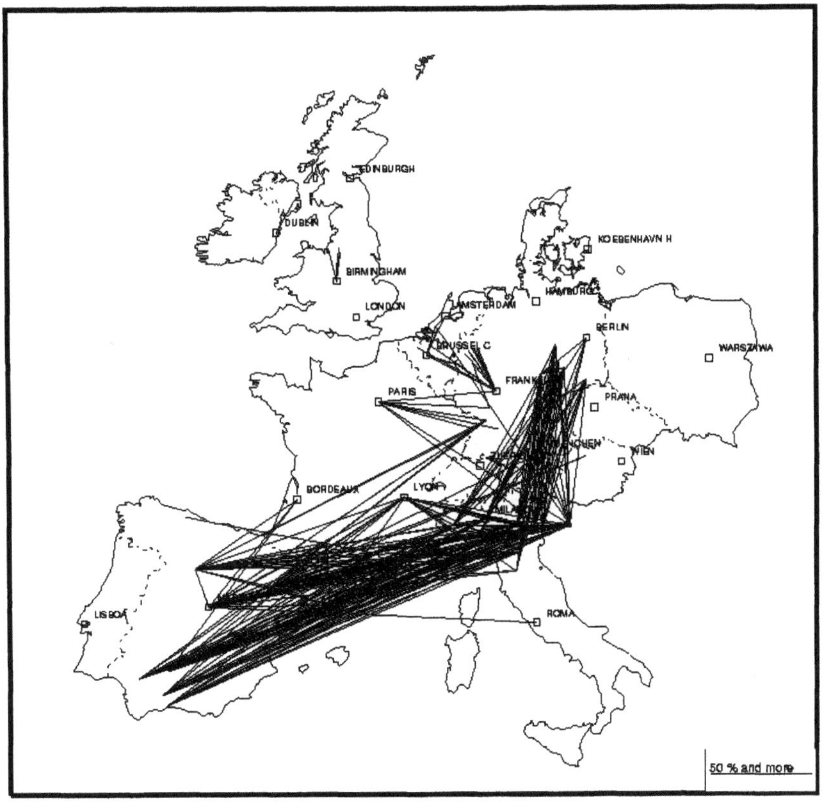

Key: —— Increases in speed of more than 50 % as the crow flies
Source: VERENA GhK (1999)

Figure 3: Quality of the transport infrastructure in the regions of West-Central Europe

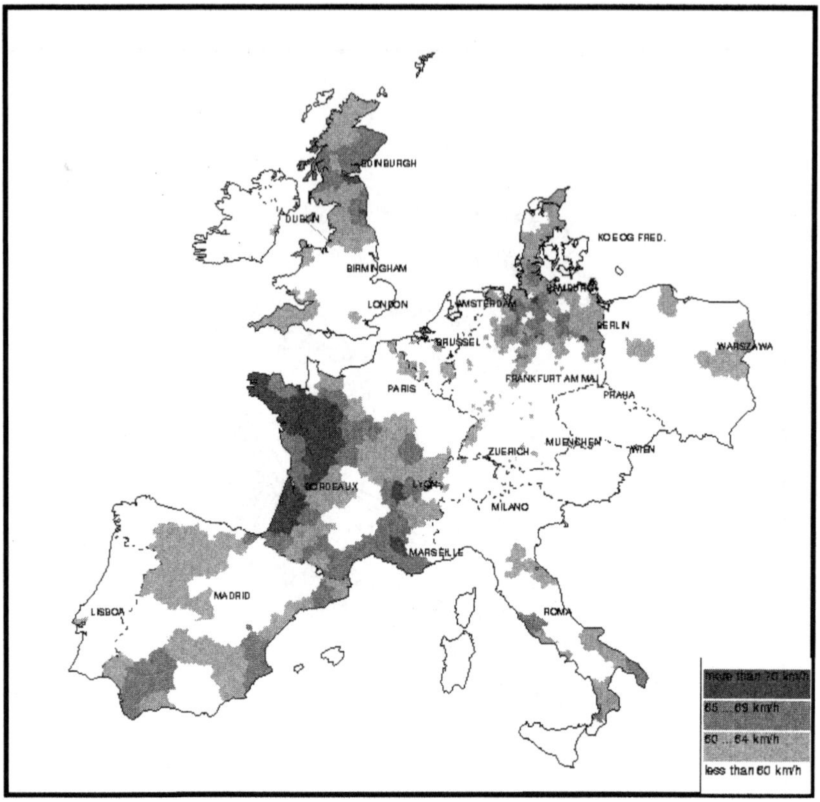

Average speed as the crow flies (in km/h) to all other regions in the area under investigation; weights according to a gravity approach. 4 Classes: >70km/h, 65-69 km/h, 60-64 km/h, <60 km/h. Source: VERENA GhK (1999)

Table 2 summarises these results and presents them for each country, with all German regions averaging 59.2 km/h. The variance of 33.5 shows the difference between all cities and administrative districts.

Furthermore, *Table 2* makes clear that:

- the development of roads is superior to the development of railways in virtually every country, with the exception of Ireland and Spain;
- there are considerable differences between countries; on average, the regions in Spain and France are the best connected, whilst those in the Czech Republic and Portugal are the worst:
- in some countries, the developmental quality is virtually the same in all regions (minimal variance) – this is especially true for the Netherlands; the qualitatively good level of development in transport, however, is concentrated in a few selected centres of special importance, especially in France.

How will this situation be changed through the building (expansion) of the Berlin–Verona route through the implementation of all the priority projects? The answer is provided by *Figures 4* and *5* in combination with *Table 2.* In *Figure 4*, we can see which regions will benefit greatly from the building (expansion) of the Berlin–Verona route. Although those regions, where the developmental quality will be most improved, lie immediately close to the route (Ingolstadt before Erfurt and Bozen), the effects will nevertheless extend through large parts of Germany, Poland, the Czech Republic, Austria and Italy. The reason for this is relatively simple: people in, for example, Poland will also use this route for journeys to the south. *Figure 4* shows that these priority projects clearly have a supranational character. *Table 2*, in turn, summarises the regional results as national results, whereby Italy enjoys the greatest benefit from these projects, with an average improvement in developmental quality of 2.8 km/h in all regions. This is followed by Austria with an improvement of 1.9 and Germany with 1.8. In comparison with the present status, the increasing variance makes it clear that these priority projects will actually increase the differences between regions. Those economic areas that are already well developed will experience the greatest benefits.

Figure 5 and *Table 2* inform us that the Spanish, Portuguese and Italian regions benefit most from all priority projects. Legovia (+23.4 km/h) is in the lead, followed by Madrid (+20.5) and Valladolid (+19.9). There is also a considerable increase in the differences in development between the NUTS-III areas. This is especially true for Spain, France and Portugal, but also applies to the whole of West-Central Europe. Thus, the priority projects of the European Union will lead to an improvement in the quality of connections between core centres, while at the same time amplifying the differences in regional accessibility.

Table 2: Quality and regional differences of the rail-transport infrastructure in the countries of West-Central Europe

Country	Number of Regions	Inhabitants (in 1000) per Region	Variants							
			A		B		C		D	
			AM	VAR	AM	VAR	Δ AM	Δ VAR	Δ AM	Δ VAR
D	440	185	59.18	33.53	66.18	7.39	1.83	5.17	6.03	-0.13
F	96	591	61.69	71.01	65.39	19.96	0.08	-0.29	7.11	16.96
I	103	552	57.04	31.32	63.75	20.61	2.84	4.34	8.67	14.20
NL	40	380	57.52	3.65	69.04	2.84	0.24	0.14	5.08	2.97
B/L	44	237	56.93	16.96	69.16	4.41	0.05	-0.02	6.78	4.63
GB	65	895	58.72	24.46	62.86	15.66	0.00	-0.02	6.43	7.29
IRL	8	568	58.13	3.61	52.59	4.46	0.01	-0.03	5.61	3.20
DK	15	346	59.21	4.96	60.04	20.83	0.69	0.04	2.36	0.60
E	48	780	61.84	25.80	61.39	21.57	0.01	-0.01	14.89	38.51
P	28	335	53.49	31.00	60.68	5.12	0.00	0.00	8.87	13.46
A	35	224	54.28	7.82	62.93	3.86	1.93	6.75	5.65	10.64
CH	27	257	57.45	15.42	64.22	3.62	0.30	-1.62	3.45	-1.09
PL	49	786	55.29	23.25	58.99	1.91	1.22	2.59	2.56	3.69
CZ	76	136	47.64	5.75	57.21	2.56	1.00	0.68	3.16	2.04
Σ	1074	372	58.35	39.69	63.59	21.81	1.00	1.14	6.99	28.77

Country	**Country name**
D	Germany
F	France
I	Italy
NL	Holland
B/	Belgium/
L	Luxembourg
GB	Great Britain
IRL	Ireland
DK	Denmark
E	Spain
P	Portugal
CH	Switzerland/Liechtenst.
PL	Poland
CZ	Czech Republic

A	Present rail network
B	Present road network
C	Present rail network + priority Project Berlin–München–Verona
D	Present rail network + all priority projects in rail transport
AM	Arithmetic Mean speed as the crow flies weighted with he help of the population figures
VAR	Variance weighted with he help of the population figures
Δ AM	Changes in AM compared to Variant A
Δ VAR	Changes in VAR compared to Variant A

Source: Own calculations

Figure 4: Changes in the quality of the rail-transport infrastructure in the regions of West-Central Europe through the building and expansion of the Berlin–Verona route.

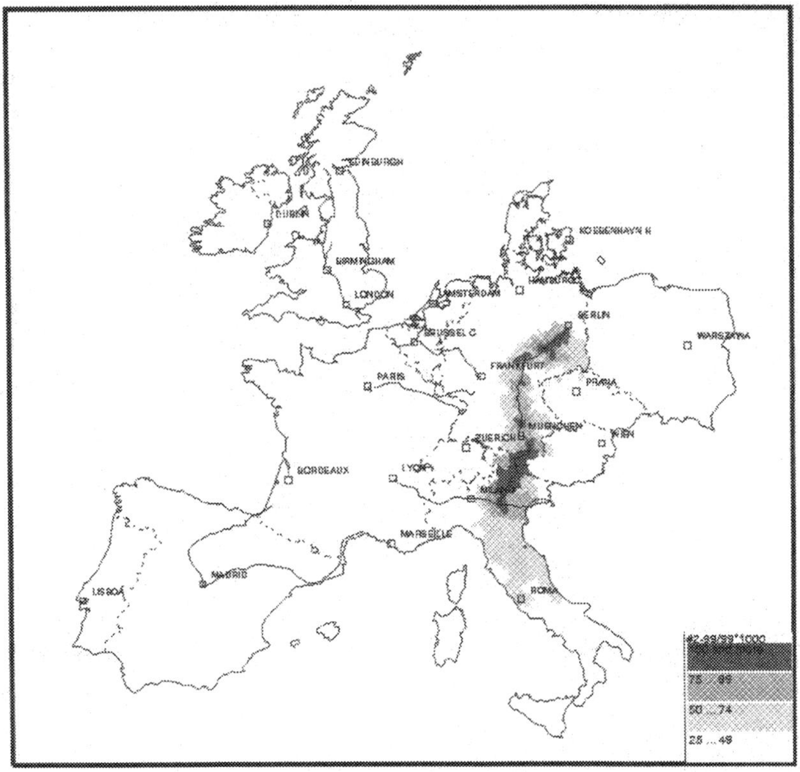

Changes in speed as the crow flies for the rest of the regions in area under investigation (in promille). Four Classes: more than 100. 75-99. 50-74. less than 50 promille. Key: — priority projects. Source: VERENA GhK (1999)

Figure 5: Changes in the rail-transport infrastructure in the regions of West-Central Europe through the implementation of all priority projects

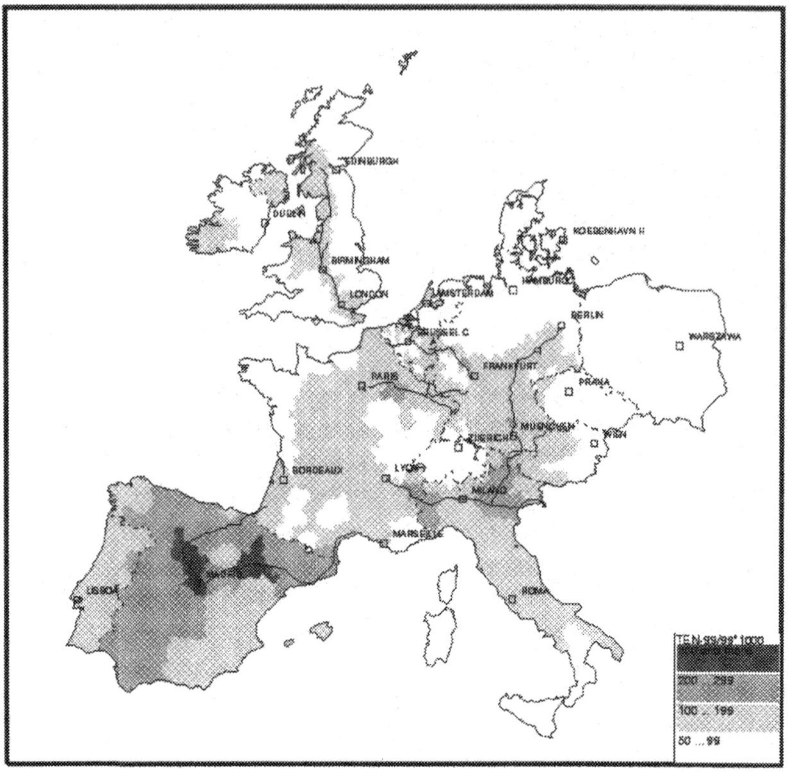

Changes in speed as the crow flies for the rest of the regions in area under investigation (in promille). Four classes: more than 300. 200-299. 100-199. less than 100 promille. Key: — priority projects. Source: VERENA GhK (1999)

3. Summary

The authority of the EU in the area of transport policy has clearly increased in recent years. This includes the task of providing an efficient international transport network (Trans-European network). Fourteen selected priority projects are seen as especially important for the increasing unity of Europe. The above elaboration addresses the questions.

- whether such a centralisation of transport policy is sensible against a background of subsidiarity and fiscal equivalence.
- how to measure the developmental quality of the regions.
- what differences can be determined in developmental quality of the economic areas in West-Central Europe.
- how these differences change through the implementation of the priority projects. and
- what effects will these projects have on a wider area.

In conclusion. we can determine that an expansion of authority in infrastructure policy in favour of the EU is only justifiable if there are considerable international spill-overs from the projects. We have demonstrated how these spatial external effects can be measured. using the example of the building and expansion of the Berlin–Verona route as well as all the priority projects in rail transport to illustrate the results.

References

Bulletin (1994) Zwischenbericht der persönlichen Beauftragten über die transeuropäischen Netze. In: Bulletin der Europäischen Union. Vol 27. Special Appendix 2

Commission of the European Communities (1993) White Paper on Growth. Competitiveness. Employment: The Challenges and Ways Forward into the 21st Century. Supplement 6/1993 to the Bulletin of the European Communities. Luxembourg: Office for Official Publications of the European Communities

Commission of the European Communities (1997) Treaty Establishing the European Community. Official Journal C 340. November 10th 1997. Luxembourg: Office for Official Publications of the European Communities. pp 173-308

Commission of the European Communities (2000) Internet Information. July 10th. 2000. www.europa.eu.int/en/comm/dg07/tentpp9807

ECMT (1995) The European Conference of Ministers of Transport: European Transport Trends and Infrastructural Needs. Paris

Erdmenger J (1996) Transeuropäische Netze im Bereich Verkehr. EUREG 3: 6-15

Laaser CF (1997) Infrastrukturpolitik der Europäischen Region: Ein Widerspruch zum Subsidiaritätsprinzip? In: Karl H (ed) (1997). Transeuropäische Netze: Die infrastrukturpolitischen Aufgaben der EU. Europa-Union-Verlag. Bonn. pp 31-58

Lutter H. Pütz T. Spangenberg M (1992) Accessibility and Perpherality of Community Regions: The Role of Highways. Long Distance Railways and Airport Networks. Bundesforschungsanstalt für Landeskunde und Raumordnung. Bonn

Schulze G (1996) Die Rolle der Europäischen Union beim Aufbau transeuropäischer Netze. In: Zippel W (ed) Transeuropäische Netze. Nomos. Baden-Baden. pp 29-43

Vickerman R. Spiekermann K. Wegener M (1999) Accessibility and Economic Development in Europe. Regional Studies 33: 1-15

Wink R (1996) Transeuropäische Verkehrsnetze: Für Wachstum oder für regionale Umverteilung? Wirtschaftsdienst VI: 301-308

Risk of Planning and Financing Infrastructure Projects: A Private-Public Nexus

Peter Nijkamp

Department of Economics, Free University

Amsterdam, the Netherlands

1. Setting the Scene

Transportation does not just mean physical movement of people or goods. It is an interlinking activity integrating the economies of our world. It acts as a driving force for development and new opportunities. Transportation fulfils a key role in modern societies. It does not only offer services to road users, but also to many other actors: public authorities, network operators, industry and society at large. In the same vein, transport is assuming a central role in the new European force field. Since the beginning of the 1990s, the context and nature of European trade and transport is entering a new era. In recent years, Europe has offered a scene with profound changes: integration of the EU market, desintegration of various nation states and more openness between all countries and regions in Europe (including Central and Eastern Europe). Countries – and increasingly also regions – within such trade-blocks are becoming part of an economic *network* with often *global* dimensions. To maximize the competitiveness of such a network and thereby to maximize its socio-economic potential and performance, the quality of European infrastructure is of critical importance, as transport has become an important component of modern production processes, amongst others because of changes in division of tasks in and between firms (often in different countries) and the logistic integration of business processes (e.g., horizontal and vertical integration, outsourcing). At the same time, large metropolitan areas appear to become poles of competition in an international context, so that also the quality of a metropolitan network plays a pivotal role in a global competitive system.

There is thus a need for a *systems-based assessment and policy strategy* approach that regards the European space as a comprehensive window of transportation opportunities which may generate a substantial value added in a competitive global economy (Bayliss 1992).

The European transport market is not only moving towards a more integrated network, but it is also becoming increasingly *liberalized.* Unnecessary regulations (e.g., regarding cabotage or protection of national industries) are more and more removed, while an increase in efficiency is strived for through more competition (e.g., in the aviation sector). The presence of more competitive – or at least contestable – markets should make transport operators more alert and induce a new situation with a higher service level at lower costs. This means that various new transport operators will play a critical role in the development of a European integrated infrastructure network for freight transport, as they govern the strategies to make networks really integrated.

Consequently, a new element to be considered in the current European transport policy scene is the changing role of actors in this field, in both the public domain (e.g., infrastructure owners or transport authorities) and the private domain (e.g., freight forwarders or logistics suppliers). A major issue is whether and how transport regulatory policy can be used to create conditions for fair competition, based on a creative division of tasks between public authorities and private actors with the aim to generate added value on using intermodal networks in Europe. This issue is once more important in the light of profound changes in decision processes of freight forwarders, new acquisitions and mergers in the freight industry, and company diversification into non-core business. In this context, also the division of roles between the private and public sector is at stake.

In the economics literature, transport is often regarded as a *derived* demand. Clearly, this is true in as far as the shipment of goods is necessary to serve the needs of the markets. But at the same time it should be realized that transport is a major industrial sector with its own indigenous target to make money out of physical movement. Thus, transport contributes significantly to GDP as a normal industry creating value added. The main challenge of the transport sector will be the creation of competitive locational conditions for regions, cities and industries to such an extent that they are able to operate at a competitive edge. That is also the main reason why in the commercial sector people are willing to pay for transport and for the use of high quality transport networks.

In light of the strategic importance of networks, it is also clear that the evaluation of investment programmes related to a network should not be based on individual projects, but on the *synergy* created by network operators in an interconnected infrastructure. This means that an infrastructure network is a cohesive set of links (edges) between concentrations of population or economic activity centres (the so-called nodes), which serve to provide all services (transportation, communication) that are necessary for an efficient transport of persons, goods or information between nodes. The assessment and the evaluation of a network should therefore not only take account of the way such a network can be designed and developed, but also *operated.*

In the past decades, infrastructure has often been managed by means of a *bureaucracy*, not as *a market-oriented service industry.* This model is characterised by poor accounting for costs, little relationship between revenues and costs or between revenue and service performance, and thus lack of accountability to the ultimate users as the "customers". Apart from the poor service quality which has often resulted from this approach, bureaucratic systems of infrastructure provision have given little regard to good management of assets (e.g., maintenance of roads, bridges, pipelines) which has often undermined their performance. Market instruments should contribute to a greater extent to the provision of infrastructure. Market instruments are here interpreted in the sense of competition and pricing. A commercial orientation (e.g., awareness of costs) and financial discipline are basic preconditions for the use of these market instruments (see also Section 4). In many infrastructure activities, the potential for applying competition and pricing has been enhanced by technological change, which has altered the nature of production and the services themselves (Frybourg, Nijkamp 1997).

Infrastructure activities which create the most significant and durable benefits in terms of both production and consumption provide a degree of reliability and quality that is desired by *paying users*. Users' charges should be based on economic prices reflecting both costs of supply and demand considerations (willingness to pay) as well as externalities. This means that new policies on network operations should be based on customer's preferences (and not modal interests), user charges and a third party access.

This approach is called *unbundling* by the World Bank in its "World Development Report" (1994). In this context, much emphasis is placed on three principles: customer driven, user charges and third party access. Public services are provided through a combination of capital and management. Infrastructure is not only a matter of *investment* (or capital stock), but also a matter of *operation and management*. The weaknesses and deficiencies in the infrastructure sector are inherent in incentives produced by the current institutional and organisational arrangements. Production inefficiency is consequently built into organisations where outputs and inputs are not carefully measured, monitored and managed. Lack of maintenance is intertwined with political and institutional bias toward new and imaginative investments. Traditionally, the interest in networks was instigated by supply side motives, but it is increasingly recognised that new competitive behaviour of firms in Europe requires to focus much more directly on those actors who co-ordinate, manage and operate flows in this network infrastructure.

For infrastructure activities which do not lend themselves to market instruments, other approaches are needed to ensure a satisfactory performance. A corollary of this is that governments must focus on and perform more effectively, the functions which should remain their responsibility, in particular certain well defined tasks of planning and regulation. The planning and financing of national highways, for example, remains a public responsibility in virtually all countries; on the other hand, many countries have adopted the goal of at least partially privatising national railroads (e.g., by privatising railway operations). As a result of various new market forces, the role of *public* (or semi-public) actors is declining and the importance of *private* operators is rising (Widlert 1995).

In view of the performance of interconnected networks for European countries, it is thus necessary to develop an appropriate analytical framework for assessment and policy evaluation, based also on a set of meaningful and practical indicators (Nijkamp, Blaas 1994). It makes sense to measure the added value and synergy of a (European) network configuration by means of a benefit criterion which will comprise both *quantitative use* indicators related to actual demand (function, fulfilment or use) in relation to capacity and *qualitative structure* characteristics which depict the cohesiveness (or synergy) of a network in terms of modes, regions, interconnectivity etc. From an economic perspective, it would be desirable to have a full insight into all costs and benefits (including the distributional implications) of extensions or improvements in network infrastructure. There is a wealth of studies on time savings and monetary evaluations of transportation, but their empirical validity is often questioned, their policy use is usually limited and their transferability to other situations is often very problematic. Transportation planning is nowadays essentially risk management, so that also the financial accountability of new transport plans is fraught with difficulties.

The above sketch of information needed for the assessment of European transport networks shows convincingly that – despite the glamour embodied in the three appealing missionary statements for European transport policy, viz. interconnectivity, intermodality and interoperability – it has to be recognized that there is still a series of analytical assessment problems. Although the needs and potentials of a coherent transportation system for both passengers and freight are widely acknowledged, the current practice offers at best examples of fragmented and project-oriented modal solutions and hardly of any successful implementation of an integrated blend of synergetic transport solutions based on solid assessment methods. This will be further illustrated in the next section which will address the issues involved in large-scale infrastructure projects in Europe.

2. Large Scale Infrastructure in Europe

The European infrastructure map has always been governed by national perspectives and interests. In many cases, the network had a centripetal configuration oriented towards the centre (e.g., France). This holds certainly for roads and even more so for railways. All these networks have a branch and tree structure towards the border, with only a few border crossing points. With the completion of the European internal market, it was increasingly recognized that economic integration would be hampered by infrastructure barriers for international trade, transport and communication. Based on the notion of missing links and missing networks (Nijkamp, Blaas 1994), the idea has grown that large investments would be necessary to create a competitive edge for the European economy. With the enry of the Scandinavian countries and the opening up of Central and Eastern Europe, policy-making bodies at the European level came to the conclusion that Trans European networks (TENs) would be a sine qua non for enhancing the competitiveness of Europe and for ensuring social cohesion in Europe.

This has provoked many research initiatives in European countries on the planning, implementation and evaluation of large scale transport investments with due interest in economic, financial, environmental and institutional issues (see the Pentagon prism discussed in Nijkamp, Blaas 1994). The question is now whether there is sufficient information on the demand for such new provisions, on the costs and revenues of infrastructure expansions, on the social costs of more mobility and on the social acceptability and institutional flexibility for planning new infrastructure. It seems worthwhile to address these issues from two sides: general design of accountability issues and case study approaches. This might also involve an integration of quantitative analysis and qualitative interpretation.

It should be added that transportation infrastructure comprises a wide diversity of different transport provisions, such as roads, railways, terminals, stations, ports, airports, bridges, tunnels etc. The financial order of magnitude of new investments in these facilities may be formidable and will for each individual project in many countries easily exceed 500 Mill Euro. Taking this as a general provisional baseline, the question is what we can learn from previous experiences in order to improve current and future practice of planning for large scale transport infrastructure. There is certainly much knowledge available among transport planning bodies in various countries, but this information is fragmented and not easily accessible. Therefore, some sort of a meta-analytic international comparative study may be helpful in generating the necessary knowledge on reliable cost assessments of large scale infrastructure in Europe. In this framework, it might be better possible to create a proper information strategy on economic-financial, environmental, institutional and urban-regional aspects of large scale transport infrastructure investment plans.

Against this background, private financing and operation of infrastructure has received much attention over the last decades. First, general devolution trends appear to prevail, and – from a ideological point of view – private sector influence should be increased (Banister, McLellan 1997). Second, government deficits are very high and should be reduced. At the same time, governments want to invest in new infrastructure, so that private financing becomes an important option. This also holds for the Trans European networks; the EU has no sources to finance these and private financing is often mentioned as a source of financing new transport investments.

The question whether the government should intervene in the market may be clarified by means of the *transaction costs* approach. Transaction costs include those of, e.g., negotiating, making contracts, control and requiring information. When no transaction costs occur, even externalities will be included in the market or government decision, because negotiations will continue until there is a Pareto-optimal allocation of goods (Coase 1988). As a result, there is no efficiency difference between provision by either the public or the private sector. An intervention causes again transaction costs, so that a trade-off has to be made between the transaction costs of the private and the public sector. However, in practice, governmental policies and outcomes of decision-making processes in society are not that simple. Also, other stakeholders play an important role, while each stakeholder has his own utility function and thus individual strategies (Rienstra, Nijkamp 1997).

3. The Changing Role of Institutions

3.1 Introduction

Since the mid 1970s, a number of Western European countries has actively been engaged in substantial regulatory reform. Unnecessary regulation has been removed from various areas of the economy in which public control was previously rigorously applied, while in other areas where regulation still remains appropriate at least the methods and the intensity of regulation are reconsidered. The process of regulatory reform has been most actively pursued in France and the United Kingdom, but it has been undertaken to varying degrees in virtually all European countries. The poor performance of many public enterprises[1] (hereafter PE) has been the main impetus for this reform movement, but reform has also been pursued to improve the performance of private firms (Amsden et al. 1994). In recent years, regulatory reform has become a big political movement in Eastern Europe (Domanski 1992; Domanski, Judge 1994).

The growing interest in regulatory reform is based on two ideas: (1) the efficiency of an enterprise – public or private – is higher as the enterprise is forced to maximize profits in a competitive market, and (2) public enterprises are more likely to deviate from profit maximization than their private counterparts. Proponents of regulatory reform argue that the *removal of market restrictions*, together with *various forms of privatization*, will improve the economic performance of both public and private enterprises and thereby of the economy as a whole (e.g., nation, region or city). Both forms of regulatory reform will be discussed here.

---

[1] A public enterprise is a government owned productive organization that (i) is expected to earn a significant portion of its revenues from the sale of goods it produces, (ii) possesses an accounting system separate from any government agency that controls or supervises it, and (iii) is a distinct legal entity.

3.2 Eliminating Market Restrictions Through Competition Policy

The notion of a "level playing field" is central to competition policy. Product markets are most efficient if all enterprises in the market place are essentially in the same position to compete. In many economic sectors, there is no such level playing field. Public enterprises often operate in sheltered markets. They enjoy distinct advantages over their competitors, such as preferential access to credit, subsidies to cover operating losses and privileges of tax exemption (in principle, private companies might enjoy similar advantages, but this is seldom the case). These public enterprises are not exposed to the discipline of the market and are therefore less motivated to increase efficiency than firms operating in competitive markets.

The aim of competition policy is in general the creation of conditions approximating those of efficient and effective private markets. Important instruments to abolish barriers to competition are the removal of regulations on prices, entry and exit, output, international trade, the amount of profit companies are permitted to earn, etc. Another instrument is the relaxation of public or private monopolies (antitrust law). In some circumstances though, competitive markets are either impossible or inefficient. But even then, competition policy can still play a role in improving the performance of PEs and private firms.

It is important to note that full competition is not essential to achieve desired competition: the threat of competition may be sufficient. A monopolist is said to operate in a *contestable* market when his behaviour approximates that of a competitive firm. If other firms can easily enter this market, the monopolist is forced to keep prices close to costs. It goes without saying that even the existence of contestable markets creates substantial transition problems to firms, which have always been operating in protected markets, as is witnessed by many experiences in Eastern Europe.

3.3 Privatization

Privatization is the general process of involving the private sector in the *ownership or operation* of a public enterprise. There are various ways in which the private sector can assume the responsibility of activities which were formerly undertaken by the public sector. In case the private sector assumes ownership of (part) of a public enterprise, a *sale* is involved. But a change in ownership is not a necessary element of privatization. *Contracting out* is perhaps the most common form of privatization, having been widely used in the local public services (such as refuse collection, catering, and cleaning). Finally, it should be noted that there is also the possibility that the private sector will assume responsibility for the management of an enterprise, which continues to be owned by the state *(lease, franchise, management contract)*. Thus, there is a wide spectrum of privatization initiatives and forms.

4. Characteristics and Risks of Transport Infrastructure Investments

Several aspects and characteristics have to be taken into account in the decision-making process on infrastructure provision. These aspects relate to characteristics of the investment, the risks involved and the expected costs and revenues of the investment. These issues will be discussed in the next Sub-Sections.

4.1 Characteristics of Transport Infrastructure Investments

We will first address specific features of transport infrastructure. For private investors, investments in transport infrastructure have characteristics which make these investments different from competing investments such as immovables and capital goods in several ways. These are in general:

- The expected *economic life* of infrastructure is rather long compared to other investments. This may vary from 20 years to more than a century. The pay-back period of infrastructure investments is also long; concessions are often granted by the government for some 15 to 30 years. Other immovables and capital goods usually have a much shorter pay-back period; the average of capital goods is usually in the order of magnitude of 8 to 9 years.
- The *operational costs* are relatively *low* in many cases, especially on longer distance infrastructure. There are some labour, overhead and maintenance costs, while a system must be exploited for selling tickets and making reservations. Compared to the construction costs of infrastructure and to the exploitation costs of other investments, these costs are low however.
- During the construction phase, a *large amount of capital* is required. Often high loans have to be attracted which makes interest costs relatively high.
- The *period, before infrastructure construction* actually begins, can be very long because of many legal decision-making procedures, resistance in society etc.
- The *construction period* is very long compared to other investments. This period may take 2 to 7 years. In this period, there are no revenues, while there are already interest and other costs.
- Once started, the investment is almost *irreversible*. If the construction is stopped, this would imply destroying capital, because it is not possible to use the investment alternatively.

From the above mentioned observations it is clear that in the beginning of a project high financial capital amounts are needed. In general, this makes private investors more reluctant, as this reduces their flexibility. The relatively high interest amounts at the start of the project are not immediately compensated by high cash-flows. Instead, often the future returns on investments are relatively low, while in most cases there are no revenues at all before the infrastructure operation starts. After the start of the operation, profits will of course get higher in due course, because repayments are made. There are, however, many risks involved, e.g., on the use of the infrastructure at hand. Clearly, when mobility on the segment concerned grows, the revenues tend to grow as well. The problem is that the rise in profits and revenues often starts many years after the initial investment, which makes the uncertainty and the risks very high compared to alternative investment options. As a consequence, the financial and legal aspects of private loans for infrastructure are often rather complicated (ECMT 1990).

In practice, however, it is even possible that the operation will run at a loss all the time. The construction costs, including interest costs, are – up to a certain level of demand/transport – fixed costs; the other costs are partly fixed and partly variable. Therefore, compared to competing investments, the fixed costs are very high for an investor, while variable and marginal costs are relatively low. When the price in this case is set according to the marginal costs (which is economically optimal), it is often not possible to make a satisfactory return on investments.

A risk premium is usually incorporated in all kinds of investment, but for investments in infrastructure it is usually particularly high for several reasons, which will be outlined in the next subsection.

In this context, it is important to acknowledge that there are differences between transport infrastructure and other types of infrastructure. User charges on telecommunication infrastructure can, for example, much easier and cheaper be levied, which may be a reason for the privatization of this sector in many countries. The same holds for public utilities, such as water and electricity infrastructure. Another reason for the more easy privatization of these types of infrastructure is that the negative externalities are much lower than of transport infrastructure.

4.2 Risks of Investments in Infrastructure

Investments in infrastructure include, like all investments, various types of risks. Because of the long term investments, these risks may be very high. The following main classes of risk may be distinguished (McKay 1989):

- *political* risks; for example, changes in transport policy, nationalization, intervention/regulation by the government, etc.;
- *financial* risks; for example, fluctuations in interest rates, fluctuations in exchange rates, false expectations about inflation, etc.;
- *construction* risks; for example, delays, unexpected and higher costs etc.;
- *operational* risks; for example, damage by accidents, vandalism, demand shortfalls, etc.;

- *commercial* risks; for example, incorrect cost estimates, wrong estimates of the traffic volume, unexpected competition, etc.

These risk categories will hereafter be discussed in more detail.

Political risks

Political risks in infrastructure policy may be significant, since a government has many reasons to interfere in the transport market. There is always a danger of changes in laws or new regulations or even nationalization, because of a changing transport policy. In the Netherlands, for example, the government has the legal right to interfere when national interests are harmed; in France, the government forced the investors in the Mont Blanc tunnel and the St. Bernhard tunnel to invest their profits in other infrastructure projects.

Since the political risks of investments in infrastructure are rather high compared to other investment opportunities, this may make these investments unattractive for private investors. As a consequence, there must be a high risk compensation. In theory, this compensation may stem from high profit expectations, as is also shown by recent road tunnel projects in the Netherlands. It would also be possible for governments to make the investments more attractive, by guaranteeing other benefits (e.g., tax exemptions) or joint-risk constructions (e.g., in guaranteeing a public subsidy if the use of infrastructure is below expectations). In the next Section, various possibilities for stimulating private involvement are analyzed.

Financial and construction risks

When the financiers of a project (private and/or public) are identified and the procedures are completed, the construction of the project can start. In this stage, it is very important that the costs are kept under control, because this may often cause many problems. It appears that often the costs of construction are higher than expected or that certain financial items have been neglected. It is also important that the construction contracts are clear about who pays for excess costs; this often leads to conflicts, which can have serious economic implications (e.g., delays, higher costs).

It appears to be very difficult to estimate the costs of construction of major infrastructure projects, however. These projects are often much more expensive than estimated beforehand; well-known examples are the Channel tunnel, High Speed Train sections or the Betuwe freight railway line in the Netherlands. This problem arises especially when the project is a completely new transport mode or when new technologies are used. Then many costs are not known at the outset of the project, and the estimates appear to be too low in almost all cases.

Another important cause of rising costs are relatively expensive solutions, chosen to cope with resistance in society, e.g., to avoid external effects (this may lead, e.g., to (half-)subterranean infrastructure and noise-shields). It is however very important that the cost estimates are made on a reliable basis, as otherwise it will be impossible to assess the economic viability of the project. And if no return on investment can be calculated, a project is not interesting for private investors.

On the other hand, it is essential to minimize annoyance to local people during the construction essential, especially when the construction takes place in densely populated areas. When the annoyance is high, the resistance in society against the construction will be high, which may again cause delays.

Operational risks

To calculate the possible revenues of a project, several issues are noteworthy, which are mainly important for the transport mode(s) which use(s) the infrastructure at hand. First, an assessment of the market in which the mode will operate is important. Therefore, the (sub-)market(s) one is aiming at should be analyzed. These sub-markets can be distinguished according to the residential zones of clients, their destinations, the reasons for travelling, etc. When, for instance, a project serves a mass transport mode, the price must be low, while the comfort, speed and service may be of lower importance. When the project is aiming at the higher level business market, the speed, reliability, service and comfort are very important, while the price may be set somewhat higher. The latter is of course also dependent on the prices of competing modes.

To maximize total revenues, it may also be important to generate other revenues than those which are directly related to transportation. Catering on long-distance travelling and tax-free shopping at airports are well-known examples of indirect revenues. But there may also be other possibilities. For example, railway stations are popular sites for several business companies like bookshops, snack bars, flower shops, travel agencies, etc. Another possibility for generating revenues is a development based on the value of the locations around transport terminals, which may arise after the construction of, e.g., a new railway station. The question here is of course whether it is possible for the investor to receive (part of) these revenues.

Commercial risks

When the transport mode is relatively new, it will be difficult to acquire a sufficient share of the transport market. In most cases, new modes will have to find a new niche in the market first, while later they may also start to compete with existing transport modes. A good marketing strategy is very important to get a profitable market share. It is common practice that ticket prices have to be relatively low at the beginning, in order to attract new travellers and to give users of alternative modes an incentive to shift. Later on, the charge may be raised towards the economic (or social) optimal level.

It appears that many risk-related barriers have to be overcome, before transport projects are interesting for the private sector.

5. Private Involvement in Transport: Regimes and Practices

5.1 A Typology

Infrastructure is characterized by a network character. This makes infrastructure a special good, which cannot simply be provided by the private sector. This does not only hold for transport infrastructure but also for other types of infrastructure, like energy grids, telecommunication infrastructure, etc. Although it should be acknowledged that there also may be private involvement in the planning, design and ownership of infrastructure (Banister et al. 1995), this is not discussed here.

When analyzing private provision of transport, it is useful to make a clear distinction between financing and operation of infrastructure. The operation is in this case defined as the operation of the infrastructure itself, the operation of the vehicles using the infrastructure are not included in this analysis. The relevant categories are indicated in *Figure 1*, although in practice the distinction may sometimes be less straightforward.

The *first category* (I) refers to a situation where infrastructure is regarded as a normal good with normal market prices. There is no public intervention. The airline sector in the US is an example of this situation.

Figure 1: Different focus of public-private sector involvement

		Financing	
		Private	Public
Fehler! Textmarke nicht definiert.	Private	I	II
Operation	Public	III	IV

The *second category* (II) refers to many new situations involving railway companies. It has the advantage that the infrastructure will be efficiently operated, while the government only has to pay the fixed infrastructure costs and not the variable operating costs. So, economically, this category may be attractive, because of the gains in efficiency. For governments, however, this option may not be very attractive, because the public budget is not relieved from the high investment costs, while the influence on the transport market may decrease. Examples of this category are the railways in Sweden and Switzerland.

The *next category* (III) concerns a situation where the private sector finances the infrastructure, but where the public sector is charged with the operating costs. This may be an appealing short-term budget solution and therefore attractive for governments, but this is more expensive, since governments mostly borrow at lower interest rates than the private sector. It is in practice also questionable whether the private sector runs sufficient risks to speak of private financing, since in practice it is often observed that the government assumes the risks in this category (e.g., by guaranteeing debts). Examples of this category are recent tunnel projects in the Netherlands, where the government had to share the risk of a lower than expected use of these infrastructure categories; guaranteeing debts has also been the case in many other projects, e.g., the new links in Denmark.

Finally, *category IV* is a common situation in conventional road and waterway infrastructure. User charges are in this case not levied and financing and operation are under control of the government.

As appears from these categories, an important question is in which cases one may speak of pure private involvement in financing infrastructure. In general, two conditions should be fulfilled:

- The private party runs all *risks*. The government should, for example, not guarantee the pay-back of loans or the amount of revenues in one way or another. Otherwise, the government runs the risks of the investments so that the economic result is equal to that of public financing (although formally and administratively this may not be the case).
- The operation of the infrastructure should be exclusively based on *user charges* so that the investment is paid directly by its users. When no user charges are levied, the government has to pay the revenues. In this case, no market situation is reached and the government pays back the investor, which is only expensive for the government in the long run – an example being the leasing of transport infrastructure by the government.

From these conditions, it is clear that most economic benefits may be found in the operation of the infrastructure; in that case, user charges are levied and the private sector runs clearly the risks. Therefore, it seems plausible that the government should aim at achieving this in the first place. The financing, however, may as a consequence (partly) be private, when the expected operational profits are high enough.

5.2 Private Provision in Practice: A Concise Historical Sketch

It is interesting to note that private sector involvement was common in the 19th century. The first canals and railways were privately financed, although the influence of the government was rather large. From this historical analysis, it becomes however clear that entirely private provision of transport is not feasible (Rienstra, Nijkamp 1997a). Networks will not come into existence, because several links are not profitable or too risky for private financiers. Therefore, the generation of network synergy will be more difficult, especially when there are several suppliers. Interestingly, certain operational and financing constructions which are currently under discussion in several European countries for the railways have been applied in the Netherlands and elsewhere in the past (Marcou 1993).

In the 20th century, however, the governments took responsibility for the financing and operation of infrastructure. In this Section, some European case studies will be presented concisely in order to analyze the possibilities of private provision in practice and to investigate whether the above observations hold.

Since 1945, almost all European transport infrastructure has been financed and operated by governments or by public organisations tied to the government. Especially in the case of railways, there is at present a trend to separate the financing and operation of infrastructure, as is the case in Sweden, Switzerland and the United Kingdom (Category II in *Figure 1*) (Hannson, Nilsson 1991; Nash 1993). In this model, the management and financing of infrastructure is the responsibility of the government. The operation takes place on a private basis, where the operator imposes user charges. In this situation there may be several suppliers of transport services, which allows competition. This model corresponds to recent EU regulations and is proposed or under discussion in several countries (Germany, Italy, Netherlands). In the United Kingdom there are also plans to privatise the rail infrastructure owner (Railtrack).

Road infrastructure is mostly the responsibility of the public sector however, although there are in several countries discussions about introducing toll or road-pricing systems. In Sweden, the official policy aims at introducing the same construction for road infrastructure as for rail infrastructure (Hannson, Nilsson 1991). Because of the so-called Mannheim treaty – forbidding user charges and protection measures on most waterways – also waterways have been financed by the public sector.

Because of the risks and characteristics of infrastructure investments, joint public-private projects are increasingly advocated as a solution for the problems of entirely private provision of infrastructure. It should be emphasized, however, that also in this case the above mentioned conditions – risks should be shifted to the private sector and user charges need to be levied – should be satisfied to make such a construction economically feasible.

An example of joint projects may be transport infrastructure franchising by the private sector (Andersen 1995). A franchise can be defined as a contract between a transport authority (the franchiser) and a private company (the franchisee), by which the latter obtains the right to operate a transport system. Under a conventional franchise contract, the franchisee pays the franchiser for using his property rights. In the case of transport infrastructure, this situation may be reversed: the transport authority may compensate the private company for an expected operational deficit. These franchise contracts may be distributed by means of tendering. There may be two different kinds of contracts: a given transport system is transferred to the company which offers to operate it at the lowest costs or the contract is transferred to the company which offers the best transport system for a given budget. Clearly, such systems need detailed agreement on service levels and operating conditions, in order to meet both efficiency and equity criteria (see also Fielding, Klein 1993).

A franchise agreement can be applicable to both existing infrastructure and new infrastructure that has to be built yet. In the former case, management responsibility has to be transferred to the private firm. In the latter case, the responsibility for financing may be transferred as well, but it is also possible that the government finances the infrastructure (partly). To achieve social goals, a franchise contract should state the conditions which have to be observed by the franchisee. For example, price setting may be restricted to prevent abuse of the monopoly power of the franchiser and for equity reasons (access to services for everyone). In the United Kingdom, a franchise system has been proposed for the rail infrastructure (Nash 1993).

6. Conclusions

The interests of the private sector clearly differ from that of the public sector. As a result, transport infrastructure is not a good which can easily be provided by the private sector (see also Newbery 1994). Governments have several reasons to take the responsibility and have influence on the provision of infrastructure in order to secure equity objectives (e.g., isolated regions or mobility-deprived people), to reduce negative external effects and to achieve positive external effects. Infrastructure is clearly a special form of network capital, which has led to the idea that in general a natural monopoly – provided by the public sector – is the most efficient market organisation. However, there are reasons to consider private financing and operation of infrastructure:

- the private sector may provide, construct, operate and maintain the infrastructure more efficiently;

- the acceptance of user charges may be higher, because a private company is the owner;
- it reduces government expenditures and may in this way help to achieve financial policy objectives; therefore, the project may also be constructed earlier.

Completely private provision of transport is possible from a theoretical point of view, although there are several arguments for public intervention. Also, in practice there seem to be many problems. Still, private influence in the transport sector may be increased. Societal views on the importance, effectiveness and acceptance of market incentives appear to change over time; therefore, in the 1960s and 1970s, the government took most responsibility for the operation and financing of railway infrastructure. In recent years, however, the earlier applied constructions seem to be introduced once again.

It should be acknowledged that these views are in the first place important for the private operation of infrastructure projects. Most gains may be achieved in this way, also because new technologies (e.g., road pricing) make levying tools easier and cheaper.

Private financing – which is only feasible when the private operation generates sufficient income – seems nowadays only possible for specific projects, since the most profitable links are already constructed. When private financing should become a feasible option, large scale changes are necessary; in scenarios such changes could of course be assumed.

It should, however, be acknowledged that large scale privatization might have negative impacts on regional development issues. It is not likely that investments in and to regions with a low population density (e.g., the TEN), relatively low average income per capita and expensive infrastructure are profitable for private investors. Because the EU has not sufficient funds available, the financing of the TENs should largely take place by national governments. It is likely that only a few profitable projects can be financed by the private sector, when the above discussed conditions are met. In practice, however, it may be likely that more pragmatic constructions will occur, in which governments take largely the risks and the operation, while officially the infrastructure is financed privately. For example: governments can get loans from the European Investment Bank up to 50 % of the investment costs. When a private construction will occur, these loans may not be counted as national debt, although the pay-back is still the responsibility of national governments. Probably, also investments in new transport modes may be lower when large scale privatizations occur, because of the high risks involved.

There is a wide range of policy measures available to stimulate the private financing and operation of transport modes – especially joint venture, in which the private and the public sector share risks may be attractive. Of course, governments can also subsidize the fixed costs of an infrastructure project, so that it becomes profitable for private investors. The same holds for giving tax exemptions and giving guarantees about compensations when future policies interfere with the profits of the project. Finally, the introduction of road pricing makes it easier to levy tolls for private operators; so this may make privatization easier to accomplish.

References

Amsden AH, Kochanowcz J, Taylor L (1994) The Market Meets its Match. Harvard University Press, Cambridge (Massachusetts)

Andersen B (1995) Franchising Alternatives for European Transport. In: Banister D, Capello R, Nijkamp P (eds) European Transport and Communications Networks. John Wiley, Chichester, pp 221-247

Banister D, McLellan A (1997) The Organisation of Transport Markets. Possum-Working Paper 25/05-97, London.

Banister D, Andersen B, Barrett S (1995) Private Sector Investment in Transport Infrastructure in Europe. In: Banister D, Capello R, Nijkamp P (eds) European Transport and Communications Networks. John Wiley, Chichester, pp 191-219

Bayliss B (1992) Transport Policy and Planning. The World Bank, Washington, D.C.

Coase RH (1988) The Firm, the Market and the Law. The University of Chicago Press, Chicago

Domanski R (ed) (1992) Space-Economy in the Transition. Policy Academy of Sciences, Warsaw

Domanski R, Judge E (eds) (1994) Changes in the Regional Economy in the Period of System Transformation. Polish Academy of Sciences, Warsaw

ECMT (1990) Private and Public Investment in Transport. Paris

Fielding JF, Klein DB (1993) How to Franchise Highways. Journal of Transport Economics and Policy. 27: 113-130

Frybourg M, Nijkamp P (1997) Towards an Evaluation Framework for Integrated European Transport Network Operations. In: Banister D, Nijkamp P, Priemus H (eds) European Transport and Communications Networks. Edward Elgar, Cheltenham

Hanson L, Nilsson JE (1991) A New Swedish Railroad Policy: Separation of Infrastructure and Traffic Production. Transportation Research 25: 153-159

Hines P (1993) Integrated Materials Management: The Value Chain Redefined, The International Journal of Logistics Management 4: 101-114

Marcou G (1993) Public and Private Sectors in the Delivery of Public Infrastructure: The Case of the Channel Tunnel from an International Perspective. Environment and Planning 11: 1-18

McKay M (1989) Möglichkeiten der privatwirtschaftlichen Finanzierung von Verkehrsinfrastrukturinvestionen in der EG. Beitrage aus dem Institut für Verkehrswissenschaft. Universität Münster

Nash C (1993) Rail Privatisation in Britain. Journal of Transport Economics and Policy, 27: 317-322

Newbery D (1994) The Case for a Public Road Authority. Journal of Transport Economics and Policy 28: 235-253

Nijkamp P, Blaas E (1994) Impact Assessment and Evaluation in Transportation Planning. Kluwer, Boston, Dordrecht

OECD (1992) Advanced Logistics and Road Freight Transport. Paris

Rienstra SA, Nijkamp P (1997) The Role of Stakeholder Analysis in Constructing and Validating Scenarios. Possum Working Paper 10/01-97. Free University, Amsterdam

Widlert S (1995) Coordinated Infrastructure Planning in Sweden. Paper WCTR Conference, Sydney

World Bank (1994) World Development Report 1994. Washington, D.C.

Regional Integration of Transport and Communications Systems in Southern Africa

Rolf H. Funck

Universität Karlsruhe (TH)

Institut für Wirtschaftspolitik und Wirtschaftsforschung

Karlsruhe, Germany

Preface

Karin Peschel's – may I say: infatuation with Southern Africa which began in the 1970s was, I believe, caused as much by a personal fascination with some of the world's most beautiful sorts of countryside as by her political desire to understand the then prevailing multicultural conflicts and evaluate the differing approaches to overcome them, and her interest as an economist in the reasons for failure or success of the efforts toward socio-economic development in the region.

The development policy of the European Union, several of whose member states represent the former colonial powers of the region, tries to imprint on the Southern African region the same principles that have proved successful in the context of European integration: deregulation, commercialization, privatization, removal of man- or rather state-made barriers to cross-border trade and travel, in order to make the various locations competitive on a level playing field. To make this approach work, creating the appropriate frame conditions is a vital task. It requires careful analysis, interactive co-operation between the European and the Southern African institutions involved in the task, and sympathetic adaptation to the local customs and possibilities.

The following may be considered as the report on a case study in this regard.

1. Reform Issues

Economic and political developments in the Southern African region have been distinctly marked by the ways in which colonial control systems were abolished and new structures established. While most of the former British colonies moved into independence peacefully during the 1960s, extended conflict occurred in the previous Portuguese colonies of Angola and Mozambique before they could achieve independence in the mid-1970s. The severe economic problems already faced by these countries were intensified by the outbreak of civil war immediately after independence.

In 1980, in order to reduce the economic dependence on South Africa – then characterized by and politically isolated through the international response to the apartheid regime – and to promote regional economic integration, the front states established SADCC, the Southern African Development Co-ordination Conference. Re-orientation began in the late 1980s, when the upcoming collapse of apartheid became visible, and led to the restructuring of SADCC into SADC, the Southern African Development Community in 1992. The SADC of originally ten – Angola, Botswana, Lesotho, Malawi, Mozambique, Namibia, Swaziland, Tanzania, Zambia and Zimbabwe – was, after 1994, extended to include Mauritius and the new, post-apartheid Republic of South Africa, and has recently admitted the Democratic Republic of Congo and the Seychelles.

In establishing and pursuing attainment of the objectives laid down in the SADC Treaty, the member states have committed themselves to the principal aims of alleviating poverty and increasing wealth generation through accelerated and regionally integrated economic and social growth. Specific actions being taken to achieve these objectives are reflected in the programmes being pursued at both national and SADC regional levels.

At national levels, from the early to mid 1990s, most SADC member states had already embarked on economic reforms with measures that principally involve pursuing sound macro-economic and monetary policies, are aimed at reducing and/or controlling inflation and entrenching liberal or market-based economic principles, as well as democratic processes of decision making. There are positive results of these policies to be registered in that, with few exceptions, average real GDP growth rates of well above 3 % (SACG 1998, Vol 3, Technical Appendices) were attained over the last several years.

At the SADC regional level, the main preoccupation since the signing of the Treaty has been the development and implementation of sector-specific protocols aimed at defining in detail the policies, strategies and modes of regional co-operation in the various sectors. While a number of protocols are still being developed – such as the Protocols on Mining, Agriculture and Food Security, Finance and Investment – and others are in the process of ratification – as the Protocols on Trade, Tourism and Education –, several are already under implementation, among them – in addition to those on Energy and Shared Water Course – the Protocol on Transport, Communications and Meteorology (in the following: *the* Protocol), which was signed by the Heads of States in August 1996 and came into effect in July 1998.

In the Protocol, the SADC member states have recognized that well-functioning transport and communications systems "are a prerequisite for the promotion of economic growth and development and the improvement of the quality of life and social interaction" (SATCC-TU 1998a, p 2). For being able to achieve success in the pursuance of these goals, to determinedly integrate, extend and strengthen the regional transport and communications systems is among the foremost requirements: sustainability and efficiency of the systems must be ascertained and improved through timely and adequate maintenance and qualified management, the capacities of the systems must be increased, and efficient interaction and co-operation between them secured. This, in addition to organizational, technical and managerial restructuring, requires attracting new and additional investment as well as skills and competence from potential sources inside and outside the region.

Obviously, creating an appropriate political and institutional framework is a necessary condition for bringing about change toward strengthening existing and introducing new technical and commercial practice and private sector involvement. Since the transport and communications sectors were early on being recognized as catalysts for regional economic development, it was already at the change of the 1980s to the 1990s, that the SADC member states began, in co-operation with the European Commission and the World Bank, to conceptualize a comprehensive study to be directed at analysing the existing transport and communications systems and their shortcomings as well as the effects on the systems of the expected future socio-economic and political integration in the region, in particular at a time when destabilization and civil disturbances in some of the region's countries would be resolved and a post-apartheid RSA would join with the other countries as a full partner. The results of this analysis should then be used to devise appropriate measures to remove the barriers toward an unimpeded movement of passengers, goods and information flows, and to deal with the challenges expected from a more rapid economic development in a regionally integrated system.

Based on these conceptual ideas, a number of detailed research tasks was defined which included: developing of a regional transport and communications data bank and data management system; analysing the state of regional and international trade in order to identify present constraints and review potential trade strategies; conducting a full regional transport and communications analysis, focussing on systems issues and strategies, in particular with regard to regulations, operations, investments, maintenance, organizations and institutions, human resources, and cross-sub-sectoral linkages; analysing investment and policy options, and recommending Investment and Policy Action Programmes, including an Immediate Action Programme.

With some delay related to determining scope and financing, the European Commission, within the Seventh European Development Fund, provided a budget of 5.8 million ECU for this "Transport and Communications Integration Study for Southern Africa" to be commenced, under the auspices of SATCC, the Southern Africa Transport and Communications Commission, in 1996. After about 35 working papers, intermediate reports, manuals and other documents, consisting of a total of some 50 volumes, had been produced by the Southern Africa Consulting Group and been discussed and reviewed in six meetings of the Steering Committee and five workshops – with a total participation of about 700 representatives of SADC member states, regional, governmental and para-governmental agencies, international co-operating partners, regional universities and the private sector – , the results were condensed into the 127 pages of the final report's main volume, published in June 1998 (SACG 1998, Vol 1).

2. Implementing Change

Parallel to the progress of the Integration Study, and following the signing of the Protocol, also in 1996, efforts began toward implementation of the Protocol: again under the guidance of SATCC and with the assistance of STEP, the SADC Transport Efficiency Project, financed by USAID, the United States Agency for International Development, annexes to the Protocol were developed concerning the technical details to be observed on the sub-sectoral levels, and their transformation into national regulations pursued within the intricate political-administrative structure foreseen in the Protocol (SATCC-TU 1998a). These initial restructuring measures gained considerable impetus through the completion, distribution and widespread acceptance of the Integration Study's final report. Also, the SADC-EU Transport Conference on Protocol Implementation, which was held in Maputo in October 1998 under the auspices of the Austrian EU Presidency, added weight and speed to the reform process.

Within the implementation process, member states are expected to condense their intended actions into a comprehensive Micro Action Plan (MICAP) which should reflect, filtered down to a national perspective, the agreed Macro Action Plan (MAP) for the SADC region as a whole. The MAP, in turn, consists of an update based on the Regional Policy Action Programme (PAP) which is one result of the Integration Study (SACG 1998, Vol 1 and 2). As of November 1999, two thirds of the twelve SADC member states (not considering Congo and the Seychelles) had finalized and published their MICAPs.

In a document presented to the SATCC Committee of Senior Officials by the SATCC-TU in 1999, the then current state of Protocol implementation is reflected in much detail across member states and sub-sectors. A general overview of activities shows that implementation has made substantial although not sufficient progress. "The share of actions completed in the total aggregate of actions necessary has, from 9.9 % in November 1998, almost doubled to 18.1 % in May 1999. Also the share of actions underway though not yet completed, has increased slightly from 22.8 % to 24.3 %. However, the share of actions not yet commenced, while reduced from 67.3 % to 57.6 %, still represents the majority of implementation activities necessary" (Funck 1999b, p 3).

While policy reform is well under way, actual implementation of policy change is hampered by the slow progress in legal reform which is, in turn, mainly due to a wide spread lack of local expertise with regard to the legal requirements specific to the transport and communications sectors. Model legislation which has been provided by the SATCC-TU with the assistance of experienced STEP staff (e.g., out of a large number of Model Legislative Provisions and Model Agreements: Model Legislation Investment in Transport Act, SATCC-TU 1998b) can only partially fill this gap, since it will always be necessary to adapt the national legislation to the requirements of the specific country.

As regards sub-sectoral achievements in Protocol implementation, it is the road transport sector where the highest degree of completed actions (34.5 %) can be stated for 1999, followed by railways, telecommunications and road infrastructure. The ranking is similar if all actions already commenced are considered: the figure for road transport becomes 65.1 %, followed by road infrastructure, railways, the maritime sector and telecommunications, all with percentages around 50 (Funck 1999a).

This reflects the fact that already since 1989 road funds have been set up in several member states, although with mixed success. The funds are raised from fuel levies and various vehicle licence and transit fees; at present, however, charges do not yet reflect social costs, and are, in most cases, not sufficiently protected from being drawn into the general budget. However, road boards that are required to manage and administer the road fund in order to secure proper accounting for the revenues, have been set up or are in the process of being established in most countries. Private sector representation on the boards that can be helpful in securing public acceptance and support of the new system are in differing stages of development (SACG 1998, Vol 1).

Based on a tradition of co-operation between the region's railways, SARA, the Southern African Railways Association, has been established in 1995 in order to clear the way for improvements. Already, "considerable progress has been made in areas such as facilitation of border crossing through joint single inspection of wagons" (SACG 1998, Vol 1, p 55), but there are still major impediments resulting from maintenance backlogs with regard to infrastructure and rolling stock, and inadequate communications facilities, resulting in high accident rates, low speed limits and unpredictable transit times. In recent years, franchising of railway operations to the private sector has evolved as a strategy for reducing government influence on rates and fares as well as on decisions regarding scope and quality of service, and reduction of over-staffing and over-equipment, in order to make operations more efficient and financially viable.

An overview of implementation activities shows that, based on the 1999 situation, South Africa is leading with 23.9 % of completed actions, with Tanzania, Mauritius and Zimbabwe following. The picture changes only slightly if we include the actions underway, but not yet completed; the highest shares are then shown again by South Africa (53.5 %), with Tanzania and Zimbabwe following at about 45 % and, displacing Mauritius, Mozambique and Swaziland with more than 40 % (Funck 1999b).

One area of concern lies in the fact that private sector participation in Protocol implementation, so far, has remained unsystematic and is, where it happens, dominated by service providers. The reasons seem to lie in the "inbred" conception throughout the SADC region that Protocol implementation is a government task, where the private sector plays a marginal role at best, and in a missing awareness even in parts of the interested public of the significance and intended impacts of the new organizational structures on the socio-economic development in the region and, thus, for transport users and consumers along with service providers and the manufacturing industry.

Already in 1997/1998, the idea was developed by the SATCC-TU that, in order to increase private sector involvement in Protocol implementation, and elicit interest in infrastructure provision, financing and management, SATCC should engage in a "Protocol awareness campaign", and stage an Investors and Donors Forum, where the investment opportunities that would arise within a new, reformed legal-institutional framework, could be properly presented to the international financing and investing community. The plan was noted and accepted in principle by the SATCC Committee of Ministers and the SADC Council of Ministers and endorsed by the EU-SADC Transport Conference in October 1998. The Forum is now expected to be held during the fourth quarter of the year 2000.

The main messages that the Forum is supposed to project to the international financing community can be summarized as follows:

With the implementation of the Protocol, the region's transport and communications sectors are changing significantly; they have seriously embarked on the process of commercialization and privatization, thus making the SADC region a suitable place for private involvement to complement or replace government and donor funding. Given the fact that the SADC countries are poised for rapid economic growth, it is clear that the transport and communications infrastructures need significant improvements in order to be able to support and reinforce these developments.

The most recent review for identifying a comprehensive programme for sector investment opportunities has been compiled in the Regional Investment Programme (IP) of the Integration Study (SACG 1998, Vol 1 and 2) where, based on a formal multi-criteria analysis (SACG 1998, Vol 3), 38 investment projects, for which financing was not yet secured, have been given high priority for inclusion in the first five year period of the programme (1998–2002), and another 56 projects have been placed in the second category (2003–2007). Financing requirements have been estimated at 506 million US Dollar and 478 million US Dollar in the two phases respectively (SACG 1998, Vol 1).

However, compilation of the IP was limited to regional projects – that is: completion of the Regional Trunk Road Network (RTRN), investments in the railways and the regional ports system (see *Figure 1*) – excluding complementary national projects, and was based on the data available at the time. Also, the civil aviation and postal services and the meteorology sub-sectors were not included for reasons of funding reductions – probably a major mistake, as delays in advance information on upcoming meteorological disasters and the consequent loss of human life and property in Mozambique have recently shown.

Figure 1: Southern Africa's regional transport system (SACG 1998, Vol 1)

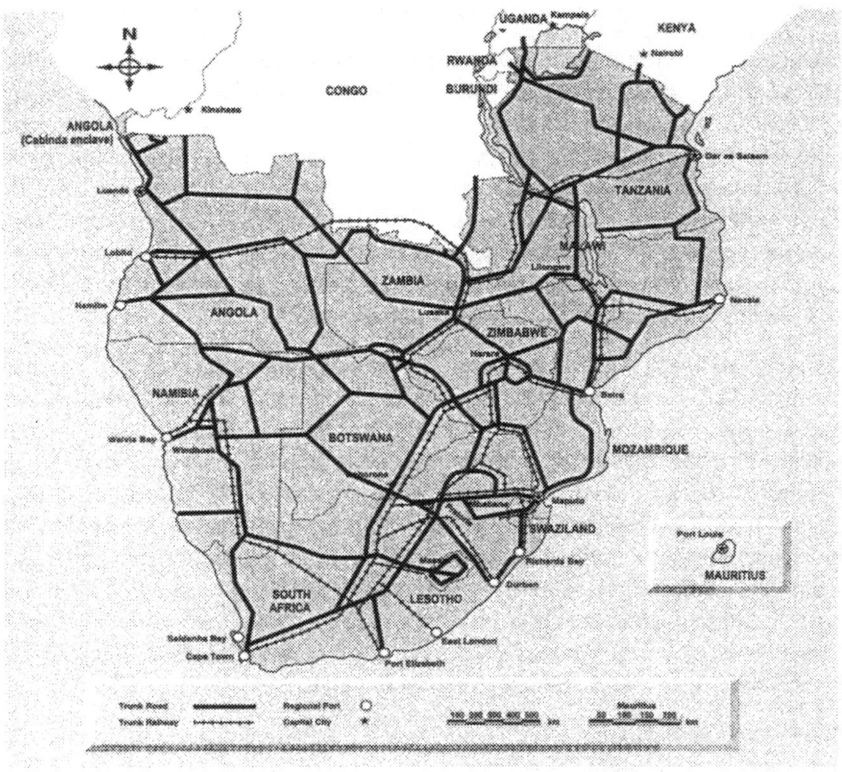

Updated information on national development perspectives, development corridors, spatial development initiatives (SDIs) and other development concepts (Kaombwe 2000) indicate that there is much more potential. Also it is expected that, once the private sector is sufficiently motivated for direct involvement in the financing, management and performance of infrastructure services in the fields of transport and communications, new opportunities will be generated that may not have been identified so far.

Including these in the multi-criteria analysis may distinctly revise the priorities, even if the criteria for investment selection do not change considerably in basic content and degree of detail – which is not likely, given the fact that, for the time being, precise information is a commodity hard to acquire in Southern Africa. At current, the criteria for regional investments fall into two dimensions, namely Regional Content – contribution to regional development and integration, capacity improvements on a regional level, efficiency improvements of the regional systems, benefits to regional traffic, institutional development and private sector involvement – and Project Feasibility – economic feasibility, availability of financing, sources of financing, financial and operational, and environmental sustainability (SACG 1998, Vol 4). In developing the IP, scoring the criteria for each project was based on a combination of quantitative and qualitative assessments.

As a result out of the total investment requirements foreseen of almost one billion US Dollar, about three quarters are considered to be necessary for improving the RTRN, with the rest almost equally divided between railways and maritime transport, after setting aside a relatively minor contribution (of less than 50 million US Dollar) to investments in the telecommunications sector. No investments in integrated transport survived the evaluation procedure. Obviously, the multi-criteria approach employed is backward rather than forward oriented: desirability of systems' improvements is measured at past statistical figures; future-directed political objectives obtain little if any weight in the procedure.

Clearly, Southern Africa's transport system was originally developed to facilitate international, i.e., extra-regional trade through the creation of arterial railway lines from a number of coastal seaports to the major mineral producing and agricultural centres inland. At that time, rail transport was "the predominant mode of freight transport in the region and...the most important mode for the movement of international trade cargo" (SATCC 1994, pp 1-2). Road transport has become the major carrier of passengers and cargo since, with the automobile dominating intercity traffic, while local and rural communication still relies heavily on pedestrian traffic and intermediate means of transport (Sieber 1996). Interestingly, however, the 1996 SATCC cross-border survey reveals that SADC cross-border traffic divides almost exactly equally between road and rail (SACG 1998, Vol 1).

At current, and updating the IP, SATCC and the EC are preparing joint efforts for improving and developing integrated regional transport (IRT) in Southern Africa. They have realized that a well developed IRT system requires not only efficiency in the individual transport modes, but also the establishing of national taxation and subsidization systems that do not favour certain and disfavour other modes of transport, the creation of a sufficient number of well-working inter-change units and efficient technical, economic and organizational operation of these units, efficient customs and other legal and documentary procedures, based on the use of regionally standardized driver, vehicle and cargo documentation and insurance, to name the most obvious and most important conditions (SATCC-TU 2000).

At present, IRT is not very well developed in the SADC region. There are a number of inter-modal container facilities working in the region, of which the "inland port" in Johannesburg is the most important and successful one, due to effective rail connections to South African ports, and to the wide range of services offered. In most transport corridors, however, rail and road aim for competition rather than co-operation. The 1996 SATCC border crossing survey and other research have shown the average waiting times for trucks at some of the most frequented border crossing points in Southern Africa to be in the range of between 28 and 60 hours. Total annual cost of border crossing delays for heavy goods vehicles was estimated at between 48 and 140 million US Dollar p.a. If such delays could be substantially reduced or even eliminated through the establishing of one-stop border posts, origin-destination times on transit routes and thus total transport cost would decline considerably.

Fortunately, progress seems imminent: pilot projects have already been designed for border post conversion to one-stop operation and infrastructure management. Also, agreement has been reached within the region and beyond on standardization and simplification of customs documentation, and awareness is growing of the need to develop working relationships among customs officials of different member states.

It should, however, be noted that improving the "processing" of transit traffic through ports, border crossings and IRT inter-change establishments will accelerate and help to optimize the flow of *existing* transit traffic, thus making a substantial contribution to better and more competitive trade. Improvements in the frame conditions for trade are, however, also necessary in order to *increase* the level of exchange in the region.

3. European Experience

European economic integration (Funck 1999a) began in 1950 with the founding of the European Coal and Steel Community, the so-called *Montane Union*. Transportation was already a sector of major concern in the Montane Treaty, mainly through setting out the rules for fair competition between rail on the one hand – which was then a totally nationalized industry in all European countries – and road haulage and inland waterways transport, covered by private business, on the other.

In 1967, when the *Montane Union*, the European Economic Community and the European Atomic Community, originally based on the Treaties of Rome (1957), were reshaped into the joint European Community, reference to transportation was inserted twice into Part One of the Treaty, where the fundamental principles for the Community are formulated (while communication – not to speak of telecommunication – was not mentioned at all).

Article 3(c) requires the creation of a single market, characterized through the abolishment of all obstacles against free trans-border movement of commodities, persons, services and capital, listed in that order. Actually, free movement of information may be considered to be included under the term "services"; still this sub-listing reflects the little attention that was, at that time, attributed to communication and the lack of foresight with regard to its huge importance in the future.

Full liberalization of commodity exchange became reality already in the mid-1960s, when the stepwise establishment of the European Community as a customs union – with unified tariffs towards third-country imports, with quantitative restrictions and internal customs borders removed, under conditions of full convertibility of European currencies – was completed. Article 3(f) requires that a common transport policy be implemented. In this respect, totally different from the fast pace in establishing free trade, practically nothing was achieved for the next three decades. The European Council of Ministers of Transport, the deciding body for European transport policy, virtually ignored all proposals placed before them by the European Commission. That is: until 1985.

In June 1985, the European Commission presented to the European Council the White Paper on completion of the European Single Market. At the end of the same month, the White Paper was accepted by the European Summit Meeting in Milan, and the date for completion of the Single Market was set for January 1, 1993. At about the same time, the European Parliament, driven by the Transport Committee and its chairman, Horst Seefeld, had filed with the European Court of Justice in The Hague, a "no-activity" suit against the Council. On May 22, 1985 – a truly historic date for European transport policies – the Court ruled that, indeed, the Council had neglected its duties to ascertain free availability of transport services in the Community, and stated it to be the Council's obligation to take the necessary action without further undue delay.

From then on matters rushed. In November 1985, the Council of Ministers decided on major guidelines for common transport policies: a free transport market without quantitative restrictions was to be established as of January 1, 1993; bilateral transport quota were to be adjusted in a stepwise procedure in order to reduce discrimination based on nationality, and to move toward common international quota; distortions in the frame conditions of the transport markets were to be reduced in order to promote Europe-wide competition. In the following years, a large number of directives on transport liberalization and harmonization – with a focus on the most difficult sub-sector: the road freight industry – was issued by the European Commission.

However, to this day, adaptation of fiscal regulations remains the most crucial link missing in the harmonization chain. As some member states rely more on vehicle taxation, others more on fuel tax, taxes on road freight vehicles and fuel still differ widely between European countries (OECD 1997): the annual vehicle tax levied on a 40 ton truck in the highest taxing country (Austria) is eight times as high as in the lowest taxing country (Greece). Although upper and lower bounds have been set for fuel tax rates, the highest rate on diesel fuel (charged in Italy) is still 176 % of the lowest rates (charged in Austria, Luxembourg and Spain). Only a minority of the countries charge motorway tolls, several others have introduced the EURO vignette system, through which heavy trucks are charged based on the period of use of the motorway, that is on a daily or up to a yearly basis.

In summing up, it can be stated that frame conditions on the European freight market continue to be quite heterogeneous. Thus, incentives are still being provided by national governments for choosing the location for establishing a company, the most suitable route for a transport service, or the place of purchase of fuel, based on monetary cost which are distorted by tax differentials and external cost arbitrage, rather than based on real cost differences. Consequently, the lack of harmonization which is still in existence, prevents the European single market from fully achieving its goal: dismissal of all artificial obstacles which hamper an unbiased and thus fully efficient use of productive factors.

Since the early 1950s, when the first efforts at shaping a common European transport policy began, about half a century has passed. For the first 35 years, until 1985, practically nothing happened. Southern Africa, on the brink of economic development, does not have that much time to waste. Although its establishing of a sound transport and communications system starts from a much lower level and cannot be supported from internal funds only, unnecessary delay in harmonising the working frame for transport and communications would, in to-day's global economy, be highly damaging if not fatal for Southern Africa's economies. Co-funding the systems development in Southern Africa lies not only in the interest of socio-economic development in the SADC region but also in the political and economic interest of Southern Africa's European partners – and, in addition, it constitutes a historic obligation.

And, before pressing for more speedy change, before lamenting the "slow" progress of transport and communications integration in Southern Africa which has, so far, taken little more than half a decade, we Europeans should look at our own history, we should recognize that integration of transport systems in Europe has already taken almost ten times that much, without fully reaching the target yet.

References

Funck RH (1999a) Relevant Experience from Europe. In: Austrian Development Corporation (ed) EU-SADC Transport Conference Report – Status of Protocol Implementation. Maputo and Vienna, pp 118-127

Funck RH (1999b) Regional Transport and Communications Integration Study for Southern Africa: Progress in Implementation of Study Results. Unpublished report, Maputo and Karlsruhe

Kaombwe SMAK (2000) Transport and Communications in Integration in Southern Africa. In: Rothengatter W, Kowalski J (eds) Soft Factors in Spatial Dynamics. Karlsruhe Papers in Economic Policy Research 7. Nomos, Baden-Baden, pp 129-136

OECD (1997) Liberalization and Structural Reform in the Freight Transport Sector in Europe. Document COM/TD/ENV(97)11, Paris

SACG Southern Africa Consulting Group (1998) Transport and Communications Integration: The Catalyst for Economic Development in Southern Africa (4 Volumes). SATCC Maputo

SATCC Southern Africa Transport and Communications Commission, EC European Commission (1994) Regional Transport and Communications Integration Study for Southern Africa: Terms of Reference. SATCC Maputo

SATCC-TU (1998a) Southern Africa Transport and Communications Commission Technical Unit (March 1998). SADC Protocol on Transport, Communications and Meteorology. SATCC Maputo

SATCC-TU (1998b) Southern Africa Transport and Communications Commission Technical Unit (May 1998). Model Legislation Investment in Transport Act. SATCC Maputo

SATCC-TU (2000) Southern Africa Transport and Communications Commission Technical Unit (January 2000). Regional Reform and Restructuring in the Transport Sector: Promoting Integrated Regional Transport (unpublished project proposal). Maputo

Sieber N (1996) Rural Transport and Regional Development: The Case of Makete District, Tanzania. Funck RH, Rothengatter W (eds) Karlsruhe Papers in Economic Policy Research 4, Nomos, Baden-Baden

List of Authors

Sule Akkoyunlu
Department of Economics
The University of Kent at Canterbury
Canterbury CT2 7NZ, United Kingdom

Siamak Baradaran
KTH - Royal Institute of Technology
Department of Infrastructure and Planning
SE-100 44 Stockholm, Sweden

Uwe Blien
Institut für Arbeitsmarkt- und Berufsforschung (IAB)
an der Bundesanstalt für Arbeit, Nürnberg
Regensburger Straße 104
D-90478 Nürnberg, Germany
Uwe.Blien@iab.de

Johannes Bröcker
Technische Universität Dresden
Institut für Wirtschaft und Verkehr
Mommsenstraße 13
D-01062-Dresden, Germany
Johannes.Broecker@mailbox.tu-dresden.de

Riccardo Cappellin
Università di Roma "Tor Vergata"
Department of Economics and Institutions
I-10133 Roma, Italia
Cappellin@Economia.Uniroma2.it

Andreas P. Cornett
University of Southern Denmark
DK-6400 Soenderborg, Denmark
Cornett@sam.sdu.dk

Dirk Dohse
Institut für Weltwirtschaft, Kiel
Kiel Institute of World Economics
Düsternbrooker Weg 120
D-24105 Kiel, Germany
Ddohse@ifw.uni-kiel.de

Hans-Friedrich Eckey
Universität Gesamthochschule Kassel
Fachbereich 7 Wirtschaftswissenschaften
Empirische Wirtschaftsforschung
Nora-Platiel-Straße 4
D–34109 Kassel, Germany
eckey@wirtschaft.uni-kassel.de

Michael Fritsch
Technical University Bergakademie Freiberg
Faculty of Economics and Business Administration
Chair for Economic Policy and Research Unit Innovation Economics
Gustav-Zeuner-Straße 8-10
D-09596 Freiberg, Germany
fritschm@orion.hrz.tu-freiberg.de

Rolf H. Funck
Universität Karlsruhe (TH)
Institut für Wirtschaftspolitik und Wirtschaftsforschung
Postfach 6380
D-76128 Karlsruhe, Germany
funck@iww.uni-karlsruhe.de

Hans-Peter Gatzweiler
Federal Office for Buildung and Regional Planning
Bundesamt für Bauwesen und Raumordnung (BBR)
Am Michaelshof 8
D-53177 Bonn, Germany
Hans-Peter.Gatzweiler@bbr.bund.de

Joachim Genosko
Katholische Universität Eichstätt
Wirtschaftswissenschaftliche Fakultät Ingolstadt
Auf der Schanz 49
D-85049 Ingolstadt, Germany
Joachim.Genosko@ku-eichstaett.de

Wilfried Görmar
Federal Office for Buildung and Regional Planning
Bundesamt für Bauwesen und Raumordnung (BBR)
Am Michaelshof 8
D-53177 Bonn, Germany

Nils Groes
Professor, Executive Director
AKF – Institute of Local Government Studies,
37, Nyropsgade
DK–1602 Copenhagen V, Denmark
ng@akf.dk

Scott Hacker
Jönköping International Business School
P.O. Box 1026
SE-551 11 Jönköping, Sweden
Scott.Hacker@ihh.hj.se

Geoffrey J. D. Hewings
Regional Economics Applications Laboratory
University of Illinois
607 S. Mathews, #236
Urbana, Illinois 61801-3671, USA
hewings@ux1.cso.uiuc.edu

Klaus Horn
Universität Gesamthochschule Kassel
Fachbereich 7 Wirtschaftswissenschaften
Empirische Wirtschaftsforschung
Nora-Platiel-Straße 4
D–34109 Kassel, Germany

Börje Johansson
Jönköping International Business School
P.O. Box 1026
SE-551 11 Jönköping, Sweden
Borje.Johansson@jibs.hj.se

Jan A. van der Linden
Policy Research Institute
Driehoekstraat 304
B-2180 Antwerp, Belgium
Jan.van.der.linden@policyresearch.be

Lars Lundqvist
KTH - Royal Institute of Technology
Departement of Infrastructure and Planning
SE-100 44 Stockholm, Sweden
Lars@infra.kth.se

Peter Nijkamp
Department of Economics
Free University
De Boelelaan 1105
NL-1081 HV Amsterdam, The Netherlands
pnijkamp@econ.vu.nl

Yasuhide Okuyama
Department of Planning
State University of New York at Buffalo
Hayes Hall, 3435 Main St.
Buffalo, NY 14214-3087, USA

Jan Oosterhaven
Departement of Economics
University of Groningen
Postbus 800
NL-9700 Groningen, The Netherlands
oosterhaven@eco.rug.nl

Lars Olof Persson
Royal Institute of Technology
Department of Infrastructure and Planning
SE–10044 Stockholm, Sweden
Larsolof.persson@nordregio.a.se

Frank Richter
Technische Universität Dresden
Institut für Wirtschaft und Verkehr
Mommsenstraße 13
D-01062-Dresden, Germany

Klaus Schöler
Universität Potsdam
Wirtschafts- und Sozialwissenschaftliche Fakultät
Lehrstuhl für Volkswirtschaftslehre, insbesondere Wirtschaftstheorie
Postfach 900327
D-14439 Potsdam, Germany
schoeler@rz.uni-potsdam.de

Michael Sonis
Regional Economics Applications Laboratory
University of Illinois and Bar Ilan University, Israel
607 S. Mathews, #236
Urbana, Illinois 61801-3671, USA

Alexandros Tassinopoulos
Institut für Arbeitsmarkt- und Berufsforschung (IAB)
an der Bundesanstalt für Arbeit, Nürnberg
Regensburger Straße 104
D-90478 Nürnberg, Germany
Alexandors.Tassinopoulos@iab.de

Roger Vickerman
Department of Economics
The University of Kent at Canterbury
Canterbury CT2 7NZ, United Kingdom
R.W.Vickerman@ukc.ac.uk

Druck: Strauss Offsetdruck, Mörlenbach
Verarbeitung: Schäffer, Grünstadt

Contributions to Economics

Simon Duindam
Military Conscription
1999. ISBN 3-7908-1203-X

Bruno Jeitziner
Political Economy of the Swiss National Bank
1999. ISBN 3-7908-1209-9

Irene Ring et al. (Eds.)
Regional Sustainability
1999. ISBN 3-7908-1233-1

Katharina Müller/Andreas Ryll/
Hans-Jürgen Wagener (Eds.)
Transformation of Social Security: Pensions in Central-Eastern Europe
1999. ISBN 3-7908-1210-2

Stefan Traub
Framing Effects in Taxation
1999. ISBN 3-7908-1240-4

Pablo Coto-Millán
Utility and Production
1999. ISBN 3-7908-1153-X

Frank Riedel
Imperfect Information and Investor Heterogeneity in the Bond Market
2000. ISBN 3-7908-1247-1

Kirsten Ralf
Business Cycles
2000. ISBN 3-7908-1245-5

Michele Bagella/
Leonardo Becchetti (Eds.)
The Competitive Advantage of Industrial Districts
2000. ISBN 3-7908-1254-4

Frank Bohn
Monetary Union and Fiscal Stability
2000. ISBN 3-7908-1266-8

Michael Malakellis
Integrated Macro-Micro-Modelling Under Rational Expectations
2000. ISBN 3-7908-1266-8

Stefan Baumgärtner
Ambivalent Joint Production and the Natural Environment
2000. ISBN 3-7908-1290-0

Henri Capron, Wim Meeusen (Eds.)
The National Innovation System of Belgium
2000. ISBN 3-7908-1308-7

Tobias Miarka
Financial Intermediation and Deregulation
2000. ISBN 3-7908-1307-9

Chisato Yoshida
Illegal Immigration and Economic Welfare
2000. ISBN 3-7908-1315-X

Nikolaus Thumm
Intellectual Property Rights
2001. ISBN 3-7908-1329-X

GPSR Compliance

The European Union's (EU) General Product Safety Regulation (GPSR) is a set of rules that requires consumer products to be safe and our obligations to ensure this.

If you have any concerns about our products, you can contact us on ProductSafety@springernature.com

In case Publisher is established outside the EU, the EU authorized representative is:

Springer Nature Customer Service Center GmbH
Europaplatz 3
69115 Heidelberg, Germany

Batch number: 10725973

Printed by Printforce, the Netherlands